HATHOR
A REINTRODUCTION TO AN ANCIENT EGYPTIAN GODDESS

HATHOR

A REINTRODUCTION TO AN
ANCIENT EGYPTIAN GODDESS

LESLEY JACKSON

Published by Avalonia
www.avaloniabooks.co.uk

Published by Avalonia

BM Avalonia, London, WC1N 3XX, England, UK

www.avaloniabooks.co.uk

HATHOR: A Reintroduction to an Ancient Egyptian Goddess

© Lesley Jackson, 2013

All rights reserved.

First Published by Avalonia, April 2014

ISBN 978-1-905-297-69-6

Typeset and design by Satori

Cover image: Photo of the *Face of the Egyptian goddess Hathor shown with cow ears* by jsp / Shutterstock.com

Illustrations by Brian Andrews, 2013

British Library Cataloguing in Publication Data. A catalogue record for this book is available from the British Library.

This book is sold subject to the condition that no part of it may be reproduced or utilized in any form or by any means, electronic or mechanical, including photocopying, microfilm, recording, or by any information storage and retrieval system, or used in another book, without written permission from the authors.

Hathor

DEDICATION

This book is dedicated to the Lady of Writing, the Mistress of the Library; and also to my parents, Mary and Peter, with love and thanks.

BIOGRAPHY

Lesley Jackson has always had an interest in, and a yearning for, the mysterious geographical; be they lost worlds, otherworlds or the sacred places of this world. A career in IT was merely a logical façade. Many years of involvement in the local archaeological society deepened her interest in ancient cultures and their religions.

Since being blessed with early retirement, Lesley has devoted much of her time to researching and writing about early religion and mythology. Ancient Egypt is an enduring passion but other paths are always beckoning from around the misty hills. She is the author of *Thoth: The History of the Ancient Egyptian God of Wisdom* (Avalonia, 2011).

She lives in the remote East Riding with a tolerant husband and an ever increasing volume of books and rocks. Any remaining spare time is spent travelling or baking and making chocolates.

ACKNOWLEDGEMENTS

No study of Egyptian religion would be possible without access to their writings. I am indebted to all of those who have studied these ancient languages and have provided translations for the rest of us to use.

I would like to thank the British Library, and the Egyptian Exploration Society and the University of Hull for the use of their libraries.

Quotes are included with permission of the following:

T.A. Allen, *The Book of the Dead or Going Forth by Day*. University of Chicago Press 1974.

C.J. Bleeker, *Hathor and Thoth: Two Key Figures of the Ancient Egyptian Religion*. E J Brill 1973. © Koninklijke Brill N.V.

J.F. Borghouts, *The Evil Eye of Apophis*. In *Journal of Egyptian Archaeology*, Vol 59 1973. © Egyptian Exploration Society.

J.F. Borghouts, *Ancient Egyptian Magical Texts*. E J Brill 1978. © Koninklijke Brill N.V.

R.O. Faulkner, *The Ancient Egyptian Coffin Texts*. Aris & Phillips 2007.

M. Lichtheim, *Ancient Egyptian Literature: Volumes I, II & III*. Publiahed by the University of California Press. © 1975 by The Regents of the University of California.

M. Poo, *Wine and Wine Offering in the Religion of Ancient Egypt*. Kegan Paul International 1995.

M. Smith, *Traversing Eternity*. Oxford University Press 2009.

TABLE OF CONTENTS

INTRODUCTION	11
NAMES & ICONOGRAPHY	13
THE COW GODDESS	27
THE SKY GODDESS	40
THE SOLAR GODDESS	46
THE TREE GODDESS	60
OBJECTS	70
ASPECTS OF HATHOR	86
MUSIC & DANCE	91
LOVE & SEX	100
LADY OF DRUNKENNESS	103
FRAGRANCE	111
FERTILITY & CHILDBIRTH	116
PROTECTING & NURTURING	121
A GEOLOGICAL GODDESS	129
GODDESS OF TRADE & FOREIGN LANDS	138
THE AFTERLIFE & REBIRTH	142
THE SEVEN HATHORS	159
SEKHMET	163
RELATIONSHIPS WITH OTHER DEITIES	183

ALTER EGOS & ASSIMILATIONS	191
THE WORSHIP OF HATHOR	198
HATHOR'S TEMPLES	229
INSIDE THE TEMPLES	256
WHAT HAPPENED TO HATHOR?	264
CONCLUSION	270

<u>APPENDICES</u>

HATHOR FESTIVALS	274
CHRONOLOGY	283
PLACE NAMES IN THE TEXT	284
SACRED GEOGRAPHY	288
BIBLIOGRAPHY	289

Lesley Jackson

1. Photograph of the face of the Egyptian goddess Hathor shown with cow ears 3rd cent. BC fragment of the capital of a column (louvre-D 2).
(c) JSP, Shutterstock.com

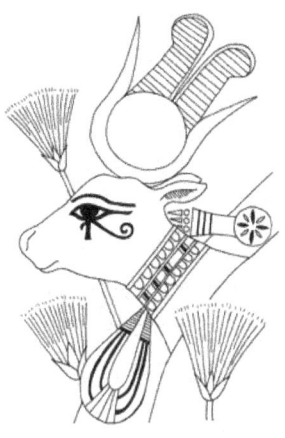

CHAPTER 1

INTRODUCTION

"The wonders that Hathor performed should be related."[1]

Hathor was once the most loved and pre-eminent goddess of Egypt. An ancient goddess, *"Hathor...who descends from the primeval age"* soon held all Egyptians in her loving embrace.[2] She was one of the most accessible of the deities so it was unsurprising that she was a favourite. Her cult, and encounters with her, were full of music, love and laughter. No stern, demanding deity she rejoiced in her followers' happiness and many could say *"she placed joy in my heart"*.[3]

---

[1] *Biographical Texts from Ramessid Egypt*, Frood & Baines, 2007:232

[2] *Hathor and Thoth: Two Key Figures of the Ancient Egyptian Religion*, Bleeker, 1973:20

[3] *Behind Closed Eyes*, Szpakowska, 2003:195

People who are aware of Hathor today usually think of her as the cow goddess but that is only one of her many faces. She is a sky and solar goddess as well as a tree goddess. Some are uncomfortable with the concept of a solar goddess, having grown up with Celtic and Greco-Roman influences. Let Hathor *"the Golden One"* persuade you otherwise.[4] She was present at birth and nurtured and protected everyone, at all levels of society, during life and then midwifed them into the afterlife. A truly universal goddess, she took merchants and travellers under her protection as well as all of the foreigners who inhabited the lesser world outside of Egypt.

Her demise brought the eclipse of a Golden Goddess. Over the millennia we have lost contact with this dynamic, independent and woman-loving Goddess. The aim of this book is to reintroduce you to *"the sovereign, the powerful goddess, whose ba is powerful, beautiful of face, sweet of loveliness, splendid of appearance among the gods"*.[5]

Sekhmet, the lioness goddess and daughter of the sun god, is covered in this book both as an aspect of Hathor and as a goddess in her own right. The cat goddess Bastet is often considered an alter-ego and benign aspect of Sekhmet or Hathor. I have chosen not to cover Bastet in detail for two reasons. Whilst she can be aligned with Hathor, I do not feel that she has the same connection as Sekhmet does. The second consideration is that a book has to have defined boundaries and the Egyptian goddesses are very fluid, flowing cobra-like from one form to the next. My focus has to remain on Hathor.

---

[4] *Pharaoh's Gold*, Reader, 2008:15-21
[5] *The Evil Eye of Apophis*, Borghouts, 1973:114-150

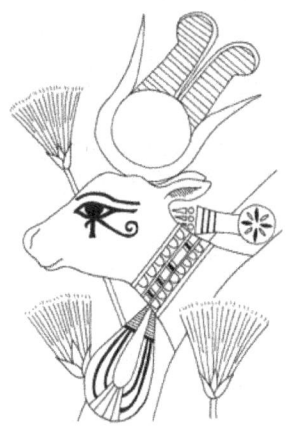

CHAPTER 2

NAMES & ICONOGRAPHY

"Oh, lady of the beginning, come thou before our faces in this thy name of Hathor, lady of emerald."[6]

Introduction

Today a name often has little value. To the Egyptians it was the essence of a person, or deity, and so names were of supreme importance. If your name survived so did you, if it was erased so were you. Names had power and if a person knew your name they had power over you. For this reason the true names of Hathor, and all the other deities, were a closely guarded secret. The Egyptians were happy to accept multiple names for their deities and the name was an important part of the deity's personality. Knowing the name of a deity gave you a

---

[6] *The Burden of Isis*, Dennis, 1910:55

connection to them. They could be worshipped by name, invoked and implored and offerings could be made specifically to them.

Many flattering, or euphemistic, names were used to deflect anger, to propitiate a dangerous aspect of the deity or even to avoid referring to them altogether so as not to call them by accident. It is always a good idea to be polite to those who are infinitely more powerful than you are regardless of your own opinions about them. It is not obvious which names these are. A kind god could be the opposite. This custom is reflected in our culture by the use of terms such as Old Nick and the Little People.

Hwt-Hrw

Hathor's name, *Hwt-hrw or Hwt-Hr*, means "*House of Horus*". There are two gods called Horus and they are often confused or combined. Horus the Elder is the son of the sky goddess Nut and is the falcon sky god. Horus the Younger is the son of Isis and Osiris, though confusingly he can also be referred to as the son of Hathor. The phrase "*House of Horus*" can be translated as the "*Womb of Horus*" which refers to Hathor's Mother aspect. It can also be seen as the sky in which Horus flies and the earth over which he presides. As Hathor is a sky goddess she is the obvious home of all flying creatures and sky deities. Her hieroglyph is of a seated woman wearing a tight dress and crowned by cow horns supporting a sun disc. Her name can also be written as a falcon inside a square representing the bounds of the palace or temple.[7]

The Greeks gave many of the Egyptian deities Greek names which were nothing like their Egyptian names. Hathor kept her own which suggests that they found it easy enough to pronounce. They allied her with their goddess Aphrodite, the goddess of sexual love.

Geographical Names

Hathor was a universal goddess worshipped all over Egypt and the surrounding lands of Nubia and Sinai. Many of her names refer to the location of her cult sites. Like all goddesses she is often just referred to

---

[7] *Hieroglyphics: The writings of Ancient Egypt*, Betro, 1996:74

as "*lady of*" or "*mistress of*". The following is a selection of some of these titles.

> "*Foremost in Thebes.*"[8]
> "*Hathor of Bhdt.*"[9]
> "*Lady of Agny.*"[10]
> "*Lady of Aphroditopolis.*"[11]
> "*Lady of Djeser.*"[12]
> "*Lady of Gebelein.*"[13]
> "*Lady of Hetepet.*"[14]
> "*Lady of Imet.*"
> "*Lady of Memphis.*"[15]
> "*Lady of Nefrusi.*"[16]
> "*Lady of Sinai.*"
> "*Lady of Sycamore-town.*"
> "*Lady of the Red Mountain.*"
> "*Lady of the temple of Herakleopolis.*"[17]
> "*Lady of the town of Atfih.*"[18]
> "*Lady of Wawat.*"[19]
> "*Mistress of Biggeh.*"[20]
> "*Mistress of Cusae.*"[21]
> "*Mistress of Dendera.*"[22]
> "*Mistress of desert borders.*"[23]

---

[8] *Valley of the Kings*, Weeks, 2010:188

[9] *Two Minor Monuments of Sety I*, el-Saady, 1990:186-188

[10] *Letters from Ancient Egypt*, Wente, 1990:196

[11] *The Bremner-Rhind Papyrus: II*, Faulkner, 1937:10-16

[12] *Senenu, High Priest of Amun at Deir el-Bahri*, Brovarski, 1976:57-73

[13] *Biographical Texts from Ramessid Egypt*, Frood & Baines, 2007:136

[14] *The Bremner-Rhind Papyrus: III: D. The Book of Overthrowing Apep*, Faulkner, 1937:166-185

[15] *The Bremner-Rhind Papyrus: II*, Faulkner, 1937:10-16

[16] *Ancient Egyptian Literature Volume III*, Lichtheim, 2006:45

[17] *The Bremner-Rhind Papyrus: II*, Faulkner, 1937:10-16

[18] *Daily Life in Ancient Egypt*, Szpakowska, 2008:138

[19] *The Bremner-Rhind Papyrus: II*, Faulkner, 1937:10-16

[20] *Adaption of Ancient Egyptian Texts to the Temple Ritual at Philae*, Zabkar, 1980:127-136

[21] *The Hereditary Status of Titles in the Cult of Hathor*, Galvin, 1984:42-49

[22] *A Reconstruction of the Triads of King Mycerinus*, Wood, 1974:82-93

> *"Mistress of Hu-Sekhem."*[24]
> *"Mistress of Libya."*[25]
> *"Mistress of Manu."*[26]
> *"Mistress of the High House, dwelling in Abydos."*[27]

The epithet *"Lady of the two egg-shells"* refers to the town of Pi-Hathor (Pathyris) near Gebelein which was a cult centre of Hathor.[28] The town was believed to be located on or near the mound of creation where the sun god was hatched from an egg laid by an ibis (a form of Thoth, the god of wisdom and writing). As the mother of the sun god Hathor was linked to this cosmology and location even though she was not the ibis in question.

There are references to *"Hathor in all her places"*[29] and *"Mistress of the sycamore shrine, in all her seats"*.[30] The term *"in all her places"* or *"in all her seats"* is used to reference less important cult centres as well as to emphasise her importance. A 20th Dynasty letter calls upon *"Hathor, mistress of Deir el-Bahri and mistress of the hills in which you are"*.[31] Wherever you go Hathor is sure to be the Lady of it.

Nwbt

Gold is strongly associated with Hathor both as a solar goddess and as the goddess of mining (see chapters 5 and 15). As well as symbolising eternity, because it does not tarnish, gold is the colour of the sun and so an appropriate epithet for a solar goddess. From the New Kingdom Hathor was often called *Nwbt "the Golden"*. Her gold epithets were particularly popular in the later periods when she was

---

[23] *Hymns, Prayers and Songs*, Foster, 1995:126

[24] *Letters from Ancient Egypt*, Wente, 1990:167

[25] *The Liturgy of Opening the Mouth for Breathing*, Smith, 1993:33

[26] *Senenu, High Priest of Amun at Deir el-Bahri*, Brovarski, 1976:57-73

[27] *The Cemeteries of Abydos: Work of the Season 1925-26*, Frankfort, 1928:235-245

[28] *Ramesside Texts Relating to the Taxation and Transport of Corn*, Gardiner, 1941:19-73

[29] *The Hereditary Status of Titles in the Cult of Hathor*, Galvin, 1984:42-49

[30] *A Reconstruction of the Triads of King Mycerinus*, Wood, 1974:82-93

[31] *Letters from Ancient Egypt*, Wente, 1990:193

often referred to simply as *"Gold"*. She was also called *"Gold of the gods in Wetjset-Hor"*[32] and *"the golden lady"*.[33] The term *"Gleaming One"* was an epithet of the sun god Ra but from the Late Period it was also an epithet of Hathor. The root of this word is *"heaven that is gleaming"* or *"radiant"*.[34] Ra was sometimes referred to as the *"Mountain of gold"* but he never had the same connection to gold as Hathor did. Hathor the *"Golden One"* was almost a personification of gold.[35]

Other Epithets

Some of Hathor's other epithets refer to aspects of her while other non-specific ones are common to other goddesses as well.

> *"August Lady."*[36]
> *"Beautiful of Face."*[37]
> *"Celestial Cow."*[38]
> *"Eye of Ra upon his disk."*[39]
> *"Goddess of drunkenness."*[40]
> *"Lady of All."*[41]
> *"Lady of Heaven."*[42]
> *"Lady of Horns."*[43]
> *"Lady of the Pillar."*[44]

---

[32] *The Significance of the Ceremony Hwt Bhsw in the Temple of Horus at Edfu*, Blackman & Fairman, 1949:98-112

[33] *The Quest for Immortality: Treasures of Ancient Egypt*, Hornung & Bryan, 2002:117

[34] *Eight Funerary Paintings with Judgement Scenes in the Swansea Wellcome Museum*, Griffiths, 1982:228-252

[35] *Pharaoh's Gold*, Reader, 2008:15-21

[36] *The Significance of the Ceremony Hwt Bhsw in the Temple of Horus at Edfu*, Blackman & Fairman, 1949:98-112

[37] *Senenu, High Priest of Amun at Deir el-Bahri*, Brovarski, 1976:57-73

[38] *Understanding Hieroglyphics: a Quick and Simple Guide*, Wilson, 1993:83

[39] *A New Temple for Hathor*, el-Sayed, 1978:1

[40] *Mistress of the House, Mistress of Heaven: Women in Ancient Art*, Capel & Markoe, 1997:95

[41] *The Evil Eye of Apophis*, Borghouts, 1973:114-150

[42] *The Gods of the Egyptians Vol I*, Budge, 1969:430

[43] *The Bremner-Rhind Papyrus: II*, Faulkner, 1937:10-16

[44] *Ancient Egypt*, Oakes & Gahlin, 2004:170

"Lady of the Sky."[45]
"Mistress of Fear."[46]
"Mistress of the Date Palms."[47]
"Mistress of all the Gods."[48]
"Mistress of the northern sky."[49]
"Mistress of the Southern Sycamore."[50]
"Mistress of the Two Lands."[51]
"Mistress of the West."[52]
"The Great One."[53]
"The Hand of Atum."[54]
"The ruler-goddess."[55]

When referring specifically to the Hathor Cow who nurses Horus she was *Sekhat-Hor "She who remembers Horus"*.[56]

Quite often Hathor was addressed by a string of epithets, as in this text from the temple of Horus at Edfu. *"Hathor, Our Lady of Denderah, Eye of Re, who sojourns in Behdet, mistress of the sky, queen of all gods, great Female Hawk in the House-of-the-Falcon, God's mother of the Falcon of Gold."*[57] Many local goddesses were assimilated with, or aligned to, Hathor. The New Kingdom *Chester Beatty* papyrus refers to

---

[45] *The British Museum Dictionary of Ancient Egypt*, Shaw & Nicholson, 2008:135

[46] *Hathor and Thoth: Two Key Figures of the Ancient Egyptian Religion*, Bleeker, 1973:20

[47] *The Goddesses of the Egyptian Tree Cult*, Buhl, 1947: 80-97

[48] *The Gods of the Egyptians Vol I*, Budge, 1969:430

[49] *The Ancient Egyptian Coffin Texts Volume I*, Faulkner, 2007:256. Spell 332

[50] *A New Temple for Hathor*, el-Sayed, 1978:1

[51] *Four New Kingdom Monuments in the Museum of Fine Arts, Boston*, Dunham, 1935:147-151

[52] *Letters from Ancient Egypt*, Wente, 1990:50

[53] *Letters from Ancient Egypt*, Wente, 1990:213

[54] *The Bremner-Rhind Papyrus: III: D. The Book of Overthrowing Apep*, Faulkner, 1937:166-185

[55] *Biographical Texts from Ramessid Egypt*, Frood & Baines, 2007:127

[56] *Hathor and Thoth: Two Key Figures of the Ancient Egyptian Religion*, Bleeker, 1973:33

[57] *The Significance of the Ceremony Hwt Bhsw in the Temple of Horus at Edfu*, Blackman & Fairman, 1949:98-112

160 Hathors which are assumed to be all the local variations and assimilations.[58]

A letter from a policeman at Deir el-Medina entrusts a workman with the care of a cow belonging to Hathor *"Mistress of the North Wind"*.[59] It is thought that this was a local manifestation of Hathor. The north wind was seen as beneficial and cooling in contrast to the hot, desiccating desert winds and so was always associated with beneficent deities.

Nicknames

Djehutiemhab on his stele refers to a vision of Hathor. He addresses her as *"the beautiful Hely"* whose *"shape being that...of mother"*. It has been suggested that Hely is a nickname of Hathor. There seem to be many layers of puns in this inscription as mother could refer to Hathor as the mother of all or to the goddess Mut (the vulture goddess whose name also means mother). This emphasises Hathor's maternal aspect. It also underlines Djehutiemhab's close relationship with Hathor. She appears to him in an understated, unthreatening form and uses an informal name.[60]

In This Her Name Of

The Egyptians didn't consider the deities to be individuals the way that people are so the specific name wasn't always as important as their characters. This made it easy for them to merge and subsume deities without encountering any theological problems. In some cases the deity could have two names or combined names such as Hathor-Sekhmet.

In one section of the *Bremner-Rhind* papyrus Hathor is referred to as *"in this her name of"* variously as Bastet, Wadjet and Sekhmet. In each case this is used to emphasise one of her particular aspects. *"Gold rises beside her father in this her name of Bastet"* is Hathor as the solar

---

[58] *The Nile, Euthenia and the Nymphs*, Kakosy, 1982:290-298

[59] *Agricultural Activity by the Workman of Deir el-Medina*, McDowell, 1992:195-206

[60] *Behind Closed Eyes*, Szpakowska, 2003:140-141

goddess. The cobra goddess Wadjet is linked to vegetation so Hathor "*makes green the Two Lands and guides the gods in this her name of Wadjet*". When her savage protecting aspect is emphasised "*Hathor has power over those who rebelled against her father in that her name of Sakhmet*".[61]

Personal Names with a Hathor Element

Names incorporating the name of a deity were popular as they invoked the deities' protection of the child. These are some of the names incorporating Hathor.

Hathoremheb means "Hathor is in festival" suggesting that the child was born at the time of a Hathor festival.[62] *Sanehat means* "son of the sycamore".[63] *Sat-Hathor* means "daughter of Hathor".[64]

Hathor was a popular name for girls, as was Isis. It was not considered irreverent to name a girl after a goddess. One diminutive of Hathor was Hunero.[65]

Iconography

The majority of Egyptian deities are only distinguishable by their animal heads or their attributes such as crown or staff. Very few had distinguishing individual features, Hathor Heads and the dwarf god Bes being the exceptions. Because of this the iconography of the deity was very important so that the viewer knew who was being referenced. However, Isis and Hathor can be identical during the later periods and only accompanying hieroglyphs can distinguish between them. Hathor has two standard depictions either as a cow or a woman. In both she wears a crown of cow horns supporting the sun disc. In addition, Hathor is also shown as a Hathor Head. This depiction is unique in Egyptian art which emphasises her importance.

---

[61] *The Bremner-Rhind Papyrus: II*, Faulkner, 1937:10-16
[62] *Ancient Egypt*, Oakes & Gahlin, 2004:459
[63] *Ancient Egyptian Religion*, Quirke, 1992:50
[64] *Dancing for Hathor: Women in Ancient Egypt*, Graves-Brown, 2010:133
[65] *Understanding Hieroglyphics: a Quick and Simple Guide*, Wilson, 1993:37

Hathor as a Woman

Like all goddesses Hathor can be portrayed as a beautiful, slender young woman. She usually wears a long wig bound by a fillet (a tie wrapped around the head to hold the hair in place). Her sheath dress is often in turquoise (reflecting her sky aspect) or red or a combination of these colours. New Kingdom paintings often show Hathor in a red patterned dress with a long narrow scarf tied at the neck. The choice of colour was not merely for artistic or aesthetic reasons. The Egyptians considered the colour of an object to be an integral part of it, the word for colour meant "*substance*". Red is associated with Hathor, particularly in her Sekhmet aspect, and at Edfu she was called "*Mistress of the red cloth*".[66] Like Hathor, red has a dual aspect in that it represents both life-giving and life-taking. Red is the colour of the Nile during the inundation which gives it connotations of fertility, it is also linked to menstruation and childbirth. Hathor has associations with all of these. Red is the colour of blood so linked with rage, injury, disease and death. For this reason it was also linked to the chaos god Seth. In all cultures, and in the natural world, red is a warning of danger. Some poisonous snakes and insects use red to advertise the fact that they are poisonous as a warning to potential predators.

Hathor is one of the few goddesses who carry the *was*-sceptre as does "*Sekhmet of the was-sceptre*".[67] This is a sceptre with a head in the form of a canine and is associated with prosperity and well being. Hathor often carries a papyrus sceptre as do Bastet and the creator goddess Neith. The *ukh* staff is a papyrus stem crowned with two feathers and was an important object in the Hathor cult. It is similar in concept to the *sekhem* sceptre.[68] This sceptre hieroglyph denotes concepts such as "*power*" and "*might*". The word *sekhem* could refer to deities, hence the name Sekhmet "*she of might*".[69] Hathor will also carry her cult object the *sistrum* (see chapter 7).

---

[66] *The Complete Gods and Goddesses of Ancient Egypt*, Wilkinson, 2003:144
[67] *The Egyptian Amduat*, Abt & Hornung, 2007:53
[68] *Reading Egyptian Art*, Wilkinson, 2011:123
[69] *Reading Egyptian Art*, Wilkinson, 2011:183

Lesley Jackson

2 - A typical portrayal of Hathor in the form of a woman with the cow horn sun disc.

Whether depicted as a cow or a woman Hathor wears a crown consisting of a pair of cow horns which support a red sun disc. The sun disc is a reference to the myth of Ra being carried by the Celestial Cow (see chapter 3). In later periods Hathor was depicted wearing the vulture cap of Mut, this might be to show her close association with this goddess. She also can wear a *sistrum* and two tall feathers. These are similar to the plumes worn by Amun, the principal creator god often merged with the sun god as Amun-Re. In her role as "*Mistress of the West*" Hathor wears the hieroglyph sign for the west, a falcon perched on a pole. Hathor may also wear the double crown of Egypt showing her royal affiliations as "*Mistress of the Two Lands*".[70]

Hathor can appear as a winged goddess. All other major goddesses such as Isis, Nephthys, Maat (the goddess of truth and justice) and Nut could appear in this form. This signifies protection particularly of the sun god. Goddess are not depicted naked, the exception being the sky goddess Nut. Usually only child gods are shown naked as a sign of their youth. Hathor is occasionally shown nude as the goddess of the West on the floors of Late Period coffins. This was to emphasis her sky aspect by aligning her more closely with Nut.

Hathor as a Cow

Domesticated cattle were important to the Egyptians but they did not choose the domesticated cow to represent the Hathor Cow instead they selected the impressive wild cow which lived in the marshes. The Goddess cannot be domesticated. Even when the Hathor Cow is depicted in desert tomb scenes she is usually shown in her home territory of the papyrus swamp. In the *Pyramid Texts* she is called "*the Great Wild Cow of the marshes*".[71] An ivory engraving from the 1st Dynasty shows a recumbent cow described as "*Hathor in the marshes of King Djer's City of Dep*".[72] Hathor appears to have been one of the first deities depicted in animal form and throughout Egyptian history retained her cow horns reflecting her origins amongst the cattle deities of the Neolithic.

---

[70] *Four New Kingdom Monuments in the Museum of Fine Arts, Boston*, Dunham, 1935:147-151
[71] *Egyptian Mythology*, Pinch, 2002:124
[72] *The Complete Gods and Goddesses of Ancient Egypt*, Wilkinson, 2003:140

From the early 18th Dynasty the Hathor Cow is often shown in a marsh setting either with papyrus or lotus. When shown with a lotus the Hathor Cow may relate to her Mehet-Weret form; the Divine Cow born from or personifying the *Nun*, the primeval chaos. It also alluded to her role as mother of Ra who was born from the lotus. Both the cow and the lotus are symbols of birth and rebirth. A cow shown with papyrus probably refers to the Hathor Cow suckling and protecting the Horus child in the marshes of Khemmis. (Both motifs are discussed in detail in later chapters.) The Hathor Cow next to a mountain is less widespread and was introduced in the 18th Dynasty. It refers to her afterlife aspects as she is standing at the entrance to the afterworld (see chapter 17).

The depiction of the Hathor Cow in the 19th Dynasty tomb of Irynefer at Thebes is in very characteristic form. She is lying down wearing a robe with a stylised quatrefoil design. Above her back is a flail and she wears a *menat* necklace and the sun disc on her horns. The Hathor Cow often sits above a pond or lake which symbolises the primeval waters.[73] The appearance of the Hathor Cow does vary. Statues from the New Kingdom often show the Hathor Cow as red-brown with star-shaped white spots. In the 18th Dynasty Theban tombs a white calf can portray Hathor. A relief from a private tomb shows the deceased worshipping a white calf wearing a red sun disc who stands between two trees, probably the two trees of the horizon through which the sun god passes (see chapter 6). The Hathor Cow is often shown wearing two feathers, or plumes, as well as the sun disc between her horns.

A Cow-Headed Woman

Only very occasionally is Hathor shown as a cow-headed woman. This is surprising as most deities have an animal headed form, indeed for Sekhmet this is her normal, instantly recognisable depiction. The reason for this is not clear. There is a depiction of a cow-headed Hathor in the Ptolemaic temple at Deir el-Medina.[74] The temple of Rameses II at Wadi el-Subua also has a depiction of Hathor with a cow's head.[75]

---

[73] *Reading Egyptian Art*, Wilkinson, 2011:59
[74] *Ancient Egypt*, Oakes & Gahlin, 2004:177
[75] *Ancient Egypt*, Oakes & Gahlin, 2004:213

Hathor Heads

Sometimes Hathor's face is shown facing forwards. This is very unusual for Egyptian deities who are invariably depicted in profile. The god Bes is shown in a similar way and he has a close association with Hathor. In this full-face form Hathor often has cow's ears. Her head is normally depicted like this when it forms the capitol of a pillar or the handle of a mirror. One explanation for this shape is that it originated in the Pre-dynastic Period when her symbol was the skull of a cow mounted on a pole. It may also be easier and more aesthetically pleasing to depict a face in this way when it is incorporated into an architectural feature rather than a statue or two dimensional painting. Whatever the reason this unique form does emphasise Hathor's special position in the Egyptian pantheon. Many deities look similar and can only be identified by what they wear or carry, but these Hathor Heads have an immediately recognisable face. Hathor Heads on columns are discussed in chapter 23.

It is possible that showing the complete face of Hathor alludes to the sun disc which is always seen as a complete disc, unlike the moon which shows distinct waxing and waning states. (The solar eclipse is the exception but this cannot be viewed with the naked eye.) Showing Hathor's face in this way would ensure that she was able to project all her energy and vitality as required whether it was to destroy, protect or revitalise.

Other Depictions

Hathor can also be depicted as a lioness, sycamore tree or a snake *"who laughs with Wadjet"*.[76] She is depicted as a lioness-headed snake goddess in the *mammisi* at Dendera.[77]

Multiple Forms

The portrayals of deities are not meant to show their appearance but to allude to an essential part of their character and aspect. As

---

[76] *The Routledge Dictionary of Egyptian Gods and Goddesses*, Hart, 2005:62

[77] *Mistress of the House, Mistress of Heaven: Women in Ancient Art*, Capel & Markoe, 1997:46

Hathor has a complex personality more than one image is needed to convey her vital essence. Her depiction will vary depending upon which aspect is emphasised and the period. According to Hornung the cow horn sun disc dates to the Old Kingdom, the suckling Hathor Cow to the 12th Dynasty and the tree goddess and cow-headed forms from the New Kingdom.[78] There are many examples in sculpture which portray Hathor's multiple forms. One example is a New Kingdom limestone statue, 67cm high (now in the Louvre, Paris). The main central image shows a cow-headed Hathor wearing the cow horn sun disc which portrays her fertility and nourishing aspects. To the left she is shown as a seated woman indicating her love and celebration aspects. On the right Hathor is a lioness-headed goddess representing her aggressive and protective aspects. Another example is found in a mould used for making vases which dates to the New Kingdom. It has four images of Hathor, two with cow heads and two with human. The latter are shown as a young girl and a woman.[79]

---

[78] *Conceptions of God in Ancient Egypt*, Hornung, 1996:113
[79] *The Gods of Ancient Egypt*, Vernus, 1998:30

CHAPTER 3

THE COW GODDESS

"The Lady of Horns is come into being with joy."[80]

The Forms of Hathor

In the temple of Horus at Edfu it was said that Hathor had as many forms as there were days of the year and in all periods the various forms of Hathor were depicted side by side to illustrate her multiple aspects. The main forms that Hathor takes are cow goddess, sky and solar goddess and tree goddess. A disconnected group at first sight but then it is impossible to force a goddess into any specific form for our convenience. Hathor has a complex personality so more than one form is needed to convey her essential essence.

---

[80] *The Bremner-Rhind Papyrus: II*, Faulkner, 1937:10-16

It is easy, and natural, to ask 'what is she goddess of' as we like to define deities by areas of responsibility or the natural phenomena that they represent. The Egyptians probably didn't think that way. To them the deities were primarily possessors of power which they would use in various ways. The Egyptians would pray to any and every deity about everything but there was a degree of specialisation which was expressed using names, appearance and roles in myths. Major deities have several spheres of interest which overlap but together make up a unique deity.

Hathor as a Cow Goddess

Hathor has her roots in the early Pre-dynastic Period. She emerges from the anonymous sky and cow goddesses of the late Neolithic Period (5500-3100 BCE). To Western minds there is no obvious connection between the sky and a cow and to some, myself included, the prospect of a cow goddess has little immediate appeal. The address "*O beauteous one, O cow*"[81] does not resonate with us especially as the term 'cow' is an insult usually prefixed by 'stupid' or 'fat'. The Egyptians, however, saw a strong connection between the two and Hathor was the Celestial Cow Goddess. To understand Hathor we have to go back to these early times and attempt to understand the importance that cattle held for the early Egyptians.

The Domestication of Cattle

The ancestor of the domestic cattle, the auroch (*Bos priigenius*), is now extinct. These huge long-horned wild cattle lived in herds in the wetlands next to the Nile and in the Delta. It is believed that they survived in the wild until the New Kingdom. They must have made a deep impression on the Egyptians. From the Pre-dynastic Period pottery jars have been decorated with wild cattle. Excavations in a number of sites in Nabta Playa and Bir Kisseibaq (in the Egyptian Sahara) and in the west of the upper Nile valley show that cattle have been venerated since before they were domesticated, for example horn cores have been found in graves.[82]

---

[81] *Ancient Egyptian Literature Volume III*, Lichtheim, 2006:108
[82] *The Complete Gods and Goddesses of Ancient Egypt*, Wilkinson, 2003:15

Hathor

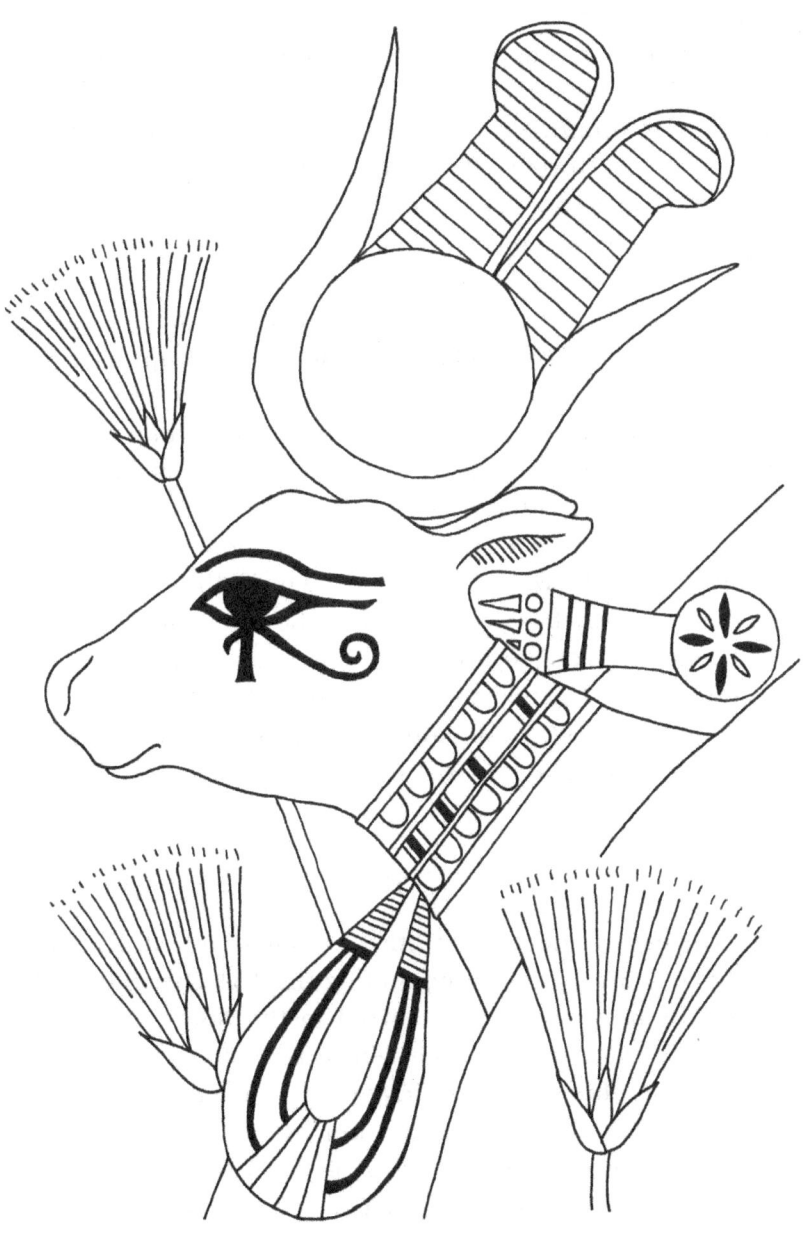

3 - The Hathor Cow emerging from a papyrus thicket at the foot of the Western Mountain.

At about 7000 BCE the predecessors of the Egyptians were hunters and cattle-herders in the Sahara and deserts west of the Nile Valley. It is believed that changing climate from 6000 to 5000 BCE brought severe droughts which forced the cattle herders to settle in the Nile Valley and eventually become farmers. The domestication of cattle is likely to have occurred as the climate became drier and droughts increased in frequency. One suggestion is that calves were captured and then kept around the homestead in the company of the women. At this time the people lived in small tribes next to transient lakes, moving in response to the herds they relied on for food. Cattle need regular water and by digging wells in the silt of dried up lakes the tribe could encourage the herds to remain in one place for longer and to associate humans with the provision of water rather than with predation. By staying close to the settlement the herd would also gain protection from other predators. Some believe cattle were domesticated in the Western Desert oasis as early as 7700 BCE others suggest that the date is nearer 5000 BCE. It is not known if the local wild cattle were domesticated by the Egyptians or if they came from domesticated stock in the Near East. Regardless of its origin cattle pastoralism was well established in many parts of Egypt before agriculture. Some of the oldest domestic cattle remains were found in the Neolithic settlement of Merimda Beni Salama in the fringes of the Delta.[83]

The Importance of Cattle to the Egyptians

The earliest domestic cattle were long-horned. By the Old Kingdom there were also short-horns and by the 18th Dynasty the humped zebu cattle. Suitable pastures occurred in the Nile Valley and especially in the Delta which became the centre for cattle breeding. Cattle were of major importance to the Egyptians providing them with draught animals, fertilizer, milk, meat and other products such as hide and bone. They were also important psychologically, an inheritance from their Neolithic cattle pastoralist ancestors. A similar attitude can be seen in today's cattle herders of East Africa and the Sudan. The people were economically dependent upon the herds that were largely maintained for milk but also provided meat and hides. They acted as a living bank account and much prestige was attached to the size of a person's herd. Cattle were used for tribute, compensation and the

---

[83] *The Animal World of the Pharaohs*, Houlihan, 1996:12

payment of taxes and because they were so valuable they were considered a very suitable offering to the deities. Beef was the food of the wealthy elite and is often portrayed in offering scenes.

Over time tribal kingdoms became agricultural chiefdoms in the Nile Valley and the Goddess, together with the early male gods, became the local tribal deities. With the unification of Egypt around 3200 BCE there was a dramatic change in ideology and the kings took part in re-enacting cosmic myths. The myths reflect the trauma of this cultural change but the Goddess as life-giving and nurturing Cow remained a constant.

The Symbolism of the Cow

As cattle were close to the hearts of the early Egyptians it is not surprising that they used the metaphors of cattle to represent the cycles of life, death and rebirth and also the celestial bodies and deities. The desert was the birthplace of Egyptian theology. Cattle, women, water and milk were sources of regeneration and nourishment. Without water or milk there was sickness and death. These associations proved to be psychologically significant and formed the foundations of the Dynastic religion with the underlying theme of birth-death-rebirth as well as linking the cow with the life providing and protecting Goddess. The inclusion of cattle related artefacts in burials suggests an association with the afterlife. Clay models of long-horn cows have been found in Amratian or Naqada I (4000-3500 BCE) graves.

There was a strong link between women and cattle despite the fact that the herders would have been men or boys. The female was seen as the source of life and nurture as opposed to the male who was the hunter-killer. Both give life and nourish through their milk and many depictions of cows, in all periods, show them nursing calves. The bond between women and the Goddess as a Cow was also emphasised by the depictions of women with their arms upraised to resemble cow horns. The cow represented fertility and motherhood both on an individual basis for humans and animals and as a symbol of the abundance and fertility of the natural world. As the cow was an archetypical symbol of motherhood it was a natural choice to represent motherhood, both in general and with reference to goddesses. The verb *"to be joyful"* has a hieroglyph determinative (a symbol used to clarify the meaning of a word but which is not pronounced) of a cow turning round to the calf at her side[84] and the hieroglyph of a nursing cow is used in the verb *3ms*, *"to show care"*.[85]

Sacred Cattle

Sacred animals represented the *ba* (the soul or manifestation) of the deity and could act as their intermediary. Cows sacred to Hathor were kept at her temple in Dendera and Cusae. The breed most sacred to Hathor was the *tjentet* cow. Middle Kingdom texts from Dendera and Deir el-Bahri refer to the *"herdsman of the tjentet cows"*. In the Hathor shrine of Djeser-Djeseru is a depiction of the Hathor Cow with the inscription *"Hathor of the tjentet cows"*.[86] In the later Memphis cult of Hathor white cows were considered sacred and were consecrated to Hathor. They were called *"she who remembers Horus"*.[87] Strabo mentions that a white cow, sacred to Hathor, was worshipped at Aphroditopolis. He suggested that the old name of the town, Tep-ihu, means *"head of cattle"*.[88] From the tomb of Tetaky at Thebes there are reliefs showing the royal family worshipping the Hathor Cow. She wears a *menat* necklace and has the sun disc on her horns; she is white with red-grey spots. Nofretari (a female relative) is censing and offering libations which are in a blue bowl in the shape of a Hathor Head. Flames are shown in the bowl. The Hathor Cow is called *"darling of Hathor"* so is probably a depiction of a sacred cow rather than a representation of Hathor.[89]

People were referred to as *"god's cattle"*. The hope was that the deities would care for their 'cattle' as attentively as humans cared for their cattle. In one *Coffin Text* spell the deceased states *"I am one of your tjentet cows, O Hathor, my lady"*.[90] This is one of a group of spells in which the deceased takes on different roles in Hathor's entourage

---

[84] *Kingship and the Gods*, Frankfort, 1948:166
[85] *Hieroglyphics: The writings of Ancient Egypt*, Betro, 1996:126
[86] *Votive Offerings to Hathor*, Pinch, 1993:173
[87] *Kingship and the Gods*, Frankfort, 1948:44
[88] *A Stele of the Reign of Sheshonk IV*, Peet, 1920:56-57
[89] *The Tomb of Tetaky at Thebes (no. 15)*, Davis, 1925:10-19
[90] *Votive Offerings to Hathor*, Pinch, 1993:173

and might be the reason for the figurines and plaques of the *tjentet* cows in tombs and as offerings.

Mummified cattle have been found but they don't appear to be associated specifically with Hathor in the way that mummified cats, for example, were offered to Bastet. This may just reflect the value of cattle. If a cow was sacrificed it would normally be used for meat offerings.

Pre-dynastic Goddesses

It is believed that the Egyptian goddesses appeared before their first gods and certainly before the first kings. Gods were present in the Pre-dynastic beliefs of the Egyptians but it wasn't until the time of kings that gods rose to dominance and the king assumed his divine role as ruler on earth.

The oldest period of Egyptian prehistory is the Badrian (5500-4000 BCE) and in a few upper class burials there are female figurines made of ivory or pottery. These are nude with an exaggerated pubic triangle and are made of clay or soft limestone and range in height from 10-36 cm. This is the forerunner of the figurines found in graves right up to the Roman period which are associated with Hathor (see chapter 22). From the next period, the Amratian or Naqada I (4000-3500 BCE), funerary vases have been found which are decorated with the earliest representations of the Goddess. These figures have upraised arms and have thinner waists and broader hips than is usual in Egyptian art. One example portrays a large figure with upraised arms. Between her legs is a zigzag pattern suggestive of a skirt. A second smaller female figure appears to be dancing before the image of the Goddess.[91]

Figures with upraised arms are commonly used to represent the Goddess. They can show dancing and worship and/or mimic the horns of the cow. The wild cattle and early domesticated cattle had long sweeping horns which curved upwards and outwards. In the Dynastic Period deities are often shown with outstretched arms in a way which mimics the hieroglyph for *ka*, two arms held at right angles, which symbolises protection. An associated hieroglyph is that of *hetep*, embrace, where the arms are more curved. Both show a similar outline

---

[91] *Burial Customs and Beliefs in the Hereafter in Predynastic Egypt*, Murray, 1956:86-96

to the horns of a cow and the protective embrace of the Divine Cow. A tomb at Naqada also yielded a vase decorated with a human head flanked by cow horns. Other vases show women dancing with their arms upraised. There is anecdotal evidence from the early 20th century explorers and anthropologists of 'cow dances' performed by the Dinka and Shilluk cattle herding tribes of Sudan. Cattle are central to their society and the dancers hold their arms raised, in the same way as the Pre-dynastic figures, to portray the sweeping horns of their cattle.

The latest period of the Pre-dynastic is the Gerzean or Naqada II (3500-3100 BCE) which provides a lot more evidence of the Goddess. There is a statuette of the Goddess with upraised arms. It is made of clay and wickerwork and her body is covered with designs which look like tattoos. Anatomically the arms are far too long and with the head broken off it is easy to discern the figure morphing into a bovine head and horns. Is this representing the cow goddess in human form? The earliest clear representation of a cow goddess is on a slate palette from this period. It is decorated with a relief consisting of a forward facing cow's head with five stars on the tip of her horns and is also the first representation of the Celestial Cow. During the Gerzean Period cow head amulets appear for the first time in graves, they are made of ivory and amethyst and have a hole drilled through them so that they can be worn. It is suggested that they represent Hathor, although this may well be the goddess Bat (another early cow goddess).

The designs on the slate palettes become increasingly complex over time culminating in the magnificent Narmer palette which commemorates the unification of Egypt by the 1st Dynasty king Narmer. On it the king is portrayed as a victorious warrior. Above the battle scenes are two forward facing human heads with cow ears. It is significant that the Egyptians chose the Goddess to preside over the birth of the nation rather than one of their early gods. Perhaps they realised that the unification of two countries was a delicate time that required nurturing and protecting rather than cementing by brute force. The cow goddess was probably a universal deity recognised and worshipped by all of the population whereas the gods may have differed in form and nature and thus proved more divisive. The illustration on the Narmer palette can be seen in two ways; either as a cow's head with horns or as a headless figure of the Goddess with upraised arms. As a cow's head there is a star marking the tuft of hair between the horns and a star on each ear. When viewed as a goddess the stars mark her head, hands and breasts. However it is viewed the stars are clearly in the form of a constellation, Orion is a possibility. The celestial cow goddess could be Bat, Hathor or Nut. Until we find hieroglyphs giving the name of the Goddess it is not easy to discern which celestial cow goddess is represented.

The Emergence of the Hathor Cow

The concept of Hathor as cow goddess was a continuation of these primeval cow goddess of the Neolithic herders who lived beyond the Nile Valley. At what point the various local goddesses coalesced into Hathor in a form that the Dynastic Period Egyptians would recognise is not clear. It is believed that she was well established before the Dynastic Period but the first written evidence doesn't appear until the 3rd Dynasty with a reference to her temple at Gebelein. By the 4th Dynasty she had become a major deity on par with the sun god Ra. There are a number of other cow goddesses. Some were originally local goddesses who became identified with and then assimilated by Hathor whilst others, such as Nut, kept their identity and cow goddess was just one of their forms. Without inscriptions or specific Hathoric symbols it is not possible to be certain whether the cow represents Hathor or one of these other goddesses.

The Celestial Cow

During the Pre-dynastic Period the link between cows and the sky had been firmly established, as seen on the Gerzean and the Naqada II palettes which show a cow's head with stars. By the end of the Pre-dynastic Period the cow had become the divine symbol of creation, fertility and rebirth with strong stellar connections. It could even be considered an embodiment of the Milky Way. The Celestial Cow straddles the earth, her legs marking the cardinal points. Her belly is the sky and she carries the sun disc between her horns. The long curved horns of the early breeds of domestic cows do suggest the crescent moon although the Egyptians did not have a lunar goddess until the Greco-Roman Period.

The connection between cow and sky might have appeared obvious to the Egyptians. Cattle were important in Egypt which was a reflection of heaven, so there must be cattle in both the afterlife and the sky. When the Egyptians worshipped a cow goddess it is likely that they placed her in the sky, or heaven, as this is where most humans locate their deities unless they specifically belong to the earth or underworld. There may have been the merging of a mother cow goddess and a celestial cow goddess at an early stage but on that we can only speculate. The five pointed hieroglyph star adorns the body, or dress, of Nut when she is represented as a woman. There seems to be a similar idea with the trefoil and quatrefoil designs on the hide of the Hathor Cow which can be seen as an imitation of the natural spotting of cows. Did such markings on the wild cows suggest the stars and thus point to a celestial link?

The celestial cow goddess is also connected to the primeval ocean, the pre-creation waters of the *Nun*. These waters surround the earth both above in the sky and underground and can take the form of a great cow. When the Creator arose from these waters creation began. In this form the Hathor Cow is aligned with Mehet-Weret the cow goddess whose name means the "*Great Flood*". She is specifically the night sky, "*the darkness in the night which is in Mht-wr.t*".[92] It is on these waters that the solar barque has to travel each night and from which the sun god is born each day. This Celestial Cow gave birth to Ra and placed him between her horns, one reason for the sun disc between the horns of Hathor. A similar myth is told in the *Book of the Heavenly Cow*. It is found in New Kingdom texts but is likely to have been written in the Middle Kingdom. After the *Destruction of Mankind* (outlined in chapter 5) Ra decides to retreat from the world, and humans in particular, because "*my heart is too weary to remain with them*".[93] The sky goddess Nut transforms herself into a Celestial Cow and lifts the weary Ra away from the scheming, troublesome humanity and into the sky. In these myths Ra sails in his barque along the belly of the Cow during the day and at night along an underground river that is sometimes identified with Mehet-Weret. The horned head of the Sky Cow became a symbol of the daily cycle of the sun; she was the mother cosmos giving birth to the diurnal and nocturnal forms of the sun.

---

[92] *Hathor and Thoth: Two Key Figures of the Ancient Egyptian Religion*, Bleeker, 1973:31-32

[93] *The Literature of Ancient Egypt*, Simpson et al, 2003:292

As the Celestial Cow the Goddess is the feeder and protector of the king and of Egypt. Hathor is often depicted as a nursing cow her coat spotted with stars. For the Egyptians, the sky is the mother and provider not the earth which was the domain of the earth god Geb. Hathor as cow goddess was renowned for her motherly care and fertility. The kings were quick to adopt Hathor as their divine foster mother. An 18th Dynasty statue from Deir el-Bahri shows Amenhotep II nursing from the Hathor Cow in her shrine. There is a similar relief from the temple at Dendera. In these works the cow is both a nurturing mother and a heavenly deity. The quatrefoil markings on her hide represent the stars.

Afterlife aspects are an important part of the Hathor Cow (see also chapter 17). Cattle had a strong link with funerary rites and so it was an ideal form for the Goddess of the West. Tutankhamun's funerary couch has sides in the shape of long, slender cows with the sun disc between their horns. As she protected the king during his life Hathor would protect him in the afterlife. The Celestial Cow will also help the deceased king to ascend to heaven because she lifted up the weary sun god between her horns. One of Tutankhamun's thrones was inlaid with ivory and ebony in imitation of a cow's hide.

Other Cow Goddesses

– Bat

Bat was an early cow goddess. She was important in the late Pre-dynastic and early Dynastic Periods. Bat is also a sky goddess, the Celestial Cow. The word *bat* means *"female spirit"* or female soul. In the *Pyramid Texts* she is called *"Bat with her two faces"* which probably refers to her ability to look into the past and the future or to see both the living and the dead.[94] She was the chief deity of Nag Hammadi and her cult centre was known as the *"mansion of the sistrum"*.[95] Bat is seldom depicted in art apart from on pillars and palettes as a human head with cow ears and horns. Her horns grow from her temples rather than from the top of the head as a cow's would and they curve inwards. Hathor's horns usually curve outwards. This depiction was the ensign

---

[94] *Myths and Legends of Ancient Egypt*, Tyldesley, 2010:177
[95] *The Complete Gods and Goddesses of Ancient Egypt*, Wilkinson, 2003: 172

of the 7th nome of Upper Egypt and during the Old Kingdom the Bat emblem was worn on crossed chest bands as a sign of rank for palace officials. Bat was later closely identified with Hathor who was the cow goddess of the neighbouring 6th nome, but she retained her importance in southern Egypt until the 11th Dynasty when her cult was absorbed by that of Hathor.

– Hesat Cow

Her name is thought to mean "*the wild one*" and she was a Predynastic cow goddess. In the *Pyramid Texts* she is referred to as the mother of Anubis (the jackal-headed god of the afterlife) and of the deceased king. Hesat provided milk for the child king and for all of humanity.[96] In the Ptolemaic Period she was associated with Isis.

– Ihet

The Ihet Cow gave birth to Horus and suckled him in the marshes of Khemmis. She is identified with either Hathor or Isis. She is often depicted in a papyrus thicket protecting the Horus child.

– Mehet-Weret

Mehet-Weret was a local Theban goddess. She was the Celestial Cow goddesses of creation who rose from the primordial waters of the *Nun* and gave birth to the sun whom she placed between her horns. She is the fertile current in the *Nun* which gives birth to everything.

Mehet-Weret was merged with Hathor, possibly during the Middle Kingdom, after which she was considered a form of the Theban Hathor. She is shown as a cow in a papyrus thicket at the foot of the Western Mountain of Thebes. Usually only her head and neck are represented and she is shown with the facial marking of the *wedjat* eye. The *wedjat* eye is a sacred sign representing the restored eye of Horus (the moon). The composition shows a human or falcon eye and the 'tear line' mark

---

[96] *The Complete Gods and Goddesses of Ancient Egypt*, Wilkinson, 2003: 173

found on the cheetah, an animal associated with the heavens in early periods due to the star like pattern of its coat.[97]

Both Mehet-Weret and Hathor stand at the entrance to the afterworld. One spell in the *Book of the Dead* mentions *"veneration of Hathor, the mistress of the West; kissing the ground before Mht wr.t"*.[98] Mehet-Weret never had an independent cult, she symbolised primeval creation and was too far removed from human affairs to be worshipped. It is not surprising that Hathor took over her attributes.

– Nut

See chapter 4.

---

[97] *Reading Egyptian Art*, Wilkinson, 2011:43
[98] *Hathor and Thoth: Two Key Figures of the Ancient Egyptian Religion*, Bleeker, 1973:32

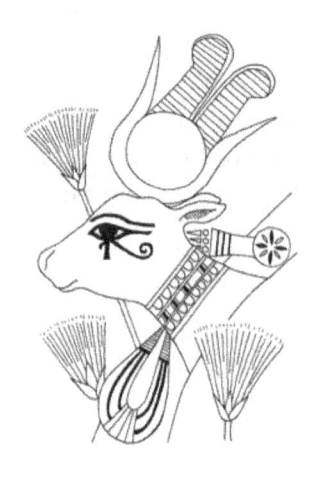

CHAPTER 4

THE SKY GODDESS

"To you has been given the sky, the deep night and the stars."[99]

Introduction

Hathor is the *"Lady of the Sky"*[100] and the *"mistress of the northern sky"*.[101] There are three definitions of sky to look at here: the blue diurnal sky through which the sun passes, the night sky studied with stars and the less tangible concept of the cosmos or universe. The concept of Hathor as the Celestial Cow has been covered in the previous chapter.

---

[99] *The Life of Meresamun*, Teeter & Johnson, 2009:32

[100] *The British Museum Dictionary of Ancient Egypt*, Shaw & Nicholson, 2008:135

[101] *The Ancient Egyptian Coffin Texts Volume I*, Faulkner, 2007:256. Spell 332

Representing the Sky

The hieroglyph for *"sky"* is a thin canopy with supports at its ends. An Egyptian word for *"firmament"* (meaning heaven or the sky conceived as a solid vault) is *bia* which is closely related to the word *biau* meaning *"marvel"* or *"wonder"* and *biat* meaning *"iron"*.[102] This was celestial iron obtained from meteorites, terrestrial iron wasn't known until much later in Egyptian history. Meteoric iron was used for ritual purposes as it was considered to be the material that the sky canopy was made of. Parts of house ceilings no doubt fell onto the inhabitants so why shouldn't parts of the sky do the same? The sun sailed beneath the polished metal canopy and the stars were seen through holes in the canopy left by the falling meteors. The concept of the sky being some sort of ceiling or canopy held up by four pillars is reflected in the temple which has a ceiling supported by columns. The temple was always seen as a microcosm of creation. The hieroglyph sign for the sky sometimes has stars sprinkled on it when the emphasis is on the cosmic sky. This is not too far away from the concept of the Celestial Cow whose body forms the sky and her legs the supports.

The Egyptians had various ways of depicting the sky but they are always viewed as goddesses. The three main celestial images are: the sky as a sea or river upon which the solar barque sails, the sky as a cow and the sky as Nut arched over the earth. Lurker suggests that these were initially geographical concepts which came respectively from the Nile, the Mediterranean and Red Sea coasts and thirdly the marshes of the Delta and the desert.[103] The hieroglyph for *"mountain"* is two rounded hills separated by a valley. This held a cosmic meaning as well as a geographical one. The universal mountain peak of the west was called *Manu* and the eastern peak was *Bakhu* and these two mountains supported heaven. They were guarded by lion deities who protected the rising and setting sun. When Hathor is shown as an emerging cow the mountain is in the shape of half of this hieroglyph.[104]

As *"Mistress of Heaven"*, Hathor is the Celestial Cow whose four legs support the vault of heaven and whose star studded belly is the

---

[102] *Through a Glass Darkly*, Szpakowska, 2006:49
[103] *The Gods and Symbols of Ancient Egypt*, Lurker, 1986:16
[104] *Reading Egyptian Art*, Wilkinson, 2011:133

night sky.[105] In the *Coffin Texts* she is described as *"the Great Lady whose horns...adorned with two stars"*.[106]

The Sky

Amongst Hathor's epithets from her temple at Dendera are the following celestial ones; *"Mistress of the sky, queen of the stars, ruler over Sirius...ruler of the sky"*.[107] The title *"Mistress of the sky"* is a very old one. The Greeks identified Hathor of Cusae with Aphrodite Urania. A foundation plaque of Ptolemy IV from the shrine of Hathor at Deir el-Medina is dedicated in hieroglyphs to *"Hathor Who-is-in-Heaven"* and in Greek to *"Aphrodite Urania"*.[108] The epithet Urania means heavenly or spiritual and was used of Aphrodite when referring to her less earthly and more spiritual aspects.

Hathor is further linked to the sky through the meaning of her name. As *Hwt-Hrw* she is the *"Domain of Horus"* the sky that the falcon god flies through. This is Horus the Elder, in some texts he is comparable to Ra. Thus Hathor contains Ra-Horus, namely she is his mother. As sky goddess she would automatically contain the sun and all celestial bodies. In the *Pyramid Texts* the domain of Horus is a specific part of the sky where the king was believed to be reborn.[109] There are many references in these funerary texts to the deceased king ascending to the sky. Most cultures fix heaven in the sky so this does not of itself prove that Hathor is a sky goddess. In one spell the word used for sky originally meant the waters of the *Nun* which may be another link to Mehet-Weret the Celestial Cow. The *Coffin Texts* reinforce this concept of Hathor as a sky goddess. *"O Hathor, may your hand be given to me, and may I be taken to the sky."*[110]

The epithet *"Lady of Turquoise"* is equally applicable to Hathor as the Goddess of the diurnal sky. In the *Book of the Dead* there is reference to Hathor as the diurnal sky, shown by the presence of the

---

[105] *Understanding Hieroglyphics: a Quick and Simple Guide*, Wilson, 1993:83
[106] *The Ancient Egyptian Coffin Texts Volume III*, Faulkner, 2007:31. Spell 846
[107] *Hathor and Thoth: Two Key Figures of the Ancient Egyptian Religion*, Bleeker, 1973:27
[108] *A Foundation Plaque of Ptolemy IV*, Hayes, 1948:114-115
[109] *Egyptian Mythology*, Pinch, 2002:137
[110] *The Ancient Egyptian Coffin Texts Volume II*, Faulkner, 2007:36. Spell 398

sun god in his three forms. *"Prepare my path to the place where Re, Atum, Kheprer and Hathor are."*[111]

The Stars

"May the Lady of the Stars be joined to you."[112] The Egyptians associated the stars with some of their most sacred images, hence Hathor's importance as a stellar goddess. The souls of the deities, deceased kings and the vindicated dead inhabited the stars.

A large fluted porphyry bowl was found in Hierakonpolis which dates to the 1st Dynasty. It is about 60cm in diameter. A relief of figures on the rim shows the Hathor Cow in a similar style to that found on the Narmer palette but here the stars are shown on the tip of each horn, on the top of the forehead and on each ear. Do the stars represent an actual constellation or is it just a reference to the Stellar Cow goddess?[113] Porphyry is black and white in colour and is associated with the night sky and hence with Hathor. It might have been filled with water and used for divination or interpreting the reflections of the stars, although this is just speculation without evidence.

Sirius

Sirius, the Dog Star, was known as Sothis by the Greeks and Sopdet by the Egyptians. It is the brightest of the fixed stars and appears in the eastern horizon just before sunrise around the time of the summer solstice. It has been suggested that the stars shown on one Pre-dynastic cosmetic palette show the rising of Sirius at midsummer. The star Sirius was associated with the inundation as its heliacal rising (where it rises at the same time or just before the sun) coincided with the start of the inundation. Isis is usually associated with Sirius and her tears of grief at the death of Osiris were said to be the cause of the inundation. However, Hathor is also associated with Sirius and the inundation. In the *Bremner-Rhind* papyrus Hathor is

---

[111] *Hathor and Thoth: Two Key Figures of the Ancient Egyptian Religion*, Bleeker, 1973:47
[112] *The Literature of Ancient Egypt*, Simpson et al, 2003:65
[113] *An Archaic Representation of Hathor*, Arkell, 1955:125-126

called *"the mistress of Sixteen"*.[114] A measurement of the inundation at level sixteen was considered ideal as this would produce the most abundant crops without causing damage. At Dendera she was called the *"ruler over Sirius, the great, who makes H'pj (the Nile) come"*.[115] Hapy is the god who personifies the inundation. The fertility that Hathor brings is thus linked to the fertility which arises from the inundation.

On an ivory palette of the 1st Dynasty king Djer the star Sirius is depicted as a cow and its appearance tied to the inundation. It is thought that this cow is Sothis or Sekhathor. She is depicted with the hieroglyph for Shu between her horns. This may be intended to form the phrase *"opening of the year"*. Shu is the god of dry air and in the *Distant Goddess* myths is interchangeable with Thoth who goes to Nubia to retrieve the Distant Goddess (see chapter 5). The feather of Shu between the cow's horns is often seen as an element of the headdress of Sopdet in astronomical depictions. It frequently has the sun disc above.[116]

Venus

Hathor as *"Mistress of the stars"* was also seen as the morning and evening star, Venus. In the *Book of the Dead* she is called *"mistress of the evening"* but this may allude to her role as protector of the setting sun.[117]

The Moon

The new moon does resemble a cow's horns. Is this why the cow was associated with the night sky? Was the Celestial Cow seen as giving birth to the stars and moon? If she was why wasn't she associated with the moon? This was probably because the moon was seen as masculine and had important gods (Thoth and Khonsu) and so wouldn't be further associated with the Hathor Cow. By the Greco-

---

[114] *The Bremner-Rhind Papyrus: II*, Faulkner, 1937:10-16
[115] *Hathor and Thoth: Two Key Figures of the Ancient Egyptian Religion*, Bleeker, 1973:27
[116] *The Egyptian Calendar A Work For Eternity*, Bomhard, 1999:49
[117] *Hathor and Thoth: Two Key Figures of the Ancient Egyptian Religion*, Bleeker, 1973:47

Roman Period Hathor, along with other goddesses, was equated with the moon but this was just a reflection of the conquerors' belief in a moon goddess and a rejection of the concept of a moon god.

Nut

Nut is the prime sky goddess. She is usually depicted as a woman arching over the earth but, as discussed earlier, she is sometimes shown in a cow form. Bleeker suggests that the difference between the two goddesses is that Nut represents the divine sky, the 'firmament seen as deity', while Hathor resides in the sky or is the physical sky that we can see. Nut was a remote goddess, she wasn't worshipped as such but formed an important part of the divine background and played a significant role in the afterlife.

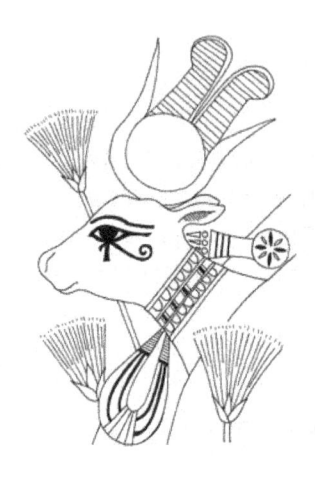

CHAPTER 5

THE SOLAR GODDESS

"Who fills the earth with golden motes of sunlight, who comes alive in the liminal east and sets in the liminal west."[118]

Introduction

From the archaeological evidence it is easy to see how Hathor developed as a Celestial Cow goddess. Her solar aspect needs more consideration but it was one of her roles from the early Dynastic Period if not before. The Egyptians recognised the link between cow and solar goddess. In the *Book of the Dead*, spell 17, it equates Hathor as the Celestial Cow to Hathor the Eye of Ra. Her strong solar connections are emphasised by the sun disc she wears which is draped by, and thus protected by, the *uraeus* cobra. It is in the role of the solar goddess that

---

[118] *Creation on the Potter's Wheel at the Eastern Horizon of Heaven*, Dorman, 1999:96

Hathor can show her more dangerous aspects. The duality of her character is emphasised, especially with the splitting off of her Sekhmet persona, reflecting the ambivalence of fire in general and the sun in particular. Although the Hathor Cow may be dangerous and unpredictable, like a wild cow, this is taken to extremes in the Solar Hathor where her protector and aggressor aspect is dominant. Like fire the sun is beneficial and dangerous, both life-giving and life-taking. It is purification and charred destruction, a nurturer of vegetation and its fierce desiccator.

Any investigation of Hathor in this role is closely entwined with the sun god Ra as she is his mother, daughter and partner. Whatever Hathor's association with Ra it is said that "*She loves Re*".[119] Hathor's triple relationship with Ra is a way of expressing the idea that Hathor represents a divine energy and potency which is essential to the life of the sun god. She continually renews him but he also generates the energy needed for creation to survive. One cannot exist without the other.

The first attestation to Ra is in the 1st Dynasty and the first mention of Hathor is on the Palermo Stone which was the annals of the earliest Dynasties. This does not tell us if either deity was present during the Pre-dynastic Period but it is likely that they were. During the reign of Userkaf (5th Dynasty) Hathor was worshipped in the sun temples and received offerings, her temples also possessed land in both Upper and Lower Egypt. In the 5th Dynasty Hathor and Ra had a close association and both deities appear to have had equal status. Hathor plays an important role in the royal sun temples in the later Old Kingdom and by then her relationship with Ra was firmly established in myth and ritual. Many of their priests had titles combining the two deities' names. Pepy I (6th Dynasty) calls himself the son of Ra and Hathor.

Some authors have suggested that Hathor was not an early goddess but was invented by the priests of Ra as a female counterpart. While I am sure that deities were invented by the priesthood and were manipulated for political reasons I do not believe this could be the situation with Hathor. She was a very popular and universal goddess and the general population would not have readily embraced a fabricated goddess. They felt no compunction to worship a goddess just

---

[119] *The Tomb of a Much-Travelled Theban Official*, Gardiner, 1917:28-38

because she was one of the state deities. It is more likely that her importance assured her a role in the official cult of Ra when it came to prominence. The dominance of the solar tradition resulted in many deities assuming solar characteristics especially during the later periods. Hathor, Isis, Horus and Khnum are worshipped as children of the sun god and as solar deities in their own right. Such an important and popular goddess as Hathor would not have been abandoned.

Amun is an early god, his name means *"the hidden one"*. At Thebes he was considered Amun-Ra, a manifestation of the sun god so Hathor can be referred to as his daughter. *"Her father Amun listens to her...propitiated when he shines bearing her perfection."*[120] He is sometimes considered the husband of Hathor. During the *Beautiful Festival of the Valley* his statue is brought to spend the night with Hathor at her temple at Deir el-Bahri. (This is covered in more detail in chapter 22.)

Mother of Ra

As a sky goddess it is an easy progression for Hathor to become the mother of the sun god. She births him *"honoured by Hathor who nurses the dawn"*,[121] protects and accompanies him on his daily journey, welcomes him at evening and provides the sky through which his solar barque can sail. *"Hail to you Re...the arms of your mother protecting you daily, every day."*[122] From a hymn to the sun from the tomb chapel of Horemheb (18th Dynasty) is *"Adoration of Ra...the young one in the Aten within the arm of your mother Hathor"*.[123] Aten is the sun disc in this context. Hathor can also be seen as the mother of the sun god in her aspect of the Celestial Cow who lifts the newly born Ra out of the waters of the *Nun*. She can also be viewed as the primeval lotus from which the child sun god emerged at dawn. Hathor is mother of all the child gods, such as Nefertem, Ihy and Harsomtus, whose birth celebrates the self-renewing cosmos.

Hathor is associated with the dawn, and the dawn barque, because she gives birth to the sun. *"The beauty of your face glitters when you*

---

[120] *Biographical Texts from Ramessid Egypt*, Frood & Baines, 2007:232
[121] *Ancient Egyptian Literature Volume I*, Lichtheim, 2006:94
[122] *Egyptian Solar Religion in the New Kingdom*, Assmann, 1995:13
[123] *Ancient Egyptian Religion*, Quirke, 1992:45

rise, O come in peace. One is drunk at your beautiful face, O Gold, Hathor"[124] The dawn and early morning sun were gentle and welcoming after the dark night and before the burning intensity of the mid-day sun. *"Hathor the lady of the evening"*[125] is associated with the evening barque as she receives the dying setting sun into her arms and also nurses him. An evening hymn to the setting sun refers to offerings to Ra and *"Hathor who suckles in the dusk"*.[126]

The Partner of Ra

Ra was considered the creator, in the Heliopolitan theology, but the stimulus to this creation is his female counterpart, Hathor. When she is referred to specifically as an aide to creation she is called Iusaas, *"she comes who is great"*.[127] In Iunu, the city of the sun, there is a prominent place in the sacred precinct of Ra for the Goddess in creation as Hathor, Iusaas and Nebethetepet *"Lady of the Field of Offerings"*. Iusaas and Nebethetepet were viewed as a single deity until the end of the Middle Kingdom. After this they are sometimes shown as separate goddesses to emphasise the two aspects of abundance and growth. The *Harris* papyrus has a painting of these two goddesses side by side with the two aspects of the solar creator Atum and Ra-Harakhti (a fusion of Ra and Horus).[128]

Daughter of Ra and the Eye Goddess

Hathor is *"The daughter of the Lord-of-All, who came forth from his body...pre-eminent in the day bark"*.[129] Hathor's main relationship with Ra is as his daughter and it is here that we see a lot of her Sekhmet persona. As his daughter she is usually referred to as the Eye of Ra and she is the sun disc, the *"Eye of Ra upon his disk"*.[130] It is Ra's love for his daughter that inspires him to cross the sky each day. Without

---

[124] *Hathor Rising*, Roberts, 2001:9
[125] *The Book of the Dead or Going Forth by Day*, Allen, 1974:86. Spell 108
[126] *The Prayers of Wakh-ankh-antef-Aa*, Goedicke, 1991:235-253
[127] *The Complete Gods and Goddesses of Ancient Egypt*, Wilkinson, 2003:150
[128] *The Cult of Ra*, Quirke, 2001:31
[129] *The Evil Eye of Apophis*, Borghouts, 1973:114-150
[130] *A New Temple for Hathor*, el-Sayed, 1978:1

Hathor's assistance there would be no sunrise each morning. *"Ra exalts without ceasing, His heart rejoices when he joins his daughter. He swims the firmament in peace."*[131]

The *Contendings of Horus and Seth* tells about their endless battles over the right to the throne once occupied by Osiris. At one stage the god Babi insults Ra by saying *"your shrine is empty"*.[132] Namely no-one worships you anymore, you are insignificant. Ra takes great offense at the slur and retires in a sulk to his pavilion. Not only does this suspend the very long proceedings, which everyone wants to get over as soon as possible, but Ra is endangering life by his withdrawal as nothing can exist without the sun's energy. It is his daughter who sets things to rights. *"Hathor, Lady of the Southern Sycamore, came and stood before her father, the Universal Lord, and she exposed her private parts before his very eyes. Thereupon the great god laughed."*[133]

Such behaviour is unlikely to further father-daughter relationships in this world however it does have parallels in other mythologies. In Greek mythology Baubo exposes herself to Demeter when she is depressed and mourning the abduction of her daughter Persephone. In addition, in many ancient cultures the display of sexual organs was used to expel evil spirits. The psychological explanation is that this intimate act is a way enticing the psyche out of its withdrawn and disconnected state so that it can communicate with life once again. As Hathor is a goddess of love and in possession of a sense of humour she would have been an obvious choice for this act regardless of her relationship with Ra. In these myths it is always a female exposing herself as this is a non-threatening gesture. A male exposing himself may be considered bawdy humour in some situations but it can also be viewed as a threat of rape.

A less sexual interpretation of the act is that Ra was in the blackness of depression and only Hathor, the radiant and loving sun goddess, could drive away this darkness and raise his spirits. The reappearance of the sun after a long duration of dreary overcast skies lifts people's spirits regardless of any deeper interpretation. Hathor's playful enthusiasm and energy are needed to uplift those weighed down by misfortune and responsibilities.

---

[131] *Hathor Rising*, Roberts, 2001:60
[132] *The Wisdom of Ancient Egypt*, Kaster, 1993:242
[133] *The Literature of Ancient Egypt*, Simpson et al, 2003:94

Retreating in a sulk is not the kind of behaviour that is expected of a major god so why did Ra behave in such a juvenile way? Babi was an unpleasant and aggressive baboon god and it probably wasn't the first time he had insulted a fellow deity. The trial between Horus and Seth had been going on for 80 years so perhaps Ra was just fed up of the whole affair and looking for a way out. It may also have been a veiled attack on the kings and other royals who had an overinflated opinion of their importance and reacted melodramatically to any perceived insult whilst not knowing what real abuse was like.

What Eyes Meant to the Egyptians

The eye needs light to see by so it is closely linked with the sun which provides this light most of the time. The word for eye, *irt*, sounds like the verb "*to do*" which makes the eye an active principle as well as feminine. The Eye is the all seeing divine power and the means by which this power was projected onto the physical world and was considered a goddess because of its grammar. This is not as trivial as it sounds. All aspects of words were considered significant to the Egyptians because words were used to create the world and held power. Words were a trail of clues left by the Creator and if the word for eye was a feminine noun it was logical, and inevitable, that its associated deity had to be a goddess. The Eye of Ra is thus a feminine aspect of the male sun god. Because he created her the Eye is his daughter.

When the Eye was dispatched it was the raging goddess and widely associated with Sekhmet. She was the righteous fury of the divine. The creative power of Ra is personified as his daughter Hathor and the Eye is an agent of illumination, renewal and creativity as well as aggression and destruction. The concept of the Eye dates to the Old Kingdom and over time she acquires an increasing amount of independence and personality.

The eye isn't just an organ of perception, it can express personality and sentiment and plays a significant role in religious thought because it can discriminate between seeing and not seeing and light and darkness. At this time it was believed that the eye gave off an energy which allowed it to see hence the eye had apotropaic functions, to repel evil, as well as the ability to cast negative energy as the evil eye. Fear of the latter was widespread. Following a parallel line of thought, the disc of the sun and moon could be viewed as divine eyes. Originally they were the eyes of the falcon god Horus the Elder, in later periods the left eye (the left eye of Horus) became the moon and the right eye (the Eye of Ra) the sun.

The Origin of the Eye and the Uraeus

In the beginning Ra (or Atum in some versions) and his Eye were one being. Ra had two children Shu and Tefnut. Shu was the god of sunlight and dry air and Tefnut the goddess of moisture. Eventually the pair wandered away so Ra sent his Eye to find them and bring them back. "*By my father Nun, the Primordial Waters, were they brought up, my Eye watching after them since the aeons when they were distant from me…They were brought back to me by my Eye which had followed after them. After I had united my members, I wept over them, and that was the coming into being of mankind, from the tears which came forth from my Eye.*" The pun, and theological significance, being *rmwt* "tears" and *rmt* "men". The Creator cried with anger and sorrow, which could explain why humans are imperfect and have too large a component of the anger and sorrow that created them.

When the Eye returned she was angry because Ra had grown another eye to replace her. To placate her Ra transformed the Eye into a cobra and placed her on his forehead where she became the rearing *uraeus*. "*It was wroth against me after it came back and found that I had made another in its place…so I advanced its place onto my brow, and when it was exercising rule over this entire land, its wrath fell away completely, for I had replaced that which had been taken away from it.*"[134] In another version of the myth the Eye gets lost and Ra sends Thoth to find her and bring her back. Thoth pacifies the Eye and gives her the place of honour upon Ra's forehead. However the Eye gets there Ra says "*I promoted it to the front of my face, so that it could rule the whole world*". Thus the cobra, or *uraeus*, became female power personified. Her mighty powers were used to protect the Creator against the formlessness and chaos of the *Nun* and to protect the king, and hence Egypt, against his enemies. In the *Pyramid Texts* the *uraeus* is referred to as Weret, the "*Great One*", or as Weret-Hekau, the "*Great of Magic*".

---

[134] *The Wisdom of Ancient Egypt*, Kaster, 1993:56

The word *uraeus* is a Latin version of the Greek *ouraicus*, taken from the Egyptian *i'rt* "*Risen One*".[135] The word for eye has a similar form, *irt*. The protective *uraeus* is depicted as a cobra encircling the sun showing both the protection of the sun and the sun's protective aspect. Although the Eye and the *uraeus* have the same origin they can be seen as having separate identities and as goddesses in their own right. There are many depictions of the *uraeus* cobras in the *Book of the Amduat* who protect Ra on his journey through the underworld. Their names are perfect descriptions of them; "*the sinuous one...the flaming one...she who is sharp in attack*".[136] Hathor herself is referred to as the "*flaming serpent*"[137] and "*the (fiery) cobra*".[138]

The Eye Goddess

The Solar Eye goddesses are intensely loyal yet they are prone to uncontrollable temper and are liable to act without any thought for the consequences. At times they even turn their anger against the sun god. Despite this they were seen as very suitable bodyguards and were considered Ra's instrument of divine retribution and protection. "*The Eye of Re appears against you...His Eye is powerful against you...She punishes you in this her name Devouring Flame.*"[139] On the sarcophagus of Ankhnesneferibre, Hathor is portrayed as the destructive Eye of the Sun. "*No man and no land sees her...if she is seen a million cubits of fire are on all her ways.*"[140] Hathor and Sekhmet are not the only Eye goddesses. Tefnut, Bastet, Mut and Wadjet are also Eye goddesses in their own right.

The Myths of the Eye Goddess

Legends of destruction tend to focus on the failing power of the sun or his Angry Eye. Despite the praises to Ra there was a deep fear of him that wasn't present with some of the other deities. The 12th Dynasty

---

[135] *The Cobra Goddesses of Ancient Egypt*, Johnson, 1990:5
[136] *The Egyptian Amduat*, Abt & Hornung, 2007:271
[137] *The Great Goddesses of Egypt*, Lesko, 1999:126
[138] *The Book of the Dead or Going Forth by Day*, Allen, 1974:162. Spell 166
[139] *Hathor Rising*, Roberts, 2001:9
[140] *Conceptions of God in Ancient Egypt*, Hornung, 1996:132

Prophecy of Neferty foretells natural disaster and political anarchy, no doubt a fear of the return of the chaos so prevalent during the preceding Intermediate Period. It mentions the pallor of the sun. *"Re will separate himself from men."*[141] The retreat of the deities allows chaos to advance, if they retreat too far then cosmic order will break down.

The Destruction of Mankind

The earliest texts referring to this myth date to the 19th Dynasty but it is believed to be a lot older. People are plotting to rebel against the ageing Ra. He did not create evil but he has to deal with it. Ra's kneejerk response is to destroy humans and start again. Ra calls the deities together to discuss what should be done. Nun (the god who personifies the *Nun*) says *"the fear of you is great when your Eye is against those who scheme against you"*. The others agree saying *"Cause your Eye to go that it may catch for you those who scheme evilly...Let it go down as Hathor"*. After the first attack on the rebels Ra is satisfied and calls back his Eye and says *"welcome in peace, Hathor"*. The goddess refuses and replies *"I have prevailed over humankind, and it is pleasant in my heart"*. So *"that is how Sekhmet came into being...to wade in their blood beginning from Herakleopolis"*. Ra then kindly thinks of a cunning plan to save the rest of mankind from the badly though out order he has given. He orders red ochre (haematite) to be brought from Elephantine, the traditional source of the Nile. This was crushed and added to beer made from barley, enough to fill 7,000 jars, and the *"fields were filled with liquid for three palms [depth]"*. When Sekhmet *"went at dawn she found this place full of water. Her face was beautiful therein. She drank, and it was good in her heart; she returned drunk, without having perceived humankind."*[142] To celebrate their lucky escape Ra orders mankind to have an annual festival. *"Make for them intoxicating drinks on the yearly feasts and entrust it to the slave girls."*[143] The ensuing beer festival was one of the most popular of Egyptian festivals, which is no great surprise. It was especially popular

---

[141] *Men and Gods on the Roman Nile*, Lindsay, 1968:205
[142] *Ancient Egyptian Cosmogonies and Cosmology*, Lesko, 1991:110-111
[143] *The Wisdom of Ancient Egypt*, Kaster, 1993:70

in Dendera *"the Place of Intoxication"* the cult centre of the *"lady of drunkenness"*.[144]

When the Nile flooded it turned a reddish colour due to the sediment it carried. This myth explains the miracle of turning water into beer as well as explaining why the river is running red. Stories of rivers turning red are always ominous due to the colour's association with blood. Like many natural forces the Nile flood has the power to save lives and to nourish, but is has an equally destructive aspect should it either fail or rise too high. Even a perfect inundation brought the dangers of strong currents, collapsing river banks and flooding. Some suggest that this myth might have been a way to explain plagues, as divine retribution that had miscarried. It also explains the origins of beer drinking at the festival of Hathor. Did the myth of Hathor and Sekhmet reflect the way that the Nile stops the Nile Valley and Delta being turned into desert? Sekhmet is called she *"who presides over the desert"* and the *"Door of the South"*.[145]

The Distant Goddess or the Angry Goddess

There are a number of variations of the Eye myths and over time they became interwoven with others. As well as associating deities the Egyptians readily absorbed local traditions into their myths and adapted them to reflect current issues and concerns. Each time the tale was told it was probably different as well as having endless local variations. The most popular deities in any area would have been substituted as long as they fitted the major theme of the story. The origins of the myths are lost but the underlying theme is constant, the Eye is separated from her father and has to be reconciled. Either she has left to put down a rebellion against him or she becomes angry for whatever reason and leaves him.

The relationship between father and daughter can be ambivalent, oscillating between strong ties of affection and rebellion which may result in estrangement. The Egyptians recognised the potential problems with such a relationship but they wanted to ensure that *maat* was followed and order and harmony restored. When the Eye is absent

---

[144] *Understanding Hieroglyphics: a Quick and Simple Guide*, Wilson, 1993:83
[145] *Men and Gods on the Roman Nile*, Lindsay, 1968:200

"*Re longed for his daughter*" and so the two must be reconciled.[146] The myths we have come from Ptolemaic temples and demotic papyrus and no doubt contain some older elements. In these stories Tefnut can take the place of Hathor and her brother Shu can take the place of Thoth.

The Eye leaves Ra and takes the form of a lioness and goes to Nubia where she transforms into a killer. The potency of the sun is transformed into a raging force, reflecting the fact that the further south in Egypt and Nubia you go the more ferocious the sun's power becomes. Ra sends Thoth to persuade his estranged daughter to return. Thoth finds her at the Eastern Mountain of the Sunrise, at *Bwgm* the "*Place of Finding*". She is very dangerous and deadly even to a god. Thoth alternately cajoles and harangues her. He tells her how depressed Egypt is without her and how there will be joyful singing, dancing and offerings when she returns. She also gets a lecture about her duty and the dignity befitting a daughter of Ra. Eventually Thoth persuades her to return but her temper still flares up and Thoth has to continually tell stories to pacify her. She is finally appeased at the borders of Egypt, at Bigeh near Philae, and returns to her peaceful benevolent aspect as soon as she comes into contact with Egyptian soil. They come home, guided by the sacred baboons, to Heliopolis via Philae, Edfu, Esna and Dendera. Her return was celebrated in these cities with music, dancing and feasting. At Heliopolis the Eye is reunited with her father Ra. A 19th Dynasty ostracon shows the baboon form of Thoth persuading the Distant Goddess, in the form of a lioness, to return to Egypt. A Late Period relief from the Dakka temple in Nubia shows the baboon form of Thoth and a lioness. Above her head is the sun disc and *uraeus*. She is walking, her tail raised to show anger, and her breasts indicate that she has just given birth.[147]

In some versions of the myth Thoth persuades Hathor to bathe in the sacred lake on the island of Bigeh. The source of the Nile, and the inundation, was traditionally believed to be in a cavern deep below this island. The water cools her rage and the reuniting of the elements of fire and water enables the waters to rise and the life-giving inundation to begin.

---

[146] *Hathor and Thoth: Two Key Figures of the Ancient Egyptian Religion*, Bleeker, 1973:123

[147] *Gifts From the Pharaohs*, Noblecourt, 2007:11

A number of explanations of these myths have been suggested. Was the myth of the Angry Goddess in the south originally an astronomical myth connected to the winter solstice where the sun appears to retreat south or was the underlying theme the battle between order and chaos? Whatever the theme Ra is powerless and lonely without his daughter. Bleeker has a different suggestion; the Distant Goddess was originally a Nubian goddess who originated in a mythical land. She represented the dangerous and mysterious aspects of the divine who can panrtially adapt to the world of humans so as not to unintentionally harm them but who cannot, or will not, entirely discard her tumultuous nature.[148]

In some of the myths the goddess bathes in the Nile which becomes red with her anger linking the story to the inundation. It has been suggested that the lioness represents the annual flood and that the baboon Thoth, as god of the calendar, is trying to avoid any delays to the inundation. The return of the Distant Goddess was celebrated at the time of the inundation. A drawing from the Saite Period shows a terracotta jar. These were filled with holy water from the new inundation and exchanged as gifts. The neck of the jar was often decorated with baboons. One example has the Hathor Cow on a barque in a papyrus swamp on one side and a *sistrum* on the other. It has been suggested that these myths are an explanation of the solar eclipse but there is nothing in the texts to support this. During the solar eclipse the moon is invisible, is this why the moon god, Thoth, is the one who searches for the missing Eye goddess?

The Uraeus and the Cobra Goddess

Cobra goddesses and *uraeus* snakes are a symbol of life, order and legitimate kingship. First attested to in the Pre-dynastic Period they are always shown as a rearing cobra with its hood extended. *"O You whose head is raised, there has been given to him the nobility of Hathor."*[149]

The *uraeus* was always a divine and royal symbol and is widespread in Egyptian art. The Egyptians were good observers of

---

[148] *Hathor and Thoth: Two Key Figures of the Ancient Egyptian Religion*, Bleeker, 1973:128

[149] *The Ancient Egyptian Coffin Texts Volume II*, Faulkner, 2007:242. Spell 673

nature and their depictions of cobras are very life like. A cobra ready to strike will have its mouth open. There are no depictions of an *uraeus* with her mouth open as she is a beneficent goddess. Poised, powerful and protective she only attacked when provoked and then with deadly consequences. A Middle Kingdom *Hymn to the Diadem* says *"She spat at the (foes)...Her might is greater than that of her foes – in her name of 'Mistress of Might'. The fear of her is instilled into them that defame her – in her name of Mistress of Fear."*[150]

An enraged cobra, rearing with its hood extended, is the determinative in the word *irt*, *uraeus*, and in virtually all names of goddesses. It is worn on the forehead of Ra, and kings, for protection against enemies and is never omitted in depictions of them. Wadjet of Buto was the divine personification of the *uraeus*. While Hathor usually wears an *uraeus* hanging from her cow horned sun disc she is not often depicted as a cobra goddess although there are references to her as *"the serpent-goddess"*.[151]

Is Hathor A Demoted Solar Goddess?

Some authors have suggested that Hathor was originally a solar goddess in her own right, an independent deity who could be considered the female version of the sun god. Certainly she has her own solar barque in which she travels *"together with her Ennead"*.[152] From the 5th Dynasty there is reference to Ra's female counterpart Raet or Raiyt. *"Raiyt, sun-goddess, mistress of cities"*. At one time she was associated with Thebes. One of the *Leyden Hymns* is to *"the goddess Raiyt and Thebes"*.[153]

As Raet's name is the female version of the name Ra it is believed that she was created to complement the sun god rather than being a goddess in her own right. Her full name Raettawy means *"the female sun of the Two Lands"*.[154] On the occasions that she is depicted it is in a similar form to Hathor as a woman with a solar crown and *uraeus*.

---

[150] *The Cobra Goddesses of Ancient Egypt*, Johnson, 1990:10-11
[151] *The Great Goddesses of Egypt*, Lesko, 1999:107
[152] *Temples of Ancient Egypt*, Shafer, 2005:213
[153] *Hymns, Prayers and Songs*, Foster, 1995:69
[154] *Egyptian Mythology*, Pinch, 2002:185

Some goddess focused works suggest that Ra was brought to Egypt from the Mediterranean or Near East and ousted the original sun goddess. Gods deposing goddesses is far too common but I have not found any specific evidence to back this up. James, in his work of the *Cult of the Mother Goddess*, states that a *"group of intruders"* from the Eastern Mediterranean settled in the Delta during the Pre-dynastic Period and that they worshipped Ra. The inference is that they, together with *"Asiatic people"* migrating in during the 1st Dynasty, changed the culture and religion of the local people ousting some of the goddesses that did not align with their beliefs but he does not quote any evidence to support this claim.[155]

---

[155] *The Cult of the Mother-Goddess*, James, 1959: 55

CHAPTER 6

THE TREE GODDESS

"*Sit yourself down under the leaves of the sycamore trees of the Goddess Hathor.*"[156]

Introduction

At first glance there seems little that connects Hathor as sky or cow goddess to tree goddess but the epithet of "*Mistress of the Sycamore*" was a very old one.[157]

---

[156] *The Living Wisdom of Ancient Egypt*, Jacq, 1999:78
[157] *Texts From the Pyramid Age*, Strudwick, 2005:420

Trees in Egypt

Egypt was a land with few trees so trees were a distinctive and welcome part of the landscape. The commonest trees in Egypt were the sycamore fig (referred to as the sycamore throughout this book), date palm, doum palm, tamarisk and acacia.

The Sycamore Fig

The sycamore fig (*Ficus sycamorus*) is the tree most associated with Hathor. Although referred to in the literature as the sycamore this is not the same species as the European sycamore (*Acer pseudoplantus*). The name derives from the Hebrew, *sycamin*, which is a mulberry. The Greeks called the sycamore fig the Egyptian mulberry.[158]

The sycamore was once widespread in Egypt but it is now confined to gardens. It only grows in the wild in Sudan. It is a large tree with an erect trunk and spreading branches and its canopy can be up to 36m in diameter. In a largely treeless land it would have been a very striking tree and the canopy would have formed a natural sacred space which was shady and cool. There are many references to the deceased sitting in the shade with Hathor or in the shade of her tree.

The sycamore's fruit is a type of fig which is a moist fruit providing both food and liquid. Classical writers said that it produced more than one crop a year. This bounty was probably a major factor in its association with the celestial tree which provides never ending nourishment for the deceased. As well as being good to eat figs were one of the commonest fruits in funerary offerings and they are offered to the deities, appropriately enough for the fruit of a sacred tree. The Egyptians produced an opiate from the sap of the sycamore which they called *besbes*. It was used in painkilling drinks amongst other things. Some objects, such as spoons and bowls, are decorated with two figures of the god Bes who was closely linked with Hathor. This may have been a pun on *besbes*. Both the fruit and cut leaves produce a milky white liquid. This *"milk of the sycamore"* would have given an immediate association with the nursing Hathor Cow.

The word for sycamore is *nht*, sometimes written *nehet*. That fact that the Egyptians associated the sycamore with protection is

---

[158] *The Sycamore and the Fig*, Wilson, 2009:41-43

illustrated by the fact that the word *nht*, when written with the house determinative rather than the tree determinative, has the meaning of "*refuge*".[159] The hieroglyph used to refer to trees in general was that of the sycamore and reflects the shape of its leaf, an oval with smooth edges.

This intriguing fragment was found on the margin of a papyrus. "*When the wind comes, it veers toward the sycamore; when you come...*" the rest is lost.[160]

Other Trees

Hathor is associated with other trees and there are references to her as "*Mistress of the Date Palms*".[161] The date palm (*Phoenix dactylifera*) was sacred to Ra probably because its ray like crown of branches looks like the sun's rays. The *ished* or persea tree (*Mimusops laurifolia*) was associated with Hathor and the sun god and with the horizon. In a letter from Thebes the sender commends the recipient to various deities including "*Hathor of the Persea-tree*".[162] The persea ripens just before the inundation and so was linked to its fertile powers and through that to Hathor. There is also reference to myrrh trees. "*May you sit under the branches of the myrrh-tree near Hathor.*"[163] This is probably due to her association with incense and with the land of Punt (see chapter 12). Hatshepsut (18th Dynasty) had the following inscribed in her tomb. "*I sought an abiding place...and found it in Punt. I built a house there on the hillside where my mother resides beneath her sycamores.*"[164] She sent a very successful expedition to the land of Punt which came back laden with exotic treasures. An inscription at the temple of Dendera refers to Hathor as the "*Lady of the Acacia*".[165] At the temple of Ra in Heliopolis was an acacia tree that grew on the "*High Sand*" which was a representation of the primordial mound. It was said

---

[159] *The Goddesses of the Egyptian Tree Cult*, Buhl, 1947: 80-97
[160] *Echoes of Egyptian Voices*, Foster, 1992:xviii
[161] *The Goddesses of the Egyptian Tree Cult*, Buhl, 1947: 80-97
[162] *Ancient Egyptian Religion*, Cerny 1952:73
[163] *The Ancient Egyptian Coffin Texts Vol I*, Faulkner, 2007:177. Spell 225
[164] *The Sycamore and the Fig*, Wilson, 2009:41-43
[165] *The Great Goddesses of Egypt*, Lesko, 1999:125

"*death and life are enclosed*" by the acacia.[166] As Hathor is the daughter of Ra it is no surprise to find one of her sacred trees next to his main cult temple.

Gardens

In hot, dry countries gardens are very much appreciated and the Egyptians were no exception. The wealthy would have had formal gardens which consisted of a pond surrounded by trees. This provided a cool retreat from the heat where they could relax and enjoy the bird song and the fragrant flowers and they wanted to ensure that they could enjoy such a haven in the afterlife. The Egyptians assumed that the afterlife would be similar to conditions in Egypt and many tombs had paintings of gardens. One example is from the tomb of Nebamum, now in the British Museum (London), which shows a pond with sycamores on three sides. These hoped for gardens for eternity could be very large. The 18th Dynasty tomb of Ineni lists 73 sycamores, 170 date palms and 120 doum palms, amongst others.[167] In the Middle Kingdom tomb of Meketra there were small models of formal gardens with sycamore trees around a pond.

Sacred Groves and Tree Cults

Many cultures have tree spirits, in Western Europe they are known as dryads. The presence and permanence of trees engender this feeling. It was a short step from tree sprit to tree goddess in the tree poor lands of Egypt. Because they were so rare, trees were very much appreciated. They provided food and shade and would have added a spiritual ambiance to the area. Precious and sacred they could easily be viewed as kindly and approachable goddesses. Egypt did not have the dense, dark forests which the Northern Europeans had to contend with and which often gave rise to ambivalent or hostile forces and beings. Even the word shade had a different meaning for the Egyptians. To us shadows can be sinister and threatening not comforting and to be in the shadow of someone implies inferiority not protection.

---

[166] *Hathor and Thoth: Two Key Figures of the Ancient Egyptian Religion*, Bleeker, 1973:36

[167] *Gardens in Ancient Egypt*, Torpey, 2010:32-37

Growing on the edges of the deserts and wetlands trees would have been a distinctive part of the landscape as well as a marker of liminal places; those in-between places where the landscape changed and the veil separating the spiritual world was thinner. The presence of trees also marked the presence of water, for life outside the Nile Valley this was a critical factor hence the association with the sycamore providing water for the deceased. In the Pre-dynastic Period tree goddesses and cults were purely local but very early in the Dynastic Period they became associated with some of the national goddesses. We no longer have the names of these local tree goddesses. Hathor became the dominant tree goddess and assimilated most of the other tree goddesses. There is no evidence of tree gods. Tree cults were probably widespread and as the Dynastic Period progressed almost every nome had at least one sacred grove. Temple gardens were also very important for providing offerings in the form of bouquets, garlands and branches.

Sycamores are long lived and the ancient ones would have been held in very high regard. Nothing else lived as long and to the Egyptian mind this will have suggested eternal life and so implied a sacred and divine connection. There was a tree cult of Hathor at Memphis where there was an ancient and much revered sycamore. Hathor was associated with this particular tree above all others. Known as the "*Southern Sycamore*" it grew in the courtyard of the Temple of Ptah (the creator god of Memphis) during the Old Kingdom. Here she was referred to as "*Mistress of the Southern Sycamore*".[168] This appears to have been one of her earliest tree cults.

Whilst Nut and Isis were also associated with the sycamore tree only Hathor has the epithet "*Lady of the Sycamore*". This epithet is an early one, an early 4th Dynasty stele refers to a priestess of Hathor "*Lady of the Southern Sycamore*".[169] There was a suburb in Memphis called Sycamore-town and Hathor was "*Lady of Sycamore-town*".[170] One of Hathor's colours is green linking her to the foliage of the tree as well as to the papyrus, the other plant strongly associated with her.

At first it appears surprising that in some depictions Hathor's sacred trees are leafless but it must be remembered that this shows an uncertain state. The tree might be dead or it might be dormant and

---

[168] *A New Temple for Hathor*, el-Sayed, 1978:1
[169] *The Routledge Dictionary of Egyptian Gods and Goddesses*, Hart, 2005:65
[170] *The Bremner-Rhind Papyrus: II*, Faulkner, 1937:10-16

either state aligns it with the afterworld. Divine life can arise from the dead and so divine life encompasses both life and death symbolised by the potentially dead tree. Without careful examination it is not always possible to know if a leafless tree is actually dead or merely dormant. The growth of leaves from an apparently dead tree will have had important symbolic associations with the concept of rebirth after death. A spell in the *Pyramid Texts* addressed to a *sacred tree* refers to a tree *"which encloses the god...the inside of which is burnt"*.[171] The god is Osiris and the burnt tree is an emblem of death compared to its counterpart the leafy tree. A wooden coffin is in effect a dead tree which encloses the deceased.

In the temple of Ptah at Memphis there is a depiction of an ancient leafless tree, perhaps the original Southern Sycamore. On one 18th Dynasty stele Hathor is depicted standing in trees growing in clay containers. She is shown as a cow-headed woman wearing the Hathor crown with two long feathers. Hathor pours water from a libation vase to a woman standing by the tree, in her other hand she holds a tray of bread. Another stele shows a leafless tree whose trunk is decorated with ribbons. It is tempting to think of the ribbons representing prayers for healing, the same way that cloth is tied to specific trees and bushes in Western Europe, but there is no evidence for this.

As discussed previously, Hathor is sometimes the goddess in the *Wandering Goddess* or *Angry Eye* myths. She has retreated into Nubia and the god Thoth goes to pacify her and persuade her to return back to Egypt. An inscription from a temple at Dakhla is for the "*House of the nbs-tree*", which seems to be the sycamore. It shows the baboon form of Thoth resting beneath the tree.[172] No doubt he is enjoying the shade at noon, as many baboons would have done, but it also reinforces his allegiance to Hathor.

The Roles of Hathor as a Tree Goddess

The Egyptians saw the divine reflected in nature and the cosmos and consequently their deities were independent beings who were closely connected with the natural world. Hathor may have been a tree goddess because it reflects some of her aspects but it did not mean that

---

[171] *The Ancient Egyptian Pyramid Texts*, Faulkner, 2007:229. Utterance 574
[172] *The Goddesses of the Egyptian Tree Cult*, Buhl, 1947: 80-97

she was the essence of the tree that had been deified. The Egyptians looked for, and found, their deities in the natural world. Just as the presence of the cow form of Hathor was detected by the rustling of the papyrus so the tree form of Hathor was present in the rustling leaves of the sycamore. As a tree goddess she can be portrayed in a number of ways. The most common is the upper part of a woman's body rising from the centre of the tree, at other times only the arms are shown. She can also be shown as a tree, with her inscription, or as a woman wearing a tree as a crown.

The Afterlife

The sycamore is an important emblem for Hathor in her afterlife role. As well as the sacred sycamores on the Eastern Horizon it was believed that another tree, the "*Sycamore of the Western Horizon*", grew at the edge of the desert at the entrance to the afterworld where it provided shade and food to sustain the newly deceased.[173] Hathor is the guardian of this tree. In tomb paintings and funerary text vignettes the deceased are often shown sitting in the shade of the sycamore. The Egyptians viewed the afterworld as a hazardous place where the deceased would need to find food, water, shelter and protection. In the same way as sycamore trees growing at an oasis in the desert provided shelter and refreshment for the traveller the Hathor Sycamore in the afterworld provided this for the deceased. Having eaten the celestial fruit the deceased would be ensured of life after death. This is in contrast to the *Old Testament* where the celestial fruit brings suffering and death. Eating the food of the afterworld might help to anchor the deceased there, indeed it might be necessary to stop them from wandering back through the veil to interact too freely with the living. We see this concept in Western beliefs with the idea that eating food in fairy lands or in the realm of the dead will bind you to that place.

The Egyptians had a terrible fear of eating faeces and drinking urine in the afterworld (see chapter 17) and there were many spells in the funerary texts to prevent this dreadful fate. A spell from the *Coffin Texts* reminds the deceased where they will find safe and nourishing food. "*Where is it granted to you to eat?...under the branches of the*

---

[173] *The Sycamore and the Fig*, Wilson, 2009:41-43

sycamores."[174] The New Kingdom tomb of Nakht at Thebes has a painting a sycamore goddess, wearing the hieroglyph *nht* (tree) as a crown and holding a lotus, who offers a grape vine to the deceased Nakht. In the tomb of Userhet, at Thebes, a similar relief shows Userhet siting with his wife and mother under a sycamore tree laden with fruit and the sycamore goddess standing in front of them.

Sycamore trees were often shown planted near tombs and models of the tree were used in funerary amulets. In paintings a stylised sycamore is often shown standing before the entrance to the tomb. These trees were unlikely to have survived in the desert necropolis unless they were regularly watered. A painting of the tree outside the tomb may have represented the physical tree, which more often than not would have died with negative repercussions for the deceased. Hatshepsut did have a grove of trees at her mortuary temple, but she had plenty of resources available to provide for a team of gardeners to keep the trees watered and cared for. Remains of trees have been found by the causeway to the mortuary temple of Mentuhotep II. There were three rows each containing seven sycamore and tamarisk trees.

Trees, whether planted physically or symbolically, would enable the deceased to have the benefits of these trees in the afterlife. They also represented the renewal of life in general. In his tomb Maya, a high ranking official of Tutankhamun, expressed his hope that *"my ba will wander in the early morning...and stroll around between his trees which he planted on earth, then his sycamore trees will supply him with bread and beer"*.[175]

The *ba* (or soul) was often depicted as a *ba*-bird. This is a human-headed bird, often a swallow, giving it a natural affinity with the Hathor Tree. The Egyptians were keen observers of the natural world and could not have failed to notice flocks of birds living in and around trees, especially those in oases in otherwise barren lands. The *ba*-birds are often shown perching in the branches of the celestial tree.

Burial in a wooden coffin would have been viewed as a return to the womb of the mother tree goddess.

---

[174] *The Ancient Egyptian Coffin Texts Volume I*, Faulkner, 2007:162. Spell 199
[175] *The Tomb of Maya and Meryt I: The Reliefs Inscriptions, and Commentary*, Martin, 2012:35

The Celestial Tree

The sycamore was considered a celestial or cosmic tree which in turn is usually considered a manifestation of Hathor. In the *Pyramid Texts* there is reference to the *"tall sycamore in the east of the sky…on which the gods sit"*.[176] This is a similar concept to the Norse World Tree but in a land of sparse and relatively small trees such a concept was not easily envisioned. In the *Book of the Dead* there is reference to two Trees of Turquoise which grow at the eastern gate of the sky. These are *"the two sycamores of turquoise between which Re comes forth"*.[177] Hathor is portrayed as a black and white cow standing between two blue-green trees.

Other Tree Goddesses

The sycamore was also the home of the tree goddess Nehet, her name being that of the tree. In the *Tale of Sinuhe* the hero Sinuhe was Sa-nehet *"the son of the sycamore goddess'*.[178] The goddess Saosis, or Jusas, was particularly associated with the acacia. She was allied with Hathor and may have been a local variation of her. Isis is also associated with trees, but this might be solely due to her assimilating the attributes of Hathor.

It is not clear why sky goddesses were depicted as trees, perhaps it was because their branches reached into the sky and thus they could act as a conduit for the power of the sky goddess to descend to the earth. Their canopy arched over the soil in an echo of the sky arching over the earth. Nut, like Hathor, was associated with the sycamore and the date palm. The tamarisk, which also symbolises rebirth, is particularly associated with Nut. In the *Book of the Dead* there is reference to *"you sycamore of the sky"* which could refer to either goddess. There are many images of Nut giving the deceased water and fruit. Without an inscription, or context, it is not always possible to determine who the sycamore goddess is. A stele in the tomb of Nakht shows two such sycamore goddesses standing beside a mound of

---

[176] *The Ancient Egyptian Pyramid Texts*, Faulkner, 2007:159. Utterance 470
[177] *The Wandering of the Soul*, Piankoff, 1972:7
[178] *100 Hieroglyphs: Think Like an Egyptian*, Kemp, 2006:30

offerings below the false door in his tomb. (The false door allowed the *ka* of the deceased to partake of the food offerings left in the tomb.)

CHAPTER 7

OBJECTS ASSOCIATED WITH HATHOR

"Put forth your hands to these beautiful things."[179]

Introduction

There are a number of objects which are closely associated with Hathor and which form part of her cult. The *sistrum* and *menat* necklace are the principal ones.

---

[179] *The Wisdom of Ancient Egypt*, Kaster, 1993:301

4 - A faience *naos*-sistrum from the Late Period.

The Sistrum

A *sistrum* is a type of rattle. There are two types of *sistra* the looped *sekhem*, or *ib*, *sistrum* and the *naos*, or *seshet*, *sistrum*. There doesn't seem to be any functional or symbolic difference between the two types and priestesses are shown holding both types at once. Hathor was so closely associated with the *sistrum* that her face usually formed the handle. The *sistrum* was a Hathoric cult object from the beginning and was often considered to be a manifestation of Hathor. It was originally confined to the cults of Hathor and her son Ihy, though in the later periods it entered the cults of other deities in particular those of Isis and Amun. The *sistrum* was only carried by priestesses unless it was being presented as an offering to Hathor.

The *sistrum* was sometimes referred to as the "*female soul with its two faces*" a reflection of one of Bat's epithets.[180] One local temple of Hathor was called *Hwt Sekhem*, Mansion of the *Sistrum*, and later gave the town its modern name of Hiw.[181]

– The Shape of the Sistrum

The *naos sistrum* was widespread from the beginning of the Old Kingdom. It consisted of an image of a small sacred building (the *naos*) supported on a papyrus column shaped handle. Above the *naos* were small transverse bars which supported metal discs. The face of Hathor was surmounted on the doorway of the *naos*. The earliest example of a looped *sistrum* is from the 18th Dynasty. It is much simpler in form; a handle surmounted by a bowed structure. The looped *sistrum* is usually made of bronze with a curved metal band supporting three or four cross bars fitted with small metal discs. The face of Hathor forms the upper part of the handle below the arch. *Sistra* are generally made of metal, although there are a few examples in faience. Snakes and *uraei* often appear as decoration on the *sistra* for added protection.

A very ornate and heavily symbolic example of a *sistrum* comes from the late Ptolemaic Period. Above the head of Hathor is a tiny temple portal. The architraves have two recumbent lions and crowned cobras behind them. A figure of Bastet stands in the doorway of the

---

[180] *The Wisdom of Ancient Egypt*, Kaster, 1993:67
[181] *Gods of Ancient Egypt*, Watterson, 2003:121

temple holding a *sistrum*, beside her is a seated cat and a crowned duck (a symbol of Amun). On the top of the *sistrum* is a cat nursing two kittens. It is believed to allude to one of the Eye of the Sun myths where the enraged Hathor assumes the form of the lioness Sekhmet but is appeased by music and becomes the pacified cat Bastet. The handle is in the form of the god Bes. He is closely associated with Hathor (see chapter 20) and is a protector deity capable of frightening demons and thus amplifying the power of the *sistrum* to dispel evil. Then there is a very small gold *sistrum* from the Ptolemaic Period. The use of gold reinforces its link to Hathor. The head of Hathor is shown as a full face with her characteristic hair style.

– Ritual Use

Vignettes from the *Book of the Dead* show priestesses shaking the *sistrum*. Hathor uses the *sistrum* as a medium for imparting blessings. It can bestow power and protect the person who carries it. Together with the *menat*, the *sistrum* was offered to people and deities as a gift and a symbol of life.

– Playing the Sistrum

The *sistrum* hieroglyph was used to create ideograms or determinatives in words related to music. It has been suggested that the rattle used in Coptic liturgical music is derived from the *sistrum*. The *sistrum* produced a tinkling sound when shaken and it is thought that its name is onomatopoeic mimicking the sound of rustling clumps of papyrus. The sound was said to imitate the Hathor Cow walking through the marshes and thus was the ideal sound to placate Hathor, reminding her of her home in the Delta swamps. Did the *sistrum* have its origin in picking papyrus flowers for Hathor and shaking them as part of a ritual? A relief from a tomb chapel at Meir shows a festival of Hathor. The High Priest holds a large elaborate *sistrum*, *ihwey*-priests use castanets and musician-priestesses shake *sistra*.

– Pacifying Qualities

The sound of the *sistrum* was said to scare the powers of darkness. "*I dispel what is hostile by means of the sistrum in my hand.*"[182] Was this alluding to the arrival of the Great Goddess? A wild cow walking through the marshes would advertise her presence with the sound long before she was visible. At the temple of Dendera the king is shown leading a procession carrying Hathor emblems up to the roof on the first morning of the New Year. Both the king and queen carry two sistra. The queen says "*I have taken the sss-sistrum, I grasp the shm-sistrum, and drive away him who is hostile to the Mistress of Heaven*". Another relief shows Harsomtus standing in front of his mother Hathor with a *sistrum*, he says "*I drive away what is hostile every day without ceasing*".[183] Plutarch commented upon the pacifying effects of the sistrum. "*They say they turn aside and beat off Typhon with sistra.*"[184] (The Greeks equated Seth with their god Typhon.)

The sound of the *sistrum* was considered soothing and there are many references to using it to pacify Hathor. The king offers Hathor a *sistrum*, a gift to "*cool her rage*".[185] A Greco-Roman inscription from Dendera says "*the naos-sistrum of your ka-spirit obliterates your fury*".[186] The sistrum "*banishes the irritation, it dispels the rage that is in the heart of the goddess and makes her affable after her grimness*".[187] These quotes imply that Hathor has a very combustible temperament, not ideal in an all-powerful goddess. This is a contrast to the other aspects of her character which are kind and reliable. Goddesses are often portrayed as dual natured. I suspect it is in part a misogynistic tendency to see women as volatile and unable to control themselves and the same characteristic was applied to goddesses. The ability of kings and gods to lose their temper and order the destruction of people is conveniently overlooked.

---

[182] *On the Position of Women in the Egyptian Hierarchy*, Blackman, 1921:8-30

[183] *On the Position of Women in the Egyptian Hierarchy*, Blackman, 1921:8-30

[184] *Plutarch: Concerning the Mysteries of Isis and Osiris*, Mead, 2002:239

[185] *Hathor and Thoth: Two Key Figures of the Ancient Egyptian Religion*, Bleeker, 1973:60

[186] *Gifts of the Nile: Ancient Egyptian Faience*, Friedman, 1998:216

[187] *Hathor and Thoth: Two Key Figures of the Ancient Egyptian Religion*, Bleeker, 1973:60

It wasn't only deities that were soothed and charmed by the *sistra*. In the *Tale of Sinhue* the protagonist returns to Egypt after a life of self-imposed exile. When he appears at court the princesses placate the king, by performing the *"offering of the menat and of the sistrum"*, so that he doesn't get angry with Sinhue.[188]

– Fertility and Energy

Shaking the *sistrum* was thought to promote fertility through its association with Hathor and its ability to direct her power into people and objects. Plutarch makes an interesting comment about the *sistrum's* symbolism and life-imbuing powers. *"The sistrum also shows that existent things must be shaken up and never have cessation from impulse, but as it were be wakened up and agitated when they fall asleep and die away."*[189] Hathor's revitalising powers, directed through the shaken *sistrum*, revive everything which is stagnant or even dead.

– Votive Offerings

Faience *sistra* were produced for votive offerings. A *sistrum* was dedicated to Hathor by the 6th Dynasty king Teti. It is about 25cm high and made from a single piece of alabaster. Its handle is in the form of an outspreading head of papyrus on bound stems. It is a replica, made specifically as an offering, as the sound it makes is almost inaudible. The *naos* is only a few centimetres wide. It is inscribed *"The King of Upper and Lower Egypt, beloved of Hathor, lady of Denderah, to whom life is given eternally"*.[190] In the 11th Dynasty tomb of Amenemhat a woman is shown playing a *sistrum*. The inscription reads *"I offer to you the menat, the looped sistrum, the naos sistrum belonging to Amun, to the Ennead and to Hathor in all her names, that they may grant you a fair and long-lasting life"*.[191]

---

[188] *Hieroglyphics: The writings of Ancient Egypt*, Betro, 1996:177
[189] *Plutarch: Concerning the Mysteries of Isis and Osiris*, Mead, 2002:239
[190] *An Alabaster Sistrum Dedicated by King Teta*, Davis, 1920:69-72
[191] *The Life of Meresamun*, Teeter & Johnson, 2009:29

The Menat

The important cult object, the *menat*, is both an item of jewellery and an instrument. The first reference we have to the *menat* occurs in the 6th Dynasty and it was always associated with Hathor. It was a popular votive offering. The Hathor Cow often wears the *menat* and one of Hathor's epithets was "*Great Menat*".[192] A depiction of Hathor in this form has her head and arms attached to a necklace. She supports a child (either Ihy or Harsomtus) and holds an *ankh* in each hand.

– The Form of the Menat

The *menat* is a multi-strand bead necklace attached to a counterpoise of metal, stone or wood. It is normally not worn but is carried in the hand. Sometimes it is carried by the counterpoise or held in the hand with a *sistrum*, at other times it is worn draped over the elbow or shoulder or worn like a conventional necklace. Priestesses are frequently depicted with the *menat*. It is thought that the *menat* originally consisted of strands of small beads tied around the neck and worn as a necklace. The counterpoise became common in the New Kingdom. It is long and thin and terminated with a round shape. This was often decorated with scenes of the birth and infancy of Horus and showed Hathor as the mother of Horus.

There is an alternate theory about the *menat's* evolution. In the Old Kingdom women wore broad semi-circular collars. To keep them in place a flat tassel was hung at the back as a counterweight. This developed into an elongated form which broadened towards the base. Small representations of the *menat* were worn as amulets and by the New Kingdom the *menat* itself was of great importance. It has been suggested that the word derives from one of the Egyptian words for life.[193] As the counterpoise lay against the wearer's back it would be the ideal object to use as an amulet to protect them from hostile forces which approached from behind.

More expensive *menats* were inlaid with gold and silver, or gems and glass. The decorations often alluded to Hathor. One example has a cow wearing a solar disc between her horns standing on a boat in a

---

[192] *The Gods and Symbols of Ancient Egypt*, Lurker, 1986:79
[193] *The Royal Gold of Ancient Egypt*, Muller & Theim, 1999:68

papyrus thicket. Above this is a representation of Hathor as a woman.[194]

– Ritual Use

From its origins the *menat* was a cultic object of Hathor and was used in rituals accompanying the major rites of passage; birth, death and rebirth. One of its main uses was as an instrument. When shaken the *menat* made a sound which, like the *sistrum*, was likened to the rustling of papyrus in the marshes. Paintings in the Theban tombs show priestesses of Hathor with a *menat* in one hand and a *sistrum* in the other. These were alternately raised and lowered to produce rhythmic music. Ihy often carries a *menat* along with his *sistrum*. Like the *sistrum* the sound made by the *menat* was said to soothe the deities. The priestesses shake "*the menat…in order to propitiate the Golden One*".[195]

As one of Hathor's symbols it was believed to contain or channel her power. A *menat* shaken whilst offering would endow the recipient with Hathor's power. In particular it was imbued with divine healing powers. Hathor is frequently depicted offering one to the king, either handing it to him or lifting up the front of the one she is wearing. The queen was considered the High Priestess of Hathor and is sometimes shown offering the *menat* to the king. One example is from a small gilt shrine of Tutankhamun. Here queen Ankhesenamun, wearing the Hathor crown, holds a *sistrum* and *menat* before the king. The *menat* is decorated with a Hathor Head, whose arms hold two *ankhs*, which visually emphasises the concept of the goddess imparting her power through the *menat*. The powers in this case relate to life, potency, fertility, birth and renewal.[196] A relief at the Hathor temple of Dendera shows her handing a *menat* to the king.

In 18th Dynasty paintings the *menat* is usually worn as an amulet or held in the hand. It was imbued with the powers of Hathor from which flowed life, protection, joy and love. The *menat* also had a favourable influence on the deceased's rebirth and afterlife. To lay a *menat* on someone, or to hold it towards them, allowed its powers to

---

[194] *The Royal Gold of Ancient Egypt*, Muller & Theim, 1999:157
[195] *A Stela of the Reign of Sheshonk IV*, Peet, 1920:56-57
[196] *Reading Egyptian Art*, Wilkinson, 2011:172-173

flow to the recipient. From the Ramesside period they were placed in tombs as an amulet. In Meir the tomb of Sonebi, the son of a nome governor in the reign of Senusret I (12th Dynasty), shows him being presented with *sistra* and a *menat*. Paintings from tombs at Meir show the deceased receiving homage from a procession of singers and dancers who wave *menat* and *sistrum* towards him. The text says *"for your vitality, the necklace of Hathor; may she bless you"*.[197]

– Votive Offerings

Offerings of *menats* have been found at Hathor temples at Deir el-Bahri, Mirgissa, Serabit and Timna. Some appear to have been made specifically as votive offerings. Roughly made wooden *menats* have been found alongside the faience ones, a cheaper option for less wealthy donors. *Menats* might have been offered as a gesture of appeasement if the donor had reason to believe that Hathor was angry for some reason either with them or just in general. As a symbol of life and rebirth the *menat* made a good symbolic offering to Hathor at all times.

Mirrors

Mirrors are strongly associated with Hathor. To the Egyptians they were obvious symbols of femininity and fertility. Are woman associated with mirrors because Hathor is, or is Hathor associated with mirrors because women are? As Hathor is a goddess of love and beauty a mirror would be an obvious accessory in many cultures regardless of any other symbolism. A mirror of gold, bronze or copper decorated with images or symbols of Hathor represented the solar Hathor by virtue of both its form and its substance. Offering mirrors to Hathor may have symbolised her authority over the sun and moon; as sky goddess the sun and moon are held and directed by her just as a mirror is held and can be used to reflect, in effect redirect, the light of the sun and moon. The shape of the mirror is the shape of the sun disc, another link to Hathor. Mirrors are also associated with Hathor in the myth of the *Destruction of Mankind*. When Sekhmet comes upon the fields flooded

---

[197] *Hathor and Thoth: Two Key Figures of the Ancient Egyptian Religion*, Bleeker, 1973:44

with beer she saw that *"her face looked beautiful therein"* which no doubt softened her anger to some extent.[198]

– The Structure of Mirrors

There are no Pre-dynastic mirrors but dark stone palettes have been found which may have served the same purpose. When wet the smooth polished stone provides a reflective surface. The earliest mirrors found date to the early Old Kingdom. They consist of a flat disc of polished bronze or copper attached to a handle of wood or bronze. By the Middle Kingdom the sun disc was the model for the mirror itself so the mirror takes the form of the sun disc and the handle is in the form of a papyrus stalk. Many have a Hathor face as a central element. Handles could also take the form of female figures. New Kingdom mirrors show a wide range of handles composed of metal rather than wood or ivory. A handle in the form of a young girl was popular. This probably represented one of the *khener* dancers who performed at funerals.

One of the most spectacular mirrors found comes from the Middle Kingdom tomb of the princess Sit-Hathor-Yunit. (The name means daughter of Hathor of Dendera.) The mirror is of polished silver with an obsidian handle in the form of a papyrus stalk. The handle is surmounted by a human-headed Hathor with cow ears, the head is double sided and has eyes of rock crystal edged with silver and lapis lazuli eyebrows. Gold inlaid collar bands attach the handle to the disc.[199] Such elaborate and expensive objects may have been for ritual use only or they may have been used in life, a way of showing wealth and status as much as wearing fine jewellery was.

– Symbolism

The fact that a mirror reflects an image gives it a symbolic as well as a functional use. We are so used to endless, perfectly reflective surfaces that it is very hard to understand the importance and symbolism of mirrors to early cultures. Is your reflection merely a reflection of you or is it a separate you that you are observing? There is

---

[198] *Ancient Egyptian Poetry and Prose*, Erman, 1995:49
[199] *The Royal Gold of Ancient Egypt*, Muller & Theim, 1999:122

the possibility that part of your soul remained in the mirror after the image had disappeared. The face reflected is somehow detached from its body suggestive of a disembodied soul. The words "*for your ka*" were associated with the offering of mirrors. Was the phrase to be taken literally and the mirror seen as a depository of the soul?[200]

The word *ankh* was also a word for mirror. This may be because the reflective qualities of the mirror were a reaffirmation of light and so life. The fact that the mirror had the shape of an *ankh* would have been seen as evidence of the connection. One of the phrases used for mirrors is "*a living one*".[201] The mirror was seen as an active object, illuminating rather than merely reflecting as we would understand it now, and so was compared to the Eye of the Sun. They were labelled "*one who sees like Re*" and "*one who sees the face*".[202]

Hathor was a conduit into other worlds both after death and at special times during this life. The mirror was a way of seeing into these other worlds. It is possible that the mirror was used for divining and as a portal into other worlds. Mirrors can distort reality, an imperfect mirror will reflect a different reality back. With a mirror you can see what would otherwise be unseen. You can see yourself, you can use them to see behind you and around corners. Extending this logic you could also use them for divining, to see into the unknown and the future.

– Ritual Use

Hathor and Mut are often shown being presented with two mirrors as part of cult rituals. Why two? Could it have anything to do with the fact that two mirrors could endlessly reflect images so connecting them with the infinite and eternal? Hathor is often shown with two faces on Hathor Head columns so necessitating two mirrors to see herself with. This is also a sign that she can see both ways, into the future and the past, in this life and the afterlife.

---

[200] *Dancing for Hathor: Women in Ancient Egypt*, Graves-Brown, 2010:167

[201] *Ancient Egyptian Mirrors from the Earliest Times through the Middle Kingdom*, Lilyquist, 1979:66

[202] *Ancient Egyptian Mirrors from the Earliest Times through the Middle Kingdom*, Lilyquist, 1979:70

Mirrors were one of the standard offerings of wealthy women to Hathor of Dendera. A bronze mirror from the Old Kingdom was inscribed for *"Royal acquaintance, Prophet/Priestess of Hathor, Mrtw"*. Hathor was especially associated with mirrors in the Old and Middle Kingdoms. Many are votive items and a number belonging to priestesses of Hathor have been found at Giza, Saqqara, Dendera and Hiw.[203]

Mirrors are found in tombs and the tomb paintings often show mirrors being brought into the tomb. They were predominantly associated with women but were still considered appropriate funerary goods for men. The Egyptians took pride and enjoyment in their appearance. Regardless of any symbolism the deceased men no doubt wished to spend eternity in a respectful and socially acceptable state of appearance. Did the mirror allow the deceased to confirm their appearance and identity? Their association with the sun may have been important and ensured that the deceased had vision, and light to see by, in the afterlife. Hathor shaped handles linked them to Hathor in her resurrection aspect. The disc of the mirror was a symbol of the sun disc and placing them in the tomb may have helped the deceased regain their vision. Many are placed to the east of the coffin to represent the rising sun. One such coffin is inscribed *"opened is the face of NN, justified, that he may see the Lord of the Horizon when he crosses the sky"*.[204] One *Pyramid Text* spell says *"may your vision be cleared by means of the light"*.[205]

Mirror dances are shown in tomb paintings. The role of the dance is not known but as a mirror can be used to reflect and direct light these dances are surely associated with the solar and light giving aspect of Hathor. In one illustration four girls hold mirrors and three of them also hold clappers terminating in hands. It has been suggested that they clap these hands and capture the actions in the mirror. The text beneath says *"the beautiful name of Hathor"*.[206] Hathor is an active goddess, the divine principle as a force or energy, so is best worshipped

---

[203] *A Bronze Mirror with the Titles rht-nsw hm(t)-ntr Hwt-hr*, Ellis, 1984:139-140

[204] *Ancient Egyptian Mirrors from the Earliest Times through the Middle Kingdom*, Lilyquist, 1979:99

[205] *The Ancient Egyptian Pyramid Texts*, Faulkner, 2007:264 Utterance 639

[206] *Ancient Egyptian Mirrors from the Earliest Times through the Middle Kingdom*, Lilyquist, 1979:72

and illustrated by movement and movement captured. The reflected images produced by the mirror is one way of doing this.

– Secular Use

Mirrors were used for personal grooming as well as for religious rituals, so for the Goddess of Beauty it is an appropriate object. A person who used a mirror would be reminded of Hathor through her form on the handle and by the polished shiny mirror echoing the sun disc both in shape and brightness. Mirrors also became an important element in illustrations representing childbirth. This might have been to emphasise the role of Hathor with childbirth. Was the mirror symbolically used to guide the baby towards the light and life?

Mirrors were used by men but were of particular significance for women. Tomb illustrations show wealthy women carrying mirrors, in their own special bags, as an accessory. They might not have actually carried them around in life but the painting has to show that they owned them. For some reason women can be shown with mirrors under their chairs. This might be to emphasise their strong bond with Hathor as well as an artistic convention. It was an aesthetic way of showing an important object which wasn't worn or carried.

Spoons

Elaborately carved wooden spoons have been found from the Old Kingdom to the Late Period. They are usually referred to as cosmetic spoons and were thought to be used to hold and mix powders and incense. With such a label their significance was originally overlooked despite the fact that many had never been used and most were very fragile and decorative and so could only have been intended as ritual objects. In fact they were important ritual objects full of religious symbolism. The majority of the symbolism relates to Hathor and then to the goddess Nut.

It has been suggested that the spoon's decoration forms a rebus, a word play using puns and double meanings, something the Egyptians were extremely fond of. A precursor of this is found in a Pre-dynastic slate dish in the form of an interlocking *ka* and *ankh* hieroglyph. This shape easily morphs into a spoon by elongating the handle, formed by the stem of the *ankh*, and rounding and elongating the square *ka* symbol.[207] The mainstay of the spoon was often shaped into the *ankh* symbol. The *ankh* forms an ideal structural base for a spoon with its looped top and long leg. It is also similar in shape to the mirror and the *sistrum*, both cult objects of Hathor. In the Theban tomb decorations the *ankh* is held by Hathor more often than it is by the other goddesses.[208]

Nude girls playing instruments were popular decorations on spoons representing the *khener* troops who played, sang and danced for the deceased in their tombs. Girls were also depicted plucking branches of papyrus. The girls' hair is shown in detail, reflecting its importance to the Hathor cult. Another popular motif on these spoons were figures of "*Asiatics*" carrying wine jars. These might have represented the "*Easterners*" whom Hathor took under her protection. The god Bes was also popular. In one example the cross bar of the spoon is formed by marsh plants and the handle by two Bes figures holding a papyrus stalk. There is a wooden spoon with a handle in the shape of a gazelle and the bowl decorated with a lake containing fish and lotus. One spoon handle shows a girl "*shaking the papyrus for Hathor*".[209] The girl's braided hair swings as she tugs at papyrus stalks and it is very delicately carved. Another spoon is decorated with a lute player in a small boat with a gazelle-headed stern. The boat is surrounded by papyrus and other marsh plants. A girl stands in the boat, her poise is similar to the familiar one of the Hathor Cow balancing on a tiny papyrus skiff so it is possible that the girl represents Hathor. The gazelle is associated with Hathor through her association with the goddess Anukis (see chapter 21).

Papyrus

Although papyrus is not a manufactured object it is very much associated with Hathor and so is included in this chapter.

---

[207] *Egypt's Dazzling Sun: Amenhotep III and his World*, Kozloff & Bryan, 1992:331

[208] *Egypt's Dazzling Sun: Amenhotep III and his World*, Kozloff & Bryan, 1992:336

[209] *Egypt's Dazzling Sun: Amenhotep III and his World*, Kozloff & Bryan, 1992:353

Perhaps surprisingly for what we consider to be a desert land, wetlands originally formed a distinctive feature of the Egyptian landscape. The main wetlands were in the Delta but there were also many marshes along the Nile. Papyrus (*Cyperus papyrus*) was the dominant plant of the wetlands. It was almost extinct by the 20th century but was later reintroduced for tourism. It is a member of the sedge family and grows in marshy soil with its roots completely submerged. The plants reach 2.25m in height, high enough to cover both humans and the wild cattle who grazed there. Papyrus, *mehyt*, has a very strong association with Hathor. It was sacred to her because it was the habitat of the wild cattle that grazed in the swamps of the Delta and the Nile. A ritual of *"picking the papyrus stalks"* was held in her honour. The relevance of the ritual for Hathor (see chapter 22) was further stressed by the pun between *sistrum* and plucking *sesheshet*.

Papyrus was a highly prized plant. As well as being used to make papyrus sheets its fibres were used to make objects such as sandals, mats, baskets and ropes. Stalks were bundled together and used in the construction of houses and boats. Egyptian culture developed in the marshland alongside the Nile and in the Delta and their sacred symbols and architecture reflected this. Early Dynastic reliefs show houses and shrines constructed from bundles of reeds and excavations have confirmed that the commonest building materials of that period were mud and reeds. The later stone buildings were often carved to imitate reed buildings and the columns to reflect papyrus stems. Papyrus pillars were thought to hold up the four corners of the sky hence the papyrus stemmed columns in temples.

The majority of the marshland was in the Delta and papyrus was the heraldic plant of Lower Egypt and was believed to have grown on the primordial mound. The wetlands were largely impenetrable and teemed with wildlife giving them a spiritual ambience. The mythical Khemmis, where Horus was born and nursed by Isis or the Hathor Cow, was said to be located in the north west Delta near the city of Buto. Papyrus was especially associated with Hathor, Bastet and Neith but many other goddesses are shown carrying a papyriform staff. The Hathor Cow sometimes has a papyrus flower between her horns, this can symbolise either the sun or the papyrus marshes of the afterlife. Papyrus was viewed as an appropriate symbol for life. Its hieroglyph was used as a symbol for green and concepts such as freshness, flourishing, youth and joy. Papyrus amulets were common and always made of green or blue-green faience.

Frankfurt suggests that the *djed* symbol might have originally represented a column of papyrus stems. This symbol is a pillar with a layered top. It is not possible to decipher exactly what the hieroglyph represents, some have suggested a tree with lopped off branches or a pole. A Late Period text calls Hathor *"the female Djed pillar which concealed Re from his enemies"*.[210] The body of Osiris was protected by a tree which grew around it and this can be symbolised by the wooden coffin enclosing the body of the deceased. A New Kingdom tomb has an illustration of the *Raising of the Djed Pillar*. This pillar contains the body of Osiris but the ritual also has reference to Hathor as sixteen priestesses hold *menats* and shake *sistra*. Beneath them men are shown using papyrus stems in a mock battle between the citizens of Pe and Dep, the two Delta cities.

---

[210] *Kingship and the Gods*, Frankfort, 1948:178

CHAPTER 8

ASPECTS OF HATHOR

"The face of the sky, the deep and the lady who dwells in a grove at the end of the world."[211]

Introduction

Hathor is an ancient and universal goddess so it is no surprise that she has a very complex and deep character with some apparent contradictions. Initially it appears that there is no link between the various aspects of her character. What could link a goddess of mines and miners to a dangerous protector of the sun god to a goddess of sexual love and drunkenness?

---

[211] *Myth and Symbol in Ancient Egypt,* Clark, 1978: 87

The Main Aspects of Hathor

Hathor is a very physical goddess, one who is definitely of the earth despite her celestial origins. She is the celebration of the good things in life and this sensual aspect is the starting point of understanding her complex character. This gives the obvious connection to love and sex, drink, dance and music. Her sensual aspect leads onto the other parts of her character. A natural consequence of living life to the fullest is fertility and procreation; of the earth and nature in general and of women. Motherhood was seen as an expected and welcome outcome of sexuality so Hathor was both a goddess of sex and of maternity, a more logical connection than the patriarchal approach which venerates motherhood while reviling the sexual act that preceded it.

At her heart Hathor is a compassionate and caring Goddess and this is shown by her association with nurturing and providing as well as protecting. Her nurturing aspect ranges from bringing the fertilising inundation, through nursing the king to the patronage of merchants and miners. It is in her protection role that her dual character is particularly obvious. Protection carried to extremes can be threatening and dangerous to those viewed as the enemy. *"She is come in peace to overthrow her foe."* Much of Hathor's protection aspect is *"in that her name of Sakhmat"* whether it is protection against the plague or protecting Ra against the chaos serpent Apophis.[212]

Hathor has an important role to play in the afterlife which mirrors her roles during life. Acting as a midwife she eases the transition between death and rebirth. She opens the doors of the afterworld and provides sustenance to the newly deceased and gives them protection as they traverse the underworld and, hopefully, participate in the pleasures of the afterlife. Hathor's love isn't austere or spiritual and it is often sexual love. Hathor's sexual power was closely connected to her role as guardian of the dead as the Egyptians drew a parallel between the womb and the tomb and early burials were in the foetal position.

Her generosity and exuberant, bountiful energy make Hathor a goddess of life before and after death and a midwife to help you through the doorways of life and death. In many ways Hathor is a link to other worlds; those of the distant mines and foreign places, the

---

[212] *The Bremner-Rhind Papyrus: II*, Faulkner, 1937:10-16

otherworldly experiences of ecstasy and drunkenness and the afterworld of death and rebirth.

Ambivalence and Contradictions

As with many deities Hathor has a dual nature and has to be continually appeased to encourage the benevolent side of her nature. Like the world around them the Egyptians believed that Hathor could be benign and nurturing or savage and destructive, sometimes both at the same time. From their world view this was a logical explanation of the root cause of suffering that wasn't a result of simple mistake or mishap. According to some authors Hathor embodies an ambivalent attitude having both the 'good' and the 'bad' mother components. This is a common comment, though none the less sexist. Ra sees fit to destroy humans yet he is never regarding as being a 'bad father'. Hathor is all that is beautiful and desirable in women and at the same time she is a goddess of bloodshed and destruction. These two contradicting aspects of Hathor are typical of other Great Goddesses such as Ishtar and Anath. Sexism placed this role on the goddesses more that it did the gods. That said, the original Mother Goddess will have had these contradictions as part of her character as she was both the preserver and destroyer, giving life and sustenance and at the same time taking them. The fact that humans and animals can only survive by killing, even if it is only vegetation, cannot have escaped their notice.

It could be said that Hathor is enamoured with life and liveliness and hates standstill. She is perfectly willing to shake things up regardless of the consequences rather than see them stagnate, however we humans wish the opposite.

All the most important deities have different names and multiple identities and some, such as Hathor, have a number of distinct roles without showing one aspect which could be considered primary. In general the greater and older the deity the wider the range of associations and identities. The Egyptians weren't worried if aspects of their deities or myths were contradictory and incompatible. They saw this as a way of understanding and approaching the mysterious and unknowable deities. Each view contained part of the truth. In any case, these tensions and contradictions made the deities more of a personality and so easier to relate to.

The Sensual Aspects of Hathor

In this context the term sensual is taken to mean something which appeals to the senses, something in the environment that can be physically interpreted and interacted with. This can be as innocent as enjoying a cool breeze or listening to bird song through to the ecstasies of sex and intoxication. Although life in Egypt was hard, especially for the poor, they come across as a people who were optimistic and who enjoyed life and its pleasures. They were too close to the very real risk of starvation and drought to disregard the blessings of abundant food and drink. They experienced no divide between the sacred and the secular and this fundamental part of their character was reflected in their religion at both the state and the personal level.

Some aspects of a sensual connection to the divine can be seen in Roman Catholic and other high churches where altars are decorated with flowers, music is an important component of the liturgy and incense is used liberally. Wild ecstatic dancing however is not appreciated although it was used by sects such as the Shakers to allow individuals to open to the divine and was frowned upon by the religious establishment for this very reason. For the Egyptians the divine could be experienced through their senses. Enjoyment was seen as worship. If you were self denying and unhappy it showed that you were dissatisfied with what the deities had provided, that their presence didn't bring you happiness. There are frequent exhortations to rejoice and be merry and to join with the cosmic song of praise. *"Heaven, sun and moon, and earth rejoice when they sense the goddess, the animals dance in exultation, Egypt and all the lands praise her, the whole world praises her."*[213]

This attitude allowed the Egyptians to enjoy life and be religious at the same time. A drink with friends or an evening with a lover could allow you to connect to the sacred powers of the world. This allowed Hathor in particular to be invoked in secular pleasures. The deities which were worshipped in this way were not the remote superior ones who set themselves apart from humanity. They were the ones such as Hathor who were part of life and regeneration, physical deities who understood and appreciated such pleasures. In the *Book of the Dead* (spell 175) Osiris complains to Atum about his non-corporeal existence

---

[213] *Enjoying the Pleasures of Sensation: Reflections on a Significant Feature of Egyptian Religion*, Finnestad, 1999:114

now that he is dead. When Atum tells Osiris to enjoy its peace, Osiris asks how given that he can no longer enjoy making love.

Some restraint is needed otherwise society will collapse and in the Moral Instruction literature there are many exhortations towards moderate behaviour. The positive energy of Hathor has to be maintained without straying into the destructive sphere of influence of Seth which leads from cheerful intoxication to self-destructive alcoholism and from making love to rape and sexual abuse. Hathor is the goddess of love, sex, the playful liveliness of games and dance and of drunken ecstasy. There is a careful balance to strike here, a tightrope between the Hathoric delight in sex and drinking and the more Sethian destructive drug-drink-sex addiction and the puritan abstinence and repression. Hathor has both positive and negative attributes and can be seen to represent the ambivalence of activities such as drinking (social lubrication or destructive alcoholism) and sex (normal enjoyment of a natural instinct or sexual abuse and pornography).

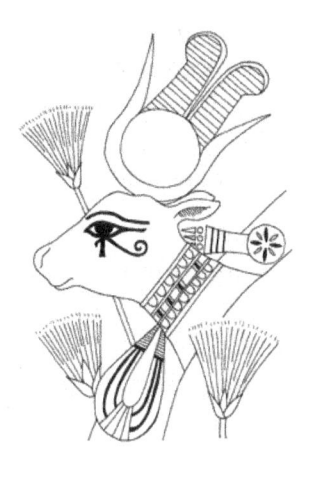

CHAPTER 9
MUSIC & DANCE

"Thou art the lady of the dance, the mistress of the songs and dances accompanied by the lute, whose face shines each day, who knows no sorrow."[214]

Introduction

Hathor's patronage of music and dance and her love of the *sistrum* were seen as a manifestation of her sexual power. While not all music can be even remotely aligned to sex, dance often can hence the puritan horror of dance and rousing music. Hathor in contrast encourages sensual joy by music and dancing.

---

[214] *Hathor and Thoth: Two Key Figures of the Ancient Egyptian Religion,* Bleeker, 1973:54

Sound has an important place in religious rituals and festivals throughout history and it was central to Egyptian worship. All deities enjoyed music and temples always had musicians, singers and dancers whose primary role was to please the deities as well as to enhance communication with the divine. Hathor seems to have enjoyed music more than the others; she was the "*mistress of music*"[215] and the "*Mistress of the songs*".[216] Even the gods Bes and Ihy played for her and so music and song played a major role in the worship of Hathor.

The deities were considered present in both the music and the song. Producing and listening to music was a way of conversing with them and allowed the divine presence to enter through the ear. Rhythmic, repetitive music might have been used to induce mild trance states, or else it was a side effect. Music pleased and soothed the deities and drove away evil. Dance, music and song are some of the oldest methods of expressing emotions and reactions so sacred dance was an important aspect of many ancient religions. They also tell stories, teach and help express religious beliefs.

Dance

Dance was probably of sacred origin and it was considered essential in both state and domestic religion. It was used in the service of the deities and especially to commune with Hathor. As dance was one of her sacred gifts it was a logical choice when it came to both worshipping and communicating with the Goddess. Dancing is a way to please Hathor, bring her joy and pay her homage. Dances were an important part of her cult. Funerary dances were designed to assist the deceased. They were also used to promote fertility and for entertainment, a gift from the "*mistress of the dance, queen of happiness*".[217]

---

[215] *Daughters of Isis*, Tyldesley, 1995:129
[216] *Hathor and Thoth: Two Key Figures of the Ancient Egyptian Religion*, Bleeker, 1973:54
[217] *Dancing for Hathor: Women in Ancient Egypt*, Graves-Brown, 2010:167

- Dance As Worship

Hathor's presence moved her worshippers to sing and dance in joyful adoration. The following is from a hymn to Hathor. *"O those lords who visit heaven. O those divine ones who visit heaven, O commoners who visit heaven, who (always) jubilate in the presence of Hathor and who (always) desire to see and support her beauty...they will repeat sacred music for Hathor...I am indeed one who (always) gives arousing, praising and music-making to Hathor every day, every hour or whenever she desires."*[218] Hathor appreciated the music and dance of her worshippers. A soapstone bowl dating to 525 BCE (in the British Museum, London) depicts a feast for Hathor. The musicians, male and female, are wearing flowers. A Late Period hymn explains why.

> *"We laud thee with delightful songs,*
> *For thou art the mistress of jubilation,*
> *The mistress of music, the queen of harp-playing.*
> *The lady of the dance,*
> *The mistress of the chorus-dance, the queen of wreath-weaving."*[219]

Another hymn to Hathor from the temple of Medamud, on the occasion of the winter solstice, expresses similar sentiments.

> *"Come, oh Golden One, who feeds on praise,*
> *because the food of her desire is dancing,*
> *who shines on the festival at the time of lighting [the lamps],*
> *who is content with the dancing at night."*[220]

The tomb of Kheruef shows dances for Hathor on the *heb-sed* festival of Amenhotep III. This festival was designed to renew the king's vitality. A relief from Deir el-Bahri shows the New Year's Day procession and a troupe of Libyans performing their dances.

Hathor personifies the effervescence of divine life and passion so it is not surprising that dances to her were often enthusiastic, tending to the ecstatic. One text at Dendera describes dances held at night. The

---

[218] *The Prayers of Wakh-ankh-antef-Aa*, Goedicke, 1991:235-253

[219] *Hathor and Thoth: Two Key Figures of the Ancient Egyptian Religion*, Bleeker, 1973:54

[220] *The Great Goddesses of Egypt*, Lesko, 1999:126

women *"entranced by wine, move their legs rapidly"*.[221] It is thought that this type of dance encouraged the dancers to enter an altered state of consciousness during the ritual. Watching their movements while listening to the loud rhythmic music may have had the same effect on others. Judging from the illustrations of the *Beautiful Festival of the Valley* some of the dances were more like acrobatic displays. Very energetic dancing took place at the fortnight long festival to commemorate the return of the Wandering Goddess from Nubia. The tomb of Antef-iker shows dancing at the Hathor festival. The erotic dances are designed to calm and propitiate Hathor. When in her Sekhmet aspect she sometimes had an inflammable temper and was easily angered.

5 - Girls performing a dance for Hathor from the Tomb of the Dancers, Thebes.

---

[221] *Hathor and Thoth: Two Key Figures of the Ancient Egyptian Religion*, Bleeker, 1973:58

– Funerary Dances

In complete contrast to Western culture, which would be disturbed by such activity, dance was an important element of funerary rites. Acrobatic dancing is depicted in the 6th Dynasty *mastaba* of Ka-gemni at Saqqara while the tomb of Mereru-ka shows the complicated steps of the dances. These scenes are usually accompanied by invocations to Hathor.[222] Priests of Hathor at Meir are shown honouring the dead with a ritual dance while women dance for Hathor. A wall painting from a 17th Dynasty tomb at Thebes gives a detailed and expressive depiction of such a dance. It is now in the Ashmolean Museum, Oxford. The female dancers are shown in various dance positions and it has the feel of a modern cartoon or comic strip. Girls in the top row are clapping the rhythm of the dance and the inscription describes them as *"making gladness"*.[223] Some of the more energetic dancers are snapping their fingers.

Hathor dances are shown in the 6th Dynasty tombs of both men and women. Those in the tomb of Iy-mery explain that the dancing was for the *Festival of Eternity* and its references to *"gold movement"* suggest an invocation to Hathor. In the tomb of Antefoker (a vizier of Senusret I) and his wife paintings show female lute players and drummers as well as dancers. The accompanying inscription states that *"the doors of Heaven open…The Golden Goddess has come"*.[224]

In the 1920's an archaeologist camping near Hu witnessed a funeral dance carried out by local women. After the funeral a band of women processed to the cemetery singing and shaking tambourines. At regular intervals they would stop, form a circle and dance jumping up and down and beating the tambourines. He debated whether this was a survival of the Hathor ceremony shown on tomb reliefs.[225]

---

[222] *Hathor and Thoth: Two Key Figures of the Ancient Egyptian Religion*, Bleeker, 1973:57
[223] *Ancient Egypt and Nubia*, Whitehouse, 2009:69-70
[224] *The Tomb of Antefoker*, Davies, 1920:24
[225] *Hathor Dances*, Mace, 1920:297

– Other Types of Dances

Female friends and relatives of the mother would dance at the birth of the baby; to aid delivery and to try and take the mother's mind off her labour and to celebrate the birth. Dances will have been performed at ordinary gatherings. Most people enjoy either dancing or watching it. As well as providing entertainment it may well have accompanied the telling of myths or traditional stories.

– The Dancers

At certain rituals the king dances in front of Hathor as part of the offerings. At the *Festival of Drunkenness* the king danced before Hathor to "*expel her anger*". To Hathor dance was the "*food of the heart*".[226]

> "*The pharaoh comes to dance*
> *He comes to sing (for thee)…*
> *His heart is sincere, his body in order,*
> *There is no darkness in his breast,*
> *O, his mistress, see how he dances,*
> *O, bride of Horus, see how he skips.*"[227]

As dancing is strongly associated with Hathor the dancers would at times impersonate her. In a number of 5th and 6th Dynasty tomb scenes dancers sing and clap and invoke Hathor by name or with the epithet "*Golden One*". Some individuals wear lion-headed masks and may be imitating Hathor, Sekhmet or Bes. The tomb of Mereuka at Saqqara shows girls playing games holding mirrors and clappers. The inscription explains that they are playing "*Hathor's dancing game*".[228]

Music

Obviously no details of the music survive, but from the inscriptions we can safely assume that a lot was enthusiastic and rhythmic. There are hints that music and dance were part of ecstatic religion and

---

[226] *The Gods and Symbols of Ancient Egypt*, Lurker, 1986:45
[227] *Hathor and Thoth: Two Key Figures of the Ancient Egyptian Religion*, Bleeker, 1973:55
[228] *Dancing for Hathor: Women in Ancient Egypt*, Graves-Brown, 2010:96

Hathor is of course closely associated with such direct communication with the divine. It would have been an amazing experience standing in a dark temple, thick with incense, whilst listening to the music although it would have been an experience that ordinary Egyptians would not have been permitted to indulge in.

Ecstatic religion is hard to prove but music, dance and intoxication are all associated with breaking down the barriers between this world and that of the divine or the afterlife. Ecstatic emotion is one means of transcending this world. Music was considered an essential part of religious ritual as it maintained cosmic order and restored balance. The *sistrum* in particular was shaken to drive away any hostile forces and to revive the deities. Certain types of music have immediate relaxing or uplifting effects and what soothed humans would do the same for the deities. One myth tells how Hathor of Philae was angry and sulking. She was appeased by Bes who played the tambourine and harp for her. He is depicted doing this on columns in her temple at Philae. [229] During the Greco-Roman Period it was said that the Egyptian priests and priestesses sang to their deities three or four times a day. Many scenes show individuals shaking a *sistrum* before a statue of a deity.

– Musical Instruments

There are references, either in word or image, to the following instruments; *sistrum*, tambourine, lyre, harp, drum, castanets and clappers. The *sistrum* was only used for cultic purposes. The *menat* necklace was also used as a percussion instrument. (The latter two have been covered in chapter 7). Clapper sticks were common and were used as percussion instruments. These were usually made in the shape of an arm and hand and were made of bone, ivory or wood. Many were decorated with the head of Hathor because she is the Mistress of Dance and Music. The divine hand had creative powers as well as protective ones and Hathor, who embodies the female creative principle, was known as the "*Hand of Atum*" (see chapter 10). Clappers were not solely used for her rituals. There are many examples of ivory clappers, particularly from the 18th Dynasty. From a cemetery near Akhmim came an ivory clapper with a Hathor Head. It is very finely carved and there are traces of red pigment on the head. One pair of clappers was

---

[229] *Ancient Egypt*, Oakes & Gahlin, 2004:477

made of ebony. This wood had been imported from sub-Saharan Africa making it a very expensive, luxury item.

Despite enjoying music very few deities actually play an instrument. Hathor's son with Horus the Elder, Ihy, personified the jubilation which came from listening to the *sistrum*. His name means "*sistrum player*" and he sometimes holds a *sistrum* and *menat* necklace. Bes, who had close ties with Hathor, was the only god who was frequently depicted playing an instrument; usually a tambourine or a harp. However, a text from the temple of Edfu tells how "*the gods play the sistrum for her (Hathor), the goddesses dance for her to dispel her bad temper*".[230]

The human voice was also highly significant. A choir accompanied the High Priest as he performed the daily rituals and made offerings. They also entertained the deity and accompanied them during processions. A Middle Kingdom song to Hathor starts "*Holy music for Hathor, music a million times, because you love music*".[231] From an inscription on the walls of the temple of Amun in Karnak is a song in honour of Hathor. "*Come that I may make for you jubilation at twilight and music in the evening. O Hathor! You are exalted in the hair of Re...for to you has been given the sky, the deep night and the stars. Great is her majesty when she is happy.*"[232]

– The Musicians

Ptolemaic reliefs show female musicians playing drums, they wear the headdress of Hathor. An inscription from the Edfu temple suggests that all Ptolemaic temples had musician-priestesses who entertained the deities; specifically they "*rattle the sistrum before them to make music for their kas*".[233] A relief on a tomb-chapel at Thebes depicts a festival of Hathor. *Ihwey*-priests click castanets and musician-priestesses shake *sistra*. A High Priest is shown holding a large elaborate *sistrum* to dispel any hostile forces.

---

[230] *Hathor and Thoth: Two Key Figures of the Ancient Egyptian Religion*, Bleeker, 1973:57
[231] *Daughters of Isis*, Tyldesley, 1995:128
[232] *The Life of Meresamun*, Teeter & Johnson, 2009:32
[233] *On the Position of Women in the Egyptian Hierarchy*, Blackman, 1921:8-30

– The Singers

In the early Old Kingdom virtually all the temple singers were female and had the title *heset*, singer. Most of these were part of the *khener*, a professional troop associated with Hathor, Bastet, Wepwawet (a jackal-headed god) and Horus. By the middle of the Old Kingdom men were included in the *khener*. During the Middle Kingdom there are references to a singer-priestess, the *shemayet*, although it is not clear how her role differed from that of the *heset*. These titles had disappeared by the New Kingdom. Originally most of the singers and singer-priestess came from the elite families. By the 19th and 20th Dynasties they came from a wider social background and included the wives and daughters of scribes and military men. They were often married to priests, though not necessarily those serving the same deity. The position of temple singer was a very prestigious one and women favoured such titles over their other ones. Like the rest of the religious orders the temple singers were hierarchical and highly organised.

"*I am he who makes the singer waken music for Hathor, every day at any hour she wishes.*"[234]

---

[234] *Ancient Egyptian Literature Volume I*, Lichtheim, 2006:95

CHAPTER 10

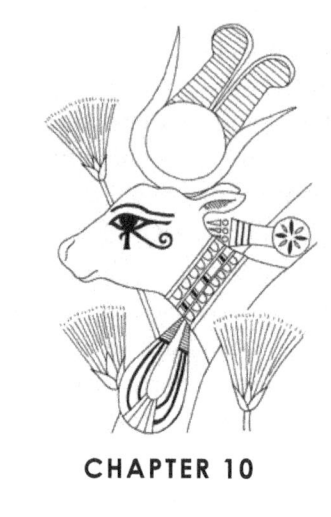

LOVE & SEX

"I worship my mistress, for I have seen her beauty."[235]

Introduction

Hathor was strongly associated with love and female sexuality and it was for this reason that the Greeks associated her with Aphrodite, their goddess of love and beauty. Hathor is the provider of sexual pleasure and joy and its usual consequence of pregnancy. The latter is dealt with in chapter 13. As well as being present in romantic love and the comfortable love of married couples she was associated with the turmoil and ecstasy of physical desire. This is another reflection of the contradictory parts of her personality as the latter can be destructive if not tempered. Her overt sexuality is seen in the *Contendings of Horus and Seth*. Ra has been insulted by Baba and withdraws and sulks but Hathor cheers him up by exposing herself. (See chapter 5.) Despite being the goddess of love Hathor was not shown naked, very few Egyptian deities were.

---

[235] *The Ancient Egyptian Coffin Texts Volume II*, Faulkner, 2007:128. Spell 484

The Hand of Atum

The Creator deity is usually considered to be composed of both the male and female principles but our language struggles with the concept so the Creator usually ends up depicted as male. In the Egyptians' creation mythology there were three principal methods of creation; intellectually by using the spoken word as by Thoth, crafted as by the potter god Khnum or biologically by Atum. The latter causes problems for a single god and Atum has to copulate with himself to begin the process of creation. Hathor represents the female creative principle and was called the *"hand of Atum"*. As the hand of Atum she is Hathor Nebethetepet or Iusaas.[236] Amongst her other directly sexual epithets was *"Lady of the Uterus"*[237] and *"Lady of the Vulva"*.[238]

Help in Matters of the Heart

Hathor *"the golden"* or the *"lady of heaven"* was invoked in love poetry and songs. She was instrumental in bringing lovers together. *"I make devotions to my goddess, that she grant me my sister...as a gift."* In this context sister and brother were used as terms of affection rather than to indicate a sibling. One happy worshipper sang *"I give adoration to Hathor; Praise to my Mistress! I called to her, she heard my plea. She sent my mistress to me"*.[239] People prayed to Hathor for success in love and marriage. In one song it says *"tell your requests to the Cow of Gold, the lady of happy life"*. As a goddess of destiny she was well placed to sort out lovers' wishes. *"O brother, I am decreed for you by the Golden One."*[240]

The Beauty of Hathor

Hathor was *"the beautiful, the lovely one, who stands at the head of the 'House of the Beautiful'; the gods turn their heads away in order to*

---

[236] *Egyptian Mythology*, Pinch, 2002:136
[237] *Votive Offerings to Hathor*, Pinch, 1993:155
[238] *Dancing for Hathor: Women in Ancient Egypt*, Graves-Brown, 2010:167
[239] *Ancient Egypt*, Oakes & Gahlin, 2004:177
[240] *The Song of Songs and the Egyptian Love Songs*, Fox, 1985:53&59

see her (better)".[241] One of Hathor's epithets is Nebet Nebed, *"Lady of the tresses"*.[242] Texts describe her hair as soft, perfumed and abundant. The typical Hathor hairstyle has a straight centre parting, the hair tucked behind the ears with a pronounced curl at the ends.

As Hathor's popularity increased so more women, especially royal ones, wanted to have their hair or wigs styled like Hathor's. Wigs in the Old Kingdom were heavy and tripartite (split into three parts). By the Middle Kingdom they had been replaced by the Hathor style. This continued to be popular into the first part of the New Kingdom after that time it was only used occasionally by queens. It was most popular during the reigns of Hatshepsut and Thutmose III. Hairdressing scenes appear on Middle Kingdom tomb paintings and it is suggested that these may be associated with Hathor worship as combs were decorated with her symbols. One such example has a figure of a kneeling ibex on the handle. The ibex is one of her sacred animals so both the comb and its decoration relate to Hathor.

---

[241] *Hathor and Thoth: Two Key Figures of the Ancient Egyptian Religion,* Bleeker, 1973:26

[242] *Egypt's Dazzling Sun: Amenhotep III and his World,* Kozloff & Bryan, 1992:335

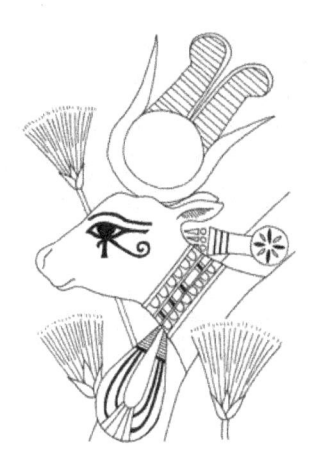

CHAPTER 11

LADY OF DRUNKENNESS

"May you be dignified through wine; may you be rejuvenated through wine."[243]

Introduction

Hathor is the *"Mistress of drunkenness"*[244] and is associated with wine and beer largely through the myth of the *Destruction of Mankind*, which has been discussed in chapter 5. As a person becomes intoxicated the persona they project to the world disappears allowing a glimpse of their true nature for a while, as summed up in the phase *in vino veritas* "in wine there is the truth". That Hathor is appeased and

---

[243] *Wine and Wine Offering in the Religion of Ancient Egypt*, Poo, 1995:161
[244] *Wine and Wine Offering in the Religion of Ancient Egypt*, Poo, 1995:129

becomes benevolent when given wine or beer is a good indication that kindness is her true nature.

The Distant Goddess

The story of the *Distant Goddess* is covered in more detail in chapter 5. Hathor for some reason becomes angry with her father Ra and leaves Egypt. She has to be persuaded to return by the god Thoth. The return of Hathor was also considered an allusion to the inundation. *"One celebrates for this goddess. It is her father Re who created it for her when she came from Bwgm, so that the inundation (Hapy) is given to Egypt...so that she may turn her back to Nubia."*[245]

There appears to be three things that tie Hathor to wine and the inundation. The Nile turns red, the colour of wine, during the inundation due to the silt is carries. One Greco-Roman story tells how the Nile once turned into wine. The flood also renews the fertility of the soil allowing a grape harvest which in turn gives wine; hence Hathor is the giver of wine. Secondly in the *Destruction of Mankind* Hathor-Sekhmet was appeased by red beer which covered the fields, an image surely inspired by the red flood water. Finally in the *Distant Goddess* the appeasement of Hathor symbolised the victory of civilisation over the untamed wilderness. A wild goddess is turned benevolent through wine, which is a product of civilisation. Arguably an excess of alcohol usually has the opposite effect, certainly amongst humans. The dual nature of Hathor is reflected in the inundation which arrives violently and is dangerous but which subsides quietly leaving its offering and blessing in the shape of newly fertilised and watered fields.

In Greco-Roman temples wine was used to pacify a wild lioness goddess in another cycle of stories about the Eye of Re in which Hathor (or Tefnut) is brought back from the Nubian deserts by Thoth. Her wild and bloodthirsty nature is not totally subdued so she has to be regularly appeased by wine offerings, music and dance and it is Thoth of Pnubs the *"lord of wine"* who is responsible for the wine offering to Hathor.

---

[245] *Wine and Wine Offering in the Religion of Ancient Egypt*, Poo, 1995:156

Beer in Egypt

May "*Hathor give you beer*".[246] Beer, *henket*, was the most common alcoholic drink and played an important part in the diet of ordinary people. It wasn't particularly alcoholic but it had a high nutritional value. Beer was made domestically from grain and was largely the work of women. The work registers at Thebes, recording details of the men working on the tombs, show days taken off for brewing beer for use at religious festivals.[247] Even the most enlightened Human Resources department today is unlikely to grant such a request for special leave. There are also records of ration payments to workers and these are of bread and jars of beer. Excavations in an 18th Dynasty palace produced a large quantity of broken beer jars decorated with three-dimensional Hathor Heads.[248]

Wine in Egypt

Wine was produced from the Pre-dynastic Period and both the cultivation of grapes and the production of wine are shown in many images. Red and white wine was made, red being the most popular. The main areas for vineyards were in the Delta, the oases of Kharga and Dakhla and in Kynopolis in Middle Egypt. Wine was held in great esteem and there were large warehouses for the storing of wine in temples and palaces. Many of the amphora and terracotta vessels had labels which gave the year, place of origin, proprietor and notes on its quality. The earliest intact wine jar has the seal of the 1st Dynasty king Den.[249] Wine was expensive and, apart from the wealthy elite, most people only drank wine on special occasions. In the Ramesside period wine was five to ten times more expensive than beer. Its price gave it prestige and made it a suitable offering to the deities and to the deceased.

Wine making and vineyard scenes were popular themes in Middle Kingdom tombs, especially in 18th Dynasty Thebes. Wine, and to a lesser extent beer, was associated with both the inundation and with

---

[246] *Letters from Ancient Egypt*, Wente, 1990:101
[247] *100 Hieroglyphs: Think Like an Egyptian*, Kemp, 2006:46
[248] *The Great Goddesses of Egypt*, Lesko, 1999:112
[249] *Wine and Wine Offering in the Religion of Ancient Egypt*, Poo, 1995:5

blood. Both of these were symbolic of the rejuvenating power of creation as well as being the intoxicating power by which Hathor, in her role as Sekhmet, could be appeased.

Ritual Offerings and Drunkenness

Graffiti at Abusir from the 19th Dynasty reads *"it is as we stand drunk before (you) [Sekhmet of Sahure], that we utter our petition"*.[250] Whilst serious and regular intoxication wasn't normally approved of 'holy intoxication' was seen as a way of connecting to the deities by entering an altered state of being. In the Middle Kingdom discourse *A Man in Dispute with his Ba* the desirability and nearness of death is described as *"like sitting on the shores of drunkenness"*.[251]

The act of turning grapes into wine is full of symbolism. The vine appears dead in winter but spring brings its rebirth when the leaves begin to bud. This leads to its association with death and rebirth in the agricultural calendar. The products of the vine, preserved as either wine or dried fruits, could survive beyond the year and the apparent death of the parent vine. Wine, like beer, could help break down social barriers and help people relax and enjoy themselves and its ability to intoxicate and to generate a feeling of otherworldliness made it a channel for communication with the divine. It also represented the dichotomy between good (the benefits of small quantities of wine) and evil (the problems of excessive consumption). Red wine had an immediate connection with blood in both its life-giving and life-taking aspects. To offer wine was to symbolically offer the creative and rejuvenating power of the world. The turning of sun warmed grapes into alcohol had divine significance. Wine was offered in funeral rites as symbols of regeneration. The grape was called *"the pupil of Horus's eye"* and wine likened to the tears in his eye.[252]

Both food and drink were an important part of worship and eating and drinking could be sacramental acts which connected people with the deities involved with this life. References to intoxication meant physical drunkenness not just spiritual intoxication. Drunkenness lowered resistance and weakened a person's grip on reality which

---

[250] *Ancient Egypt*, Oakes & Gahlin, 2004:479
[251] *Dancing for Hathor: Women in Ancient Egypt*, Graves-Brown, 2010:168
[252] *Hieroglyphics: The writings of Ancient Egypt*, Betro, 1996:146

permitted the presence of the deity to be felt. The deities thus invoked where those connected to the regenerative aspects and life in all its messy glory, of which Hathor was perhaps the greatest. These deities were not the remote, perfect, superior ones who disdained human bodies they were ones who expected people to enjoy physical pleasures. Another suggestion is that drunkenness might be a metaphor for the physical world which Hathor was mistress of. *"All the gods live on incense burning, she (Hathor) lives on drunkenness."*[253]

Offerings to Hathor

Wine was considered a particularly suitable offering to Hathor. The following quotes are from liturgies inscribed in the Ptolemaic temples. *"May your heart reckon the product of Khargeh; may your divine ka rejoice with its sweet smell of the mistress of drunkenness; repeat drinking as one begins to celebrate for your divine ka."* Another says *"O Hathor…may you be filled with it as you wish; may you be powerful through it; may you drink it"*.[254] A common expression in wine offering was *"may you be powerful through it"*. This may have been a pun on the name Sekhmet *"Powerful One"* as well as referring to the rejuvenating power embodied in wine. Ptolemy IX offers wine to Hathor saying *"I appease your ka with the Green Horus Eye"*.[255] In the Greco-Roman Period the term *"Green Horus Eye"* is used for wine, in the Pharonic period the term was only used for offerings of green fruit. This doesn't appear to be a particular type of wine and was unlikely to have been green in colour, the word was used to denote freshness. It was written using the hieroglyph of the papyrus plant which further linked it to Hathor.

Wine and beer were offered to Hathor to appease her. *"May anger be driven away from your heart…may anger be removed from your face."* An inscription from Dendera says *"the vineyards prosper in the district of Dendera…their wine is presented as your provision"*.[256] Wine was offered in a special vessel, a shallow bowl decorated with papyrus and lotus buds which often has a Hathor Cow in the middle. Such a bowl is

---

[253] *Wine and Wine Offering in the Religion of Ancient Egypt*, Poo, 1995:93
[254] *Wine and Wine Offering in the Religion of Ancient Egypt*, Poo, 1995:97-99
[255] *Wine and Wine Offering in the Religion of Ancient Egypt*, Poo, 1995:129
[256] *Wine and Wine Offering in the Religion of Ancient Egypt*, Poo, 1995:159-162

shown placed before the Hathor Cow in illustrations. Large Hathor and Bes jars have been found, probably for storing wine in. They are too large to be poured from and would have been used to fill smaller jars. The contents may have been used as offerings but these deities are associated with wine so they were probably viewed as an appropriate decoration, although filling and drinking the wine even in a domestic context might have been seen as an offering to Hathor.

The king's drunkenness at the festival was a ritual act of worshipping Hathor allowing him to come into the presence of the divine (and an excellent excuse). On a stele in Sinai Hatshepsut and Thutmose III (18th Dynasty) offer wine to Hathor to commemorate the success of a mining operation. The deceased also symbolically offer wine to Hathor. In his tomb Horemheb is depicted offering wine to Hathor, Anubis (the jackal-headed god of the afterlife) and Osiris. Wine offerings to Hathor are depicted nine times in her temple at Dendera. On the southern wall of the outer vestibule is a hymn to Hathor which calls her *"Mistress of wine"* and alludes to the *Destruction of Mankind*.[257] A hymn to Hathor on the wall of her temple at Philae refers to the *Festival of Intoxication* and says that the perfect year starts with drunkenness.[258] Not much has changed in the intervening millennia.

Offerings to the Deceased

Wine was an important funerary offering. During the *Valley Festival* alcohol was used to lift the veil between the living and the deceased. Relatives of the deceased feasted in or near the tomb so that the deceased could join in. In the 18th Dynasty tomb of Nakht a girl is shown offering wine to her deceased parents during the *Valley Festival*. *"To you health! Drink this good wine, celebrate a festive day."* Another girl presents wine to the deceased User *"for your ka! Drink, be happily drunk, and make holiday"*.[259] Tomb scenes often portray guests the worse for drink at banquets. Such drunkenness was meant to indicate the abundance of the feast. Both men and women are shown drunk, unlike in other cultures where drunken women are seen as inherently

---

[257] *Wine and Wine Offering in the Religion of Ancient Egypt*, Poo, 1995:66
[258] *Ancient Egypt*, Oakes & Gahlin, 2004:479
[259] *Wine and Wine Offering in the Religion of Ancient Egypt*, Poo, 1995:32

worse and more disgraceful than drunken men. Here women were apparently allowed to enjoy themselves as much as the men.

The Festival of Drunkenness

This festival was held on the 20th day of the first month of the year (*Thoth*). It is first attested to in the Middle Kingdom but was most popular during the Greco-Roman Period. Wine was drunk in honour of Hathor and the resulting drunkenness wasn't seen as ordinary intoxication but a state of ecstasy in honour of the goddess. Sacred drunkenness was believed to be calming in a reflection of the myth of the *Destruction of Mankind*. At this festival her followers were also meant to get rid of anger, negativity and resentment. A song to Hathor during her festival says "*Come, walk in the place of drunkenness, that pillared hall of diversion...Drunkards serenade you by night*".[260] Menou-jugs were filled with wine and offered to Hathor "*Lady of Drunkenness in the Place of Drunkenness*".[261]

Secular Drinking

Alcohol was drunk for the same reasons as it is now. Both wine and beer were used in medicine and acted as a solution for drugs.

The Issue of Excess

There are plenty of warnings in the literature about over indulgence. "*He who drinks too much wine lies down in a stupor*" and "*when you speak, nonsense comes out of your mouth*".[262] No doubt many people overindulged at times and some too much of the time. The Egyptians did have a balanced attitude towards drinking.

Wine and beer was fundamental for offering, for enjoyment and communing with the divine but excessive drunkenness leading to anti-social behaviour was discouraged. This type of drunkenness was

---

[260] *100 Hieroglyphs: Think Like an Egyptian*, Kemp, 2006:46
[261] *Dancing for Hathor: Women in Ancient Egypt*, Graves-Brown, 2010:168
[262] *Wine and Wine Offering in the Religion of Ancient Egypt*, Poo, 1995:34-35

associated with Seth. His drunkenness was different because, in line with his nature, it brought turmoil and social problems.

CHAPTER 12

FRAGRANCE

"The incense comes, the incense comes. The scent is over thee."[263]

Introduction

Perfume was a gift from the deities, they were recognisable by their pleasing scent, so perfumed oils and unguents played a very important role in rituals in all temples. Deities were thought to be present in flowers, because of their perfume, and this made them an ideal offering. Incense was burnt because it pleased the deities and made them feel at home. The rising smoke acted as a conduit for communication between the worlds. *"Incense is laid on the fire...your*

---

[263] *Sacred Luxuries*, Manniche, 1999:34

perfume reaches me, O you gods, as I hope my perfume reaches you."[264] All pleasant fragrances were believed to come from the deities' bodies. Inhaling it allowed a person to breathe a divine, life-giving substance as well as being able to enjoy the sweet perfume. The relationship between scent and air is very close and smelling is in effect the same as breathing, further emphasising the life-giving powers of perfume.

The Egyptians seem to have been compulsive perfume and incense users. The Greeks and Romans said that Egyptian perfume was the best in the world. Hathor brings erotic undertones to fragrance in her aspect of goddess of love and sexuality. Bastet is the goddess of perfume and her hieroglyph is the unguent jar used in funerary offerings. This is a tall alabaster jar whose lid is fastened with a cord. The jar was called a *bas* giving Bastet her name of "*She of the perfume jar*".[265]

Sacred Use

Huge quantities of flowers and scents were used in temples. Billowing clouds of incense were offered daily at every shrine in Egypt. The early Christians in Egypt particularly hated this pagan indulgence. Sufficient amounts of intoxicating scent can produce altered states of consciousness as well as evoke powerful memories and emotions. The large amounts of incense used will have added a magical and mystical ambiance to the dark temple illuminated by torches and oil lamps. A text from the temple of Edfu describes the offering of myrrh to Hathor. "*Myrrh belongs to your hair, hekenu-oil to your head...the richer you are in myrrh, the more repelled are your enemies.*"[266] A Harpist's song said "*anoint yourself with the true wonders of the divine offering*".[267]

Use for the Deceased

Even in the Pre-dynastic Period perfumes were found in graves. They were used lavishly in burials in the Old Kingdom and many paintings show the deceased inhaling perfumes or the scent from

---

[264] *A Sense of Smell*, Wilson, 2010:32-33
[265] *Oils and Perfumes of Ancient Egypt*, Fletcher, 1999:36
[266] *Hymns to Isis in Her Temple at Philae*, Zabkar, 1988:44-45
[267] *Sacred Luxuries*, Manniche, 1999:94

flowers. The deceased lived off the offerings of incense and myrrh the same way that the deities did. On a statue of a priest musician of Hathor at Deir el-Bahri is the request *"place unguents on my brow and sermet-beverage to my mouth"*.[268] Myrrh was used in purification rituals. The deceased were anointed with myrrh on the mouth and lips allowing them to consume the sacrificial food. Hathor also anointed the deceased so that they might live like Ra and eat from his offering table. Elaborate bouquets in the shape of *ankhs* were made as offerings. The word for bouquet had the same components as that for *"life"*, so a bouquet was considered a symbol for life emphasising the revitalising aspects of scents. *Ankh* bouquets were particularly popular in the *Feast of the Valley* (see chapter 22) where they were offered to Hathor, Mut, Ptah, Amun and Khonsu.

Secular Use

Hathor's hair was described as sweet and perfumed. Men and women at all levels of society perfumed their hair. The Egyptians must have been a very clean and pleasant people to be amongst. Perfumed oils were used in aphrodisiacs and love spells. One spell invokes Hathor and asks her to send the sun's power into the scented oil. A fish was soaked in the oil and Isis invoked with an incantation seven times a day for a week. The fish was then buried and the head anointed with the oil. All this so your loved one would come to you, assuming that the smell from the fish oil wasn't too overpowering.[269]

Ingredients

Cedar and myrrh were two of the seven sacred oils and they were used extensively. Myrrh, which was imported from Punt, was a prized offering and was sacred to Hathor. It was used to purify the deceased as well as to anoint the statues. *"I have given you these offerings which Hathor, Lady of Punt, has given you; she gives you myrrh."*[270]

The white lotus, *seshen*, and the blue lotus (*Nymphea caerulea*) were amongst the most popular flowers. The blue lotus is particularly

---

[268] *Hymns to Isis in Her Temple at Philae*, Zabkar, 1988:45
[269] *Oils and Perfumes of Ancient Egypt*, Fletcher, 1999:40
[270] *The Ancient Egyptian Coffin Texts Volume I*, Faulkner, 2007:42. Spell 47

sweet smelling. Its scent was said to be protective and restorative. Both species were associated with creation and rebirth and were considered to be the *"flower which came into being at the beginning"*.[271] They were sacred to the young son of Hathor, the god Nefertem. He was occasionally depicted seated in the lotus. His usual form is as a man or lion-headed man with a lotus headdress. He was called *"Great Lotus"* and *"Lotus-flower at the nose of Ra"*. Not surprisingly he was the god of perfume making. The sun god was said to have been born when a blue lotus emerged from the primeval waters and so the flower could be associated with the Goddess giving birth to her son, the sun. The child gods Horus, Ihy and Nefertum were associated with the solar child in the lotus. Ihy was called *"the child who shines in the lotus"*.[272] The opening of the lotus flower became a symbol for the unfolding of life and was linked with creation. The lotus grows in still water and the buds only rise above the surface of the water and open when the sun shines. It is pollinated by beetles which further emphasises its link to the dawn sun god Khepri who was depicted as a scarab beetle. Lotus flowers were important offerings. Rameses III (20th Dynasty) gave over 3,000 bouquets of lotus to Amun alone.

In funerary art the deceased often hold a blue lotus to their nose, a symbol of the granting of new life. A 5th Dynasty painted relief from the tomb of Ihat, a priestess of Hathor, shows her smelling a lotus flower.

Recipes

In the temple of Hathor at Dendera recipes for unguents and other sacred preparations are inscribed on the walls of the inner chambers. The texts, from the *"Book of Unguent"*,[273] are extensive and also contain reliefs showing the preparation work. In the temple of Horus at Edfu there is reference to a *"Hathor unguent"*.[274] Sadly it can't be replicated as one of the ingredients, *Aspalathos*, is an unknown species. In the temples of Horus at Edfu and of Hathor at Dendera there were workshops where the incense, perfumes and unguents were manufactured. There is a recipe for *"Tisheps made of ab resin"* which

---

[271] *Oils and Perfumes of Ancient Egypt*, Fletcher, 1999:18
[272] *Egyptian Mythology*, Pinch, 2002:158
[273] *Sacred Luxuries*, Manniche, 1999:37
[274] *Sacred Luxuries*, Manniche, 1999:15

was used for *"anointing the golden goddess Hathor, the great mistress of Dendera...with its fragrant liquid"*.[275] It took 241 days to make and was then left to mature for 240 days. One ritual blend of oil took 93 days to prepare, a quick recipe compared to one of the sacred oils which took 365. Kyphi is the most famous Egyptian perfume known today, made using recipes from the temples of Edfu and Philae.

Storage and Presentation

From the New Kingdom perfume containers were made of glass. Cat forms were popular because of the association with Bastet. One highly decorated perfume jar has a cat or lioness on the lid and Hathor columns on two sides.[276] A small (12cm) early 12th Dynasty alabaster container for perfumed oil is in the shape of a wildcat with eyes of rock crystal set in copper. Wildcats were admired for their eagerness to fight snakes and were seen as the embodiment of Bastet.[277] A Late Period perfume vessel in a serpentine shape with a lion on it was found in Leontopolis.[278] In the entrance to the New Kingdom tomb of Rekhmire at Thebes was a bronze bowl with a small Hathor Cow in the centre. From illustrations elsewhere we know that lotus blossoms were floated in it.[279]

---

[275] *Sacred Luxuries*, Manniche, 1999:41
[276] *A Sense of Smell*, Wilson, 2010:32-33
[277] *Sacred Luxuries*, Manniche, 1999:82
[278] *Oils and Perfumes of Ancient Egypt*, Fletcher, 1999:51
[279] *Oils and Perfumes of Ancient Egypt*, Fletcher, 1999:38

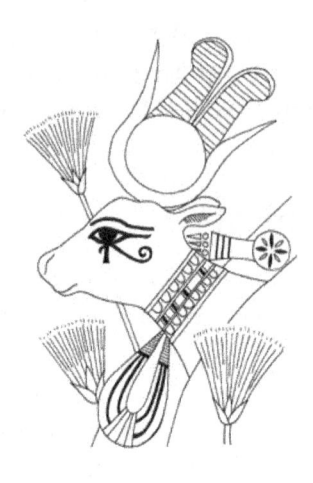

CHAPTER 13

FERTILITY & CHILDBIRTH

"May a birth be given to your daughter."[280]

Introduction

The fertility of animals and crops was primarily a function of the earth gods Geb and Osiris. Human fertility tended to be the function of the goddesses; in particular Hathor, Isis, Heket (the frog goddess of birth) and Renenutet. Hathor can also be considered the goddess of procreation and abundant life. She ensures the survival of creation by enabling a continuation of life in all its forms.

---

[280] *Votive Offerings to Hathor,* Pinch, 1993:218

Fertility in Nature

Hathor promotes the fertility of the world in general. She is *"the one who makes the plants germinate"*. It is Hathor who *"brings forth the bread"* and who *"brings abundance in all Egypt"*.[281] This is largely as a result of her connection with the life bringing inundation. The New Year festival can be seen as a celebration of the inundation and the subsequent fertility of the land and later the harvest. Whilst this isn't a festival dedicated specifically to Hathor she is at its heart as it is she who brings the inundation and enables the growth of vegetation. *"The ruler over Sirius, the great one who makes Hpj (the Nile) come."*[282]

During the *Festival of the Beautiful Embrace* the statue of Hathor of Dendera spends the night with the statue of Horus of Edfu where they celebrate their marriage. Opinion is divided as to whether this was a classic example of *heiros gamos*, the sexual union between the goddess and the god to ensure the fertility of the land. Union between the earth goddess and the sky god, such as Inanna and Tammuz from Babylonian myth, results in the procreation of life. The Egyptians don't appear to have had such a concept and nothing in the texts suggests this. They certainly had fertility gods such as Osiris and Min and connected the rising of the Nile with the ensuing fertility of the land. On balance it is probably that the union between Hathor and Horus was a celebration, and promotion, of fertility rather than regeneration via *heiros gamos*.

The Fertility of Women

A goddess of love and sex leads naturally into pregnancy and childbirth. As in most pre-industrialised societies large families were the norm in Egypt. The most important role a woman could have was that of a mother and men wanted many children, to assert their virility if nothing else. Infant mortality was very high so many pregnancies were necessary to ensure a few surviving children and labour intensive work encouraged large families. Without access to contraceptives, and few roles apart from that of mother, women had no choice but to

---

[281] *Hathor and Thoth: Two Key Figures of the Ancient Egyptian Religion*, Bleeker, 1973:40

[282] *Hathor and Thoth: Two Key Figures of the Ancient Egyptian Religion*, Bleeker, 1973:90

acquiesce to their culture's delight in and demand for many children. Whilst women in Egypt had a lot more freedom than in other cultures of the time, and indeed over history, bearing children was still essential to a woman's social standing and the security of her marriage.

Hathor received many gifts from her followers. (These are discussed in more detail in chapter 22.) Popular votive offerings left as part of prayers for fertility were wooden and stone phalluses. In at least one of her festivals a model phallus was carried in the procession, this was in allusion to fertility rather than sex.[283] A festival on the 5th of the month of *Paophi* was a procession for Hathor in celebration of *"the phallus, which makes all that exists fertile"*. Another on the 30th of the month of *Hathyr* was a procession and ritual called *"opening of the bosom of the women"* in which Hathor was asked for the blessings of children.[284] Another common type of votive offering was a clay box in the shape of an elaborate bed which again references fertility and or the protection of babies and children.

This song from the temple of Medinet Habu expresses the desire for fertility.

> *"Thy wives (praise) Hathor, the mistress of the fort of the West,*
> *In order that the goddess has your wives*
> *Give birth to boys and girls,*
> *In order that they become not sterile*
> *And you not barren."*[285]

The base of the Valley of the Queens is marked by a cave, and a waterfall during occasional rains. The cave is a deep crevasse of distinctive shape. It became a symbol of fertility and in the cave is graffiti of Hathor in both human and cow form.[286]

---

[283] *The Complete Gods and Goddesses of Ancient Egypt*, Wilkinson, 2003:145

[284] *Hathor and Thoth: Two Key Figures of the Ancient Egyptian Religion*, Bleeker, 1973:99

[285] *Hathor and Thoth: Two Key Figures of the Ancient Egyptian Religion*, Bleeker, 1973:40

[286] *Valley of the Kings*, Weeks, 2010: 278

It is said that in recent history the local women would visit some of the crypts of the Dendera temple if they were having problems conceiving.[287]

Childbirth

Hathor protected pregnant women and helped them during labour, assisted by the dwarf god Bes and also Ihy who soothed them with his music. Midwives may have been Hathor priestesses but there is no direct proof of this. In the *Westcar* papyrus there is a story which tells how Ra sent four goddesses to help the queen give birth. They are recognised as midwives as they carry *sistrum* and *menats* and these are cult objects which were carried by the priestesses of Hathor. Hathor isn't one of these goddesses but women in labour were often associated with Hathor or Isis.

Childbirth was a very dangerous time for both the mother and the baby. Childbearing goddesses such as Hathor allowed the mother to identify with a goddess and hopefully to transfer some of her pain. A drawing on a birth-brick from Abydos, dating to about 1750-1650 BCE, shows a mother, baby and two female helpers flanked by Hathor Heads mounted on branches. Both the masks and the women's hair are turquoise, a colour associated with divine beings and especially with Hathor. The Hathor Heads on branches may refer to the two sycamores of the Eastern Horizon through which the sun god is born each dawn.[288]

One spell from the *Leyden* papyrus identifies the labouring mother with Hathor and the last line of the spell affirms that it is Hathor of Dendera who is giving birth. This is a spell for "*speeding up giving of birth*". "*Open for me! I am the one whose offering is large, the builder who built the pylon for Hathor... Hathor, lady of Dendera is [the] one who is giving birth!*" The refrain "*it is Hathor who is giving birth*" was repeated a number of times creating a temporary link between the divine and human realm. The deities would then assist the mother and baby as they would the goddess and her divine baby. The continually chanted refrain may have been designed to provide much needed psychological support to the mother.

---

[287] *Magic in Ancient Egypt*, Pinch, 2006:130
[288] *Magic in Ancient Egypt*, Pinch, 2006:128

This is another spell for a woman *"nearing her time"*. *"The wife of a man had cried for a statuette of a dwarf of clay: 'come, let somebody betake himself to Hathor, the lady of Dendera. Let her amulet of health be fetched for you, that she may cause the one in childbirth to give birth!"* Another is the spell of *"the dwarf"*, namely Bes. *"Oh good dwarf, come, on account of the one who sent you…See, Hathor will place her hand on her [as] an amulet of health."* The words are to be said four times over a clay model of a dwarf which is then placed on the head of a woman who is *"giving birth (under) suffering"*.[289]

Laying hands on a patient was associated with healing and it allowed the divine healing energy to flow from the deity to the patient via the medium of the healer. One spell refers to Hathor laying her hand on women suffering in childbirth. Ivory rods which terminated in hands, representing the divine hand, were part of the magician-healer's equipment for this reason.[290]

Hathor was believed to determine the destinies of new-born children particularly in her guise of the Seven Hathors, see chapter 18.

---

[289] *Ancient Egyptian Magical Texts*, Borghouts, 1978:39-40
[290] *Magic in Ancient Egypt*, Pinch, 2006:84

CHAPTER 14

PROTECTING & NURTURING

"I give thee everything that the sky provides, that the earth creates, and the Nile brings from his source."[291]

Introduction

The aspects discussed in this chapter may appear like a collection of the remaining aspects of Hathor which don't fit neatly elsewhere. In one sense they are, and they certainly aren't her major aspects, but they can all be grouped under a general tendency of Hathor to want to provide nourishment and protection.

---

[291] *The King of Egypt's Grace Before Meat*, Blackman:57-73

Nursing the King

Hathor as cow goddess is the divine midwife and nurse of the king. Showing the royal child suckling from Hathor emphasises her care of him but, of paramount importance, it is her divine milk which makes the child the true king and confirms his right to rule. Queen Hatshepsut emphasised her legal and moral right to the crown in this way, her need to show divine authority was more pressing than that of the kings. Reliefs in Hatshepsut's tomb at Deir el-Bahri show Hathor handing the new born girl to her mythical father Amun for a blessing. She is then shown suckling from the cow goddess. Hathor tells Hatshepsut, "*I am thy mother who formed thy limbs and created thy beauty*".[292] (Hathor's relationship with the king is discussed in more detail in chapter 22.)

The precedence of suckling the king comes from the myth of the childhood of Horus. Although normally considered the son of Isis the infant Horus can be the son of Hathor and is suckled in the marshes of Khemmis by the Hathor Cow, who is also called the Ihet Cow or the milk goddess. From the Middle Kingdom kings associated themselves with the infant Horus in the marshes. Eventually non-royal tombs show the deceased sheltering beneath, or suckling from, the Hathor Cow.

Provision of Food and Drink

The Egyptians lived on a knife edge in terms of food security, being largely dependent upon an inundation of the right height to ensure a successful food harvest. Failure of the Nile flood meant crop failure. Those living away from the Nile Valley in the desert areas would have been all too familiar with drought and the problems of water provision. This insecurity is reflected in their funerary literature, the issue of what food and drink the deceased consume is a recurring theme. Food offerings to the deities and the deceased are a grateful sharing with the knowledge that food might not always be that plentiful. For the wealthy elite banquets were a much appreciated part of life which they expected to continue with in the afterlife. Hathor is "*Mistress of the viands,*

---

[292] *Hathor and Thoth: Two Key Figures of the Ancient Egyptian Religion*, Bleeker, 1973:51

possessor of abundance".[293] Through her fertility the earth can produce everything needed to sustain human life. It was Hathor who "*opens the sand causing the vegetation to grow...the inundation comes at her word*".[294]

Healing and Hathor

Perhaps surprisingly for a compassionate goddess Hathor has only a minor healing role outside that of midwifery. It is in her aspect of Sekhmet that she is a healer. This is because Sekhmet was seen as the cause of many diseases and so could be persuaded to remove them.

One of the few healing myths associated with Hathor is in the *Contendings of Horus and Seth*. In one of their many battles Horus and Seth turn into hippopotami. During the fight Isis gets involved and prevents Seth from being killed. The chaotic powers of Seth are needed by Ra in his daily battle with the chaos serpent Apophis and the power of both Horus and Seth has to be balanced and brought under control, the destruction of either one of these gods would disrupt *maat*. In his fury at this apparent betrayal by his mother Horus beheads Isis and then flees in fear to the Western desert. Seth tracks him down, attacks him and gouges out his eyes and buries them. Hathor finds Horus weeping in the desert. She catches a gazelle and milks it, then applies the milk to Horus' eye sockets and restores his sight. As Hathor is mostly associated with the cow it is at first surprising that she should use gazelle's milk. The drama did take place in the desert and the audience would know that there wouldn't have been any cows in the vicinity. The gazelle is associated with Hathor in her role as Mistress of the Desert and also because Hathor was aligned with the goddess Anukis whose sacred animal is the gazelle. As a desert dweller the gazelle was connected to Seth. Using one of Seth's sacred animals would have been a fitting antidote to the damage that he had caused. "*Thanks to her power, the Eye of Horus was found on the eastern mountain.*"[295]

---

[293] *Hathor and Thoth: Two Key Figures of the Ancient Egyptian Religion*, Bleeker, 1973:27

[294] *Hathor Rising*, Roberts, 2001:15

[295] *On Fear of Death and the Three Bwts connected with Hathor*, Frandsen, 1999:135

The damaged eyes were buried and grew back as lotus flowers. The eyes of Horus can be seen as the sun and moon which need to be restored to wholeness to ensure the survival of creation. As a solar goddess and Eye of Ra, in itself the sun, Hathor is ideally placed to restore and regenerate the solar powers. The sun was considered to have been born when the first lotus flowered hence the damaged eyes are regenerated as the lotus which bore them.

Horus has absorbed Seth's malevolent energy which has extinguished his divine light and goodness. He has become an unthinking physically and sexually aggressive man. The loss of his eyes is symbolic of this. It is only Hathor's healing and revitalising solar energy that can reignite this divine spark and enable Horus to be restored to wholeness and *maat*. Not content with decapitating his mother some texts tell how Horus raped Isis. Horus is never demonised as a result of his appalling behaviour and soon it is conveniently forgotten and written off as 'part of growing up'. Thoth heals Isis by giving her the cow head of Hathor (see also chapter 25). In doing so he may have partially healed Isis using the loving restorative energy of Hathor.

On many occasions Thoth finds and heals the left Eye of Horus, the moon, damaged during these battles. Consequently he is associated with eye diseases but for some reason Hathor doesn't appear to have been. Perhaps her healing aspect just wasn't that strong. This might be due to the fact that she has little *heka* (magical energy). Why this is so is not clear, perhaps it was all focused into her Sekhmet persona and the *uraeus* cobra. Most deities had areas of specialisation and as others had major healing aspects it wasn't necessary for Hathor to be a healer as well.

Like all deities, regardless of their aspects, Hathor was invoked during healing spells. One of the many New Kingdom spells against a scorpion sting invokes various deities and aligns them with different parts of the body. *"Thou shalt not take thy stand in his buttocks; Hathor is against thee – Lady of the Buttocks."* Some spells require the magician to make threats against the deities to force them to acquiesce to his demands. These rather severe threats come from a charm to drive away a headache. *"I will cut off the head of a cow taken from the

Forecourt of Hathor...I will cause the Seven Hathors to fly up to the sky in smoke."[296]

Hathor the Protector

Protection can be an elastic concept depending whose side you are on and many governments have called their aggressive stance a form of defence. Even our immune system, designed to protect the body, can turn against it under certain conditions. Hathor is a protector in many forms. In a benevolent form Hathor is a protector of children and young girls. A votive inscription from an 18th Dynasty tomb refers to *"Hathor, who hears the requests of all maidens who weep"*.[297] She is a protector of miners and merchants and in doing so is a provider as these people provide goods for Egypt, in particular the king.

It is as a protector of Ra and the king, and by inference the state of Egypt, that Hathor becomes a potentially destructive force especially in her name of Sekhmet. *"Hathor overpowereth the enemy of her father by this her name of Sekhmet."*[298] When angry the mild-mannered Hathor transforms into Sekhmet the uncompromising, fire-breathing lioness with her weapons of plague and pestilence. Her destructive anger is put to good use as the protector of the king and of Egypt. She is skilled with the bow and arrow and closely associated with the army. Details of Sekhmet's protective aspect are covered in chapter 19.

Hathor is a great protector but she is not known for her magical powers. Her protective power comes from the energy behind her solar aspect. Hathor is seldom referred to as using magic in the Pharonic period. Isis is *"Great of Magic"* and it was only in the Ptolemaic Period when Hathor was closely associated with Isis that her magic power was emphasised. *"I ensnare for you the rebel[s] with the magical spells on my mouth."*[299]

---

[296] *The Wisdom of Ancient Egypt*, Kaster, 1993:147&152
[297] *The XIth Dynasty Temple at Deir el-Bahri Volume 32*, Naville, 1913:8
[298] *The Burden of Isis*, Dennis, 1910:55
[299] *The Evil Eye of Apophis*, Borghouts, 1973:114-150

Protector of Ra

As Hathor is *"fearless among the gods"* she is their protector.[300] Her major protection role is as the Eye of Ra; indeed Ra is dependent upon the protective power of his daughter. *"Hathor has power over those who rebelled against her father in that her name of Sakhmet."*[301] A text from Dendera describes her as *"The Unique One, flourishing of appearances...the Eye of Re...protecting her father, while chasing away his enemies...She is the flaming goddess, the great one who is powerful through her strength, who beholds the slaughtering of Apophis."*[302]

The Eye is invoked in the *Book of Overthrowing Apep*, in the *Bremner-Rhind* papyrus. *"The Eye of Re shall appear against you...it shall consume you and chastise you in this its name of 'Devouring Flame'; it shall have power over you in this its name of Sakhmet; ye shall fall to its blast, and fierce is the flame which comes forth from its blast."*[303] Another invocation states *"Thou art (condemned) to this fire of the Eye of Re; it sends forth (?) its fiery blast against thee in this its name of Wadjet; it consumes thee in this its name of 'Devouring Flame'; it has power over thee in this its name of Sekhmet."*[304]

The *"powerful one of the dawn-boat"*[305] is also present in her multiple forms, including that of Sekhmet, during Ra's night-time journey though the underworld. The Egyptians could see the sun grow old and its power fade as it sank into the west. The next morning it rose anew, miraculously rejuvenated, and began its ascension of the heavens to its maximum ferocity and height at midday.

The funerary text known as the *Amduat* describes the journey of Ra through the night. It dates from the New Kingdom. Originally royal, Thutmose III had it in his tomb, it was used by non-royals by the 21st Dynasty. The text is also recommended for the living as it gives insight into psychic transformation and renewal. In the *Amduat* Hathor is *"Mistress of the barque"*. She is shown as a woman wearing cow horns

---

[300] *Ancient Egyptian Literature*, Foster, 2001:170
[301] *The Bremner-Rhind Papyrus: II*, Faulkner, 1937:10-16
[302] *The Evil Eye of Apophis*, Borghouts, 1973:114-150
[303] *The Bremner-Rhind Papyrus: III: D. The Book of Overthrowing Apep*, Faulkner, 1937:166-185
[304] *The Bremner-Rhind Papyrus: IV*, Faulkner, 1938:41-53
[305] *The Tomb of a Much-Travelled Theban Official*, Gardiner, 1917:28-38

and a sun disc and is present at every hour. During the first hour Hathor is in the solar barque with the ram-headed Ra. She is his guide as well as representing all aspects of regeneration. Also depicted are the twelve hour goddesses who guide Ra along the dark paths of the underworld. These are all aspects of Hathor and represent the female principle. It is their protection, and directed anger against the sun's enemies, that allows Ra to overcome all obstacles in his way. Their names reflect their roles.

> *"She who smashes the brows of her foes."*
> *"Wise One who protects her Master."*
> *"She who cuts Ba-souls."*
> *"Great One in the Netherworld."*
> *"She who is in the midst of her barque."*
> *"She who arrives."*
> *"She who repels the gang of Seth."*
> *"She of the midnight."*
> *"She who protects her Eye."*
> *"She who rages."*
> *"The starry one."*
> *"She who beholds the Perfection of her Lord."*[306]

In the second hour Ra passes through the fertile region of Wernes and Hathor is shown in the third boat with Isis and Nephthys. Hathor represents the plenitude of life and its continual renewal, this is emphasised by the scarab on the prow of her boat as it sails through the *Amduat*. Its creative power and its urge to be reborn make it a good companion for Hathor. The image of self-creation, it points to the regeneration of all beings.[307] At the tenth hour the bodyguard of Ra is the baboon-headed Thoth who holds the *Wedjat* Eye facing eight lion-headed aspects of Sekhmet the *"divine fury"* who both protect and heal the Eye.[308]

---

[306] *Knowledge for the Afterlife*, Abt & Hornung, 2003:28
[307] *The Sungod's Journey Through the Netherworld*, Schweizer, 2010:51
[308] *The Cult of Ra*, Quirke, 2001:50

The Battle Against Apophis

The Chaos Serpent Apophis is the arch-enemy of Ra and hence the enemy of creation because if he succeeds in destroying Ra, the sun, then he will manage to annihilate all of creation. Fortunately there are some powerful deities on the side of creation such as Thoth and Seth (despite his chaotic character) as well as Hathor who *"who punishes Apophis"*.

The ritual of *Hitting the Evil Eye of Apophis* was first attested to in the 18th Dynasty but most references to it are from the Greco-Roman Period. The king holds a long thin staff and a large ball and the game he plays is with the eye of Apophis. The Eye of Ra is the source of life, light and order so it is fitting that the eye of the enemy is the part that is shown as being defeated or destroyed. The Eye of Ra is also the Eye Goddess (see chapter 5) so it is appropriate that the goddess portrayed in the ritual is one of the Solar Eye goddesses. Of the seventeen Greco-Roman temples studied Hathor is shown thirteen times, Sekhmet three times and Tefnut once. These scenes are placed next to ones showing the king killing an oryx or tortoise (both sacred animals of the chaos deities) or Apophis. At Edfu Ptolemy IV, taking the part of Horus, says *"I have bent down the pupil of the rebel"*. Hathor replies *"I give you your eyes while bringing you joy, so you may illuminate that which is hidden in the darkness"*.[309] The Emperor Augustus is also portrayed carrying out the ritual at Dendera. Did Augustus understand what he was doing or was he just reciting a text given to him by the priests?

---

[309] *The Evil Eye of Apophis*, Borghouts, 1973:114-150

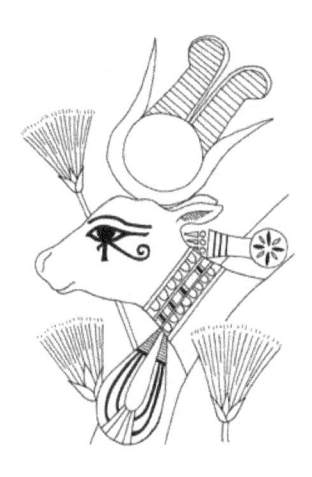

CHAPTER 15

A GEOLOGICAL GODDESS

"He makes lapis-lazuli for her hair and gold for her limbs."[310]

Introduction

Hathor was the goddess of all precious metals and gemstones and was particularly associated with those that have brilliance like the celestial bodies; such as gold, silver, copper, turquoise and malachite. An inscription from the New Kingdom says *"The heaven is gold, Nun is lapis lazuli, and the earth is covered with turquoise when he rises"*.[311] (He being the sun god.)

From earliest times Hathor was a goddess of prospecting and mining. She was the divine force who protected mines and quarries and

---

[310] *Biographical Texts from Ramessid Egypt,* Frood & Baines, 2007:232
[311] *Egyptian Solar Religion in the New Kingdom,* Assmann, 1995:91

those who worked in them. Why should a solar or sky goddess be associated with mining and minerals? Hathor has no chthonic aspects. The colour of the material might align it to Hathor but is there any reason why she is patron of the prospecting, extraction and production? The answer seems to be that it is an extension of her providing and protecting aspect.

The Egyptians associated mines with mountains as their mines and quarries were in the mountains and Hathor was the "*controller of the mountains, the eminent, possessor of precious stones*". She was linked to the Western Mountains of the sunset and the entry to the afterlife so this is a natural extension of these roles. As "*the beautiful, the lovely one*"[312] Hathor will have liked her jewellery and adornments of gold and precious stones but her kindness made her aware of the deadly dangers men faced in extracting these gifts for her so she took the men who mined and worked them for her under her care. All minerals were considered to be her gift. Harkhuf, leader of one expedition, received a letter from Pepy II (6th Dynasty) which referred to "*All sorts of great and wonderful tribute*" which it was understood that Hathor had given to the king.[313] One Middle Kingdom stele, dedicated to Hathor by the leader of an expedition, refers to "*bags full of the precious gifts of the Mistress of Turquoise*".[314]

Mining in Egypt

The Egyptians had mines and quarries outside of Egypt, in Sinai, and in the mountainous desert regions to the east and west of the Nile Valley. Hathor escorted the voyages and expeditions to Sinai and many stelae dedicated to her by the expedition leaders have been found. The cult of Hathor was well established in the mining regions of Sinai. First the mines and quarries had to be located. This was no easy task as they were in remote and arid lands. Many important mines were only worked during the cooler months and getting to them was a major exercise even before extraction started. Hathor was there to encourage the prospectors and leaders of the mining expeditions. Horurre, the

---

[312] *Hathor and Thoth: Two Key Figures of the Ancient Egyptian Religion*, Bleeker, 1973:26-27
[313] *Texts From the Pyramid Age*, Strudwick, 2005:332
[314] *Ancient Egypt*, Oakes & Gahlin, 2004:178

leader of a quarrying expedition in the reign of Amenhotep II (18th Dynasty), left a stele in the Hathor temple at Serabit el-Khadim. It explained how Hathor had guided and protected his expedition despite them having arrived, for some reason, in the summer months. He then goes on to advise other leaders who were having misfortune in prospecting not to be disheartened but to make offerings and prayers to Hathor who would reverse their fortune.[315]

As soon as they began mining the Egyptians started building chapels and temples in the area. A Middle Kingdom stele from Wadi el-Hudi was dedicated to Hathor by Sareru, Keeper of the Treasure Chamber. Here she is addressed as "*Mistress of Amethyst*", a common appellation in this area where amethyst was mined. Sareru says that he "*gave water to every thirsty man who was on this mountain/desert while I was performing rituals in the temple*".[316] In Serabit el-Khadim there are rock carved stelae and temple complexes dating from the Middle to New Kingdoms. There are inscriptions to virtually every king from Hatshepsut to Rameses IV (20th Dynasty) and all are described as being the beloved of the Mistress of Turquoise. Numerous stelae were dedicated by the mining expeditions. There are also dedications to Sopedu (the falcon god of the desert borderlands) who was "*guardian of the desert ways*".[317] The first excavation of the temple at Serabit el-Khadim produced fragments of New Kingdom glass vessels left as votive offerings to Hathor. These may have contained scented ointments.

The el-Markha plain in Sinai was a New Kingdom anchorage and copper smelting camp next to the Red Sea. The plain gave access, via wadi systems, to the southern Sinai mountains where they mined copper and turquoise. A small shrine to Hathor, Mistress of Turquoise, was found at Gebel Abu Hassa.[318]

---

[315] *Voices from Ancient Egypt*, Parkinson, 1991:98

[316] *A Newly Identified Stela from Wadi el-Hudi*, Espinel, 2005:55-70

[317] *The British Museum Dictionary of Ancient Egypt*, Shaw & Nicholson, 2008:336

[318] *Pharaonic Ventures into Southern Sinai, el-Markha Plain Site 346*, Mumford & Parcak, 2003:83-116

The Desert

To the Egyptians their land, apart from the Delta, was basically a river valley surrounded by mountainous deserts. The hieroglyph for desert was three round hills separated by a deep valley. It was used as a determinative sign for places outside of Egypt regardless of the terrain of the particular country. The word for desert, *khaset*, could mean hill country and foreign land as well as desert. To the Egyptian mind they were all the same, the somewhat scary 'other place out there'. Fortunately Hathor was present as *"Mistress of the desert"*.[319] One *Coffin Text* spell refers to *"Hathor who dwells in the beautiful desert"*.[320] A stele from the 18th Dynasty tomb of Nakht, a gardener at Thebes, shows the deceased offering to various deities including *"Hathor who resides in the desert"*.[321] Pahery addresses his prayers to *"Mistress of the desert borders, fearless among the gods"*.[322]

A red sandstone sphinx was found in one Middle Kingdom temple site. The inscriptions were in both hieroglyphics and a proto-Sinaitic script and were dedicated to the Mistress of Turquoise.[323] The compassionate Lady of Mining was important not only to the Egyptians but also to the local tribesmen who worked at the sites.

Specific Rocks and Minerals

Precious stones were more important for their colour and brilliance than they were for their rarity value. They too were seen as magical and the colour had important symbolism and power. This was equally applicable to the substitutes of glass and faience.

Gold

The Egyptians were fortunate in having access to gold in their own country as this gave them much wealth and power. They were the only

---

[319] *Ancient Egyptian Literature Volume II*, Lichtheim, 2006:16
[320] *The Ancient Egyptian Coffin Texts Volume III*, Faulkner, 2007:43. Spell 874
[321] *The Tomb of Nakht, the Gardener, at Thebes (no. 161) as Copied by Robert Hay*, Manniche, 1986:55-78
[322] *Hymns, Prayers and Songs*, Foster, 1995:126
[323] *Cracking Codes: The Rosetta Stone and Decipherment*, Parkinson, 1999:182

civilization in the area who had rich gold deposits; in the eastern desert of Upper Egypt, the Red Sea coast and Nubia. The other Near East civilisations of the time had to get their gold from areas such as Iran and the Caucasus Mountains which were outside of their sphere of influence.[324] One envious king wrote to Amenhotep III saying that *"in Egypt gold is more plentiful than dirt"* and could he please share in some of this blessing.[325]

As well as being important economically gold was highly symbolic and in great demand for use in the temples and for other religious artefacts. Gold doesn't tarnish so it represented purity and eternity, and the eternal life of the sun, and was called the *"flesh of the gods"*.[326] As well as being the same colour as the sun, gold was believed to be composed of the same material. For this reason it was strongly associated with the solar deities. Through its symbolism it was ideal for making amulets and figurines of the deities. Gold was also easy to work making it the preferred substance for jewellery. It is no surprise that the extraction and working of gold was strictly controlled by the state.

Gold was the substance of deities and kings and as such it had sacred and magical powers. Its symbolism and power was similar to that of the later alchemists' gold. As well as decorating the king and appearing to make him shine and dazzle, it protected him and gave him magical power. Only in a country rich in gold could the divine power of kings be emphasised with such splendour and certainty. Some of the Egyptian gold had a high percentage of silver and was called electrum. It was similar in appearance to our white gold which is an alloy of platinum and nickel.

One of the earliest known maps in the world is a map of the gold mines in Egypt which dates to around 1200 BCE. It was drawn on papyrus and gives accurate geographical and geological information marking the location of the mines. It is comparable with modern maps and even uses different colours to show geological information.

Gold bearing quartz was quarried in the late Pre-dynastic Period. During the Old and Middle Kingdoms gold mining was concentrated in the eastern desert because there were more water sources along the

---

[324] *The Royal Gold of Ancient Egypt*, Muller & Theim, 1999:36
[325] *Pharaoh's Gold*, Reader, 2008:15-21
[326] *The Quest for Immortality: Treasures of Ancient Egypt*, Hornung & Bryan, 2002:118

trails and near the mines. Nubt (present day Nagada) was called *"the city of gold"*.[327] It developed as a gold trading centre at the mouth of Wadi Hammamat which was the key route leading to the gold rich areas in the desert. During the reign of Senusret I (12th Dynasty) Nubian gold begins to appear. It has been suggested that the name Nubia derives from *nb*, gold. During the Middle Kingdom the Egyptians began to advance into Nubia and that country's gold resources were probably a major factor influencing that decision.

Turquoise

Turquoise was mined from the Pre-dynastic Period. Jewellery incorporating turquoise has been found dating to the Gerzean Period. As she provided access to the precious stones Hathor was *"Mistress of Turquoise"*.[328] Turquoise is a suitable stone for Hathor in her role as sky goddess. A *Coffin Text* spell refers to Hathor when *"she ascends in turquoise"*.[329] This refers to the sky turning blue as the sun rises. The celestial trees of the afterworld, closely aligned with Hathor, are described as being turquoise (see chapter 6). Wearing turquoise was believed to bring good luck.

Known as *mefkat*, turquoise was mined near Serabit el-Khadim and Wadi Maghara for nearly 4,000 years. *Nebet Mefkat "Mistress of Turquoise"* was Hathor's main epithet in Sinai, where most of the turquoise was mined.[330] In the Middle Kingdom the mining expeditions sailed across the Red Sea to Sinai from a point level with Fayum. By the New Kingdom the route appears to have changed. They went parallel to Thebes, via Wadi Hammamat to Port Kosseir then sailed to Sinai. This is probably because they were quarrying greywacke and mining gold in Wadi Hammamat making it an easier and safer route to travel.

---

[327] *Pharaoh's Gold*, Reader, 2008:15-21
[328] *The Complete Gods and Goddesses of Ancient Egypt*, Wilkinson, 2003:143
[329] *The Ancient Egyptian Coffin Texts Volume II*, Faulkner, 2007:130. Spell 486
[330] *Gifts From the Pharaohs*, Noblecourt, 2007:103

Malachite

Hathor was *"Mistress of the malachite country"*.[331] Green malachite is relevant to Hathor in her tree goddess aspect and through her association with papyrus. The colour green symbolised vegetation and thus fertility and life. It also expresses joy. The latter connection would have been appreciated far more by the Egyptians living on the edge of drought than it is by those of us living in lush and wet lands. Green is an appropriate colour for Hathor in her aspects of goddess of love, music and happiness.

Stone

Equally important to the economy was stone quarrying due to the huge building programmes of temples and monuments. Egypt had a wide range of workable stone in the deserts on either side of the Nile. Quarries have been found dating to the Pre-dynastic Period and Hathor was the patron of quarrymen. At the entrance to the sandstone quarries of Qertassi was a *kiosk* (a small open temple) dedicated to her. It has since been moved to New Kalabsha, about 40km north of the Aswan dam.[332]

Galena

At Gebel el-Zeit, on the northern Red Sea coast, galena (lead sulphide) was mined. There was a sanctuary to *"Hathor, mistress of galena"*.[333]

Flints

Iron pyrites, flint nodules, fossils and meteorites (the latter correctly as it happens) were all thought to be of celestial origin. They

---

[331] *Hathor and Thoth: Two Key Figures of the Ancient Egyptian Religion*, Bleeker, 1973:73

[332] *Ancient Egypt*, Oakes & Gahlin, 2004:181

[333] *The British Museum Dictionary of Ancient Egypt*, Shaw & Nicholson, 2008:126

were called *bi3*, which roughly translates as marvel or miracle and as such were associated with Hathor as sky goddess.

Flint nodules found within the rock were seen as curiosities of divine origin. Because they could be struck to produce a flame they were associated with solar forces. The sparks produced would show the link to the fiery Eye of Ra. The flint nodules appeared to emerge out of a completely different type of rock and were compared to creation emerging out of the primeval mound. The nodules come in an infinite number of shapes and it wasn't hard to find those whose form suggested a sacred symbol. Many flint nodules were found as votive offerings at the Hathor shrine of Mirgissa. One stele from Deir el-Medina had a flint nodule cemented into its top. This has now been lost but a sketch from a notebook shows that it was shaped like a sun disc. The emergence of the flint nodules could also be equated to Hathor in her afterlife aspects where she is portrayed as the Hathor Cow emerging out of the mountain. This theme of emergence could also be applied to the concept of birth and rebirth. In Thebes such flint nodules were associated with the Hathor Cow and rebirth.[334]

Quartz

Quartz has a wide range of colour from white through yellow, red and purple. With its sparkling texture it is the most solar of stones. The Egyptians favoured it for high quality sculpture and reliefs. One area of quarrying was the large mountain of Gebel Ahmar, named Red Mountain after its colour which is particularly noticeable where the geology changes from limestone to sandstone and quartzite. Rameses II (19th Dynasty) set up a roadside stele near to one of the purple quartzite quarries. On it Ra-Harakhti offers a sceptre to the king watched over by "*Hathor, lady of the Red Mountain, lady of heaven, mistress of the Two Lands*".[335] The inscription relates how the king was wandering over the mountain by the shrine of Hathor when he found a vein of purple quartzite.

---

[334] *Through a Glass Darkly,* Szpakowska, 2006:47-52
[335] *The Cult of Ra,* Quirke, 2001: 76

Lapis Lazuli

All precious stones and metals became the province of Hathor, either through her role as protector of the miners or the traders. She was "*Mistress of the lapis lazuli*" which was imported from Afghanistan both directly and via the Near East.[336] Lapis lazuli was prized as its deep blue colour speckled with gold was a symbol of the night sky, the *Nun* and the deities in general.

Faience

Faience is a ceramic substitute for gemstones made of crushed quartz, lime and ash. Evidence for its manufacture is found from the late Pre-dynastic Period. It was a luxury product with divine meaning and associations. The Egyptian word for faience, *tjehnet*, translated as brilliant like the light of the sun, moon or stars. As it glittered like celestial bodies it was a reflection of them and thus could symbolise life, rebirth and immortality. The epithet *tjehnet* was given to Hathor, Thoth and Horus - all deities associated with celestial light. In Late Period and Ptolemaic texts Hathor is called the "*scintillating one*" and from the 21st Dynasty there are references to the Eye of the Sun as *Tjehnet*.[337]

Faience was used as a cheaper substitute for turquoise, although it could be just as magnificent. Another one of Hathor's epithets was "*lady of faience*".[338] Was this a continuation of her role as goddess of precious and beautiful objects because it was made with sand from her desert domain or because it was made to resemble her precious stones? Whatever the reason many faience objects were dedicated to her and left as votive offerings.

---

[336] *Hathor and Thoth: Two Key Figures of the Ancient Egyptian Religion*, Bleeker, 1973:73

[337] *Gifts of the Nile: Ancient Egyptian Faience*, Friedman, 1998:20

[338] *The British Museum Dictionary of Ancient Egypt*, Shaw & Nicholson, 2008:136

CHAPTER 16

GODDESS OF TRADE & FOREIGN LANDS

> "You are like the swallow in her flight wide wandering with her fledgling brood; and when you reach the Delta in your great migration, you run with foreign Asiatic birds."[339]

Introduction

Foreign lands were regarded as being under the jurisdiction of, and the personal domain of, Hathor and goods or tribute from them seen as her gift. Hathor was a universal goddess; not only was she the most widespread and best loved goddess in Egypt but her domain covered the entire creation. As Hathor is a sky and solar goddess she must be

---

[339] *Echoes of Egyptian Voices*, Foster, 1992:57

universal as the sky and sun are the one constant over all lands. In an inscription from the temple of Dendera the king asks Hathor to look upon him from the sky, *"from Asia, from Libya, from the Western Mountain, from the Eastern Region, from every land, from every place, where your majesty shines"*.[340]

Protector of Sailors

Hathor adopted this role to become the protector of all Egyptian shipping whether at sea or on the Nile. In some ways this wasn't a completely new role for Hathor as she was the pilot of the solar barque. In the *Book of the Amduat* she is called the *"Mistress of the barque"*[341] and it is she who steers the ship carrying the deceased. In the *Texts of the Sarcophagi* there are many references to Hathor and boats. She holds the *"oar of the ship of command"* and *"fixes the cables on the rudders"* because she *"created the ship for the passage of the just."*[342]

A Greco-Roman papyrus from Saqqara refers to Hathor as *"the great one of the sea"*.[343] It appears to be recounting a myth but unfortunately the text is incomplete. Hathor was the only Egyptian deity who had a connection with sailing and navigation until the Greco-Roman influence on Isis who became Isis *Pelagia*, *"Isis of the Sea"*.[344]

Goddess of Merchants

As well as protecting the shipping Hathor also looked after the interests of the merchants and so was the goddess of trade. All precious imports became her gifts, thus she became the *"Mistress of Punt"* where the Egyptians traded for the incense so critical for their offerings to the deities including the *"Mistress of the incense"*.[345] It is believed that Punt was in northern Eritrea.

---

[340] *The Great Goddesses of Egypt*, Lesko, 1999:126

[341] *The Quest for Immortality: Treasures of Ancient Egypt*, Hornung & Bryan, 2002:40

[342] *The Living Wisdom of Ancient Egypt*, Jacq, 1999:147

[343] *Excavations East of the Serapeum at Saqqara*, el-Khouly, 1973:151-155

[344] *Isis in the Ancient World*, Witt, 1997:166

[345] *Hathor and Thoth: Two Key Figures of the Ancient Egyptian Religion*, Bleeker, 1973:73

The balance depicted in the *Weighing of the Heart* judgement scene would have been very familiar to merchants. It was the same as the ones used in the market place, workshops and temples. A silver balance was found in a cache of votive offerings to Hathor at her temple at Dendera. The pan is inscribed to "*Hathor, Lady of Iunt*".[346]

Hathor of Byblos

Egypt had major trading links with Syria from the time of unification. By the 3rd millennium BCE Egyptian merchants and diplomats had settled in the city of Byblos (modern Jebail in Lebanon). This country was an important source of timber from the start of the Dynastic Period. Here Hathor was identified with the local goddess Baalat Gebal to become Hathor of Byblos. (Baalat was a form of the goddess Anat, see chapter 21). Did the Egyptians give Hathor a territory in Syria or did they look at the characteristics of the local goddess and decide that she was Hathor by another name?

Amongst other functions Baalat was the patron goddess of sailors and merchants which is not surprising as Byblos was a major port. By the 5th Dynasty Hathor appears in the local art of Byblos in the Egyptian form of a woman with cow horns and a sun disc. Some of the Byblos rulers were shown being suckled by the Hathor Cow. In the temple to Baalat the Lady of Byblos was an obelisk dedicated to her inscribed with hieroglyphs. "*Hathor, Lady of Byblos*"[347] did not remain in Syria, there are references to her in Egypt. She was taken home by those who had lived or worked in Byblos and soon became popular in Egypt.

Hathor in Nubia

Hathor was present in Nubia in the New Kingdom. She was "*Hathor, Lady of Ibsk*" (Abu Simbel).[348] Unlike Hathor of Byblos, Hathor of Ibsk was not worshipped in Egypt. Again we need to consider whether this was an exported Hathor or the local goddess assimilated

---

[346] *Journey Through the Afterlife: Ancient Egyptian Book of the Dead*, Taylor, 2010:224
[347] *Ancient Egyptian Religion*, Cerny 1952:125
[348] *Egyptian Religion*, Morenz, 1992:242

with Hathor. Possibly it was a bit of both. In a polytheist society deities are fluid. A 5th Dynasty official, Harkhuf, came back from an expedition to Nubia with 300 donkeys laden with leopard skins, incense and ebony all of which were viewed as a gift to the king from Hathor.

Other Places

Sinai wasn't officially part of Egypt but it was almost regarded as a province and was certainly under its sphere of influence. Of all foreign lands Hathor is most closely associated with Sinai. In the 12th - 13th Dynasty Theban tomb of Akhthoy, who was responsible for transport to Sinai, it says of Hathor *"Thy might has reached the Mediterranean islands, Re goes up so that he may see thy beauty"*. The islands are likely to be Crete or Cyprus, both were long established trading partners. Hathor was also known as the *"Mistress of Libya"*.[349]

---

[349] *The Tomb of a Much-Travelled Theban Official*, Gardiner, 1917:28-38

CHAPTER 17

THE AFTERLIFE & REBIRTH

"May you come up to heaven, may you sail across the firmament, may you join the stars."[350]

The Goddess of the West

As Hathor gave nourishment, protection and abundant life on earth it was expected that she would perform the same role in the afterlife. 'The west' was a euphemism for the afterlife as, like many cultures, the Egyptians located it in the direction of the setting sun. Hathor is *"Guardian of the West"*.[351] From the Old Kingdom Hathor was called *"Mistress of the western dead"* a reference both to her role as guardian of the necropolis, usually sited on the west bank of the Nile, and of the

---

[350] *The Tomb of Maya and Meryt I*, Martin, 2012:34
[351] *An Ancient Egyptian Book of Hours*, Faulkner, 1958:16

Hathor

realm of the dead. She was particularly venerated as an afterlife goddess in Thebes where she was *"foremost in Thebes"* in her role as protector of the Theban necropolis.[352] Here she is shown on numerous stelae and papyrus as the Hathor Cow leaving the desert where the tombs are cut to go into the papyrus marshes. This gave a visual link between death in the tomb and life which continues in the valley.

Hathor is referred to as *"the sovereign of life, guide of the light on the beautiful roads"* in the *Texts of the Sarcophagus*.[353] She can be shown in one of three forms in this role; as a tree goddess, as the Hathor Cow or as a woman who wears the hieroglyph for *"the west"* as a crown. This is a falcon perched upon a round topped standard sometimes accompanied by an ostrich feather. As the Hathor Cow she is often shown emerging from the Western Mountains which marked the border of the afterworld. The mountainside represented the necropolis because tombs tended to be built into the sides of the Nile Valley. Hathor emerges from her mountain and comes to protect the deceased and give them safe passage to the afterlife. This form was particularly popular during the Ramesside Period.

Egyptian Beliefs About the Afterlife

Like all aspects of Egyptian theology beliefs in the afterlife vary. Kings expected to become gods (and may have been sorely disappointed). For the rest of the population there were two views probably held simultaneously. One was that life would continue as it had done in Egypt hopefully without the unpleasant aspects. Fields would be ploughed, crops harvested, banquets held and trips into the marshes arranged. The rich would have had more to look forward to than the poor in that case. During the Middle Kingdom the concept of the *shabti* became popular. These are model figurines, placed in the tomb, who would carry out any work demanded of the deceased. The other belief about the afterlife was that the vindicated deceased could join the retinue of their favoured deity and play a part in the re-enactment of sacred myths. A number of the funerary spells are to be *"in the following of Hathor"*.[354]

---

[352] *Valley of the Kings*, Weeks, 2010:188
[353] *The Living Wisdom of Ancient Egypt*, Jacq, 1999:147
[354] *The Gods and Symbols of Ancient Egypt*, Lurker, 1986:59

The Funerary Texts

The various funerary texts from the Old Kingdom onwards show how the Egyptians perceived the afterlife and how this view changed over time. The *Pyramid Texts*, so called as they are found on the walls of pyramids, were for the king only. The Middle Kingdom brought slightly more democracy to the afterlife assuming that you had the money for a proper burial and appropriate rituals. These are the *Coffin Texts* which were written on the coffins themselves. One variation is the *Book of Two Ways* named for the map which accompanies it. Here there are two paths through the afterlife, one of fire the other of water. This may reflect the dual aspects of the divine as seen in the raging Sekhmet and the benign Hathor. Similar contradictions are found in the *Island of Flame* which will consume those who are evil but refresh those who are worthy. Hathor was a minor deity in the *Pyramid Texts* but, reflecting her rise in popularity, she was a powerful goddess in the *Coffin Texts*. The most well known funerary text is the New Kingdom *Book of the Dead*. More people were buried with the *Book of the Dead* but it was still under ten percent of the population who could afford such a document. In later periods it was superseded by a variety of shorter texts such as the *Opening of the Mouth for Breathing* and the *Book of the Amduat*.

All these texts are a collection of spells designed to help the deceased be reborn and to guide them through the dangers of the afterlife. It is impossible to know how the majority of ordinary people felt about having to face the unknown perils of the afterlife without the benefit of a magical guidebook. Was it a major terror that overshadowed their lives and those of the bereaved or did they have their own beliefs and rituals which they trusted, knowing that their household deities would look after them regardless of the circumstances of their burial? They would have had good justification for their optimism as the two major deities who had roles in the afterlife, Hathor and Thoth, were known to be as welcoming and helpful towards commoners as they were to the rich elite and royals.

Becoming an Oriris

The Egyptians believed that all worlds and actions were a reflection of one another, in the words of Hermes Trismegistus *"as above so below*". Egypt was an image of the world of the deities and so anything one deity did for another they would also do for a person. If something happened to a deity then the same thing could happen to a person. Identifying with the myths and the deities was common medical and magical practice and was used extensively in the funerary texts. As Osiris had been killed but was brought back to life so every person could hope for this destiny. The deceased were referred to as "*Osiris N*".

Originally "*becoming an Osiris*" meant the deceased was admitted into the following of Osiris and became one of his devotees in the afterworld. Women could become an Osiris as it related to adherence to cultic principles rather than just being the same sex as Osiris. At some time before the Ptolemaic Period the idea that women could also aspire to be at one with Hathor developed as an alternate option in the afterlife choices. The first reference to this dates from the 7th – 4th centuries BCE where a woman was referred to as "*Hathor N*". Sometimes the composite "*Osiris-Hathor N*" was used. It is not clear why this came about. Hathor was not ruler of the afterworld like Osiris was and she never died to be reborn. Perhaps it was a reflection of her midwife role. Some authors have suggested that the deceased woman became a devotee of Hathor in the afterlife rather than one of Osiris but it is not clear. All the funerary texts refer to serving, or becoming at one with, a number of deities in the afterlife and this seems to have been the deceased's choice. Most of the funerary texts we have are for men and they show that they wanted to be in the following of Hathor just as the women did.

The identification of the deceased with Osiris, and in later periods Hathor, does not imply that the Egyptians expected to become gods in the afterlife with the exception of kings. They were well aware of the chasm that separated people from deities, but they hoped that the deceased would be able to participate in the creative and renewing life of the divine and become as one with their favoured deity.

Mummification and Burial

The Egyptians believed that a person consisted of a number of distinct components; the physical body, its shadow, the *ba* or soul, the *ka* or life-force and the *akh* the celestial subtle body. All these components had to be reassembled after death if the deceased was to be reborn. Equally important was the *ren*, the person's true name.

Hence the importance of remembering the deceased, mummification of the body and the many spells to reassemble and reconfigure the component parts.

The first step was mummification and Hathor will *"grant you a rich and efficacious mummification"*.[355] Many deities were invoked during this process which was overseen by the gods Anubis and Thoth. *"The band of Hathor... [place] upon his face."*[356] An effigy of Hathor was sometimes placed around the neck of the mummy to ward off evil. Button seal amulets are found in late Old Kingdom and 1st Intermediate Period cemeteries, particularly in Middle Egypt. Virtually all are associated with female or child burials. They are oval in shape, suggesting the back of a scarab, and are placed on the neck of the deceased either by themselves or at the centre of a bead necklace. There is some controversy over their origins with some researchers suggesting a Near East design influence. They have a variety of designs such as lions, falcons, Seth animals (a composite animal), human figures and also a Hathor monogram. This consists of a Hathor Head surmounted by two lions and the forequarters of a cow emerging from either side of the neck. While the design components are Egyptian some argue that the fusing of the individual components suggests a foreign influence. The horns of Hathor, for example, merge into the legs of the lions.[357]

There are also Late Period amulets for placing on the body of the deceased. They do not carry any inscription but show a kneeling cow whose horns carry the sun disc and two feathers. From a 26th Dynasty Theban tomb of a young girl, Tasheritenkhonsu, is a 20cm amulet disc made of linen and plaster. Among the illustrations is the Hathor Cow. The inscription is taken from spell 162B of the *Book of the Dead* and is a spell for *"kindling heat in the afterlife"*. The instruction says to place a *"drawing of [an ihet-cow] on a new papyrus scroll"* under the head of the deceased.[358]

The mummified body was then placed in a series of coffins. The deceased in the coffin is identified with Osiris-Ra who is reborn within the cosmos and the coffin can be identified with the sky goddess Nut,

---

[355] *Traversing Eternity*, Smith, 2009:581
[356] *Traversing Eternity*, Smith, 2009:231
[357] *The Origins of Egyptian Design Amulets*, Ward, 1970:65-80
[358] *Ancient Egypt and Nubia*, Whitehouse, 2009:106

who is mother of all the dead. Symbolically the deceased becomes a child in the womb of the sky goddess. They enter into her embrace and are reborn within her as a celestial being. Thus Nut is often portrayed on the coffin. The divine mother of the deceased can also be Hathor and Neith by the same principle. After the New Kingdom Hathor is often shown in this way on coffins.[359] On coffins from the 21st Dynasty Hathor is frequently depicted as the tree goddess providing sustenance for the deceased.

"*O Hathor, remember the man at his burial*" begs Khabekhenet on his stele.[360] To the Egyptians the tomb wasn't just a place to hold the body and to give the living a focus for remembering the deceased. As well as showing status it explained what would happen in the afterlife and emphasised the relationship between the dead and the living. Through its texts, illustrations and grave goods it helped the deceased survive in the afterlife. "*They [have made] for your ka, by the decree of the mistress of the four supports of the sky, a burial, excellent, perfect and efficacious.*"[361] The location and layout of the tomb was important and the wealthy and elite would have made extensive plans for this before their death. One Ramesside official, Djehutyemheb, had engraved on his Theban tomb the story of how Hathor appeared to him in a dream and gave detailed instructions regarding his burial. Hathor tells him "*I have made a shrine for your mummy, and I have sanctified a place for your body*".[362] His tomb contains a rock-cut stele engraved with a hymn to Hathor. Djehutyemheb was an official serving in the temple of Amun but this did not stop him being devoted to Hathor, there was no contradiction between working for one deity and worshipping another.

Tomb decorations were essential if you could afford them as they depicted the deceased's journey through the afterlife and the anticipated conditions. In the tomb of Tias and his wife is a stele which is covered with offering texts to Osiris, Anubis, Ra-Harakhti, Atum and Hathor "*Lady of the Southern sycamore*". The author points out that the monument was at Deir el-Medina but Hathor is given her Memphis title suggesting that the owner originated from Memphis. In a lower register

---

[359] *Death and the Afterlife in Ancient Egypt*, Taylor, 2001:215-216
[360] *Ancient Egypt*, Oakes & Gahlin, 2004:177
[361] *Traversing Eternity*, Smith, 2009:532
[362] *Ancient Egyptian Tombs*, Snape, 2011:228

two men worship the Hathor Cow on a pedestal. The *"Lady of the West"* has a sun disc and two plumes and wears a *menat* necklace. *"Hathor, Lady of Heaven, Mistress of the gods. Making adoration to the Lady of Heaven by the scribe Rudef."*[363]

Nefertari, the favourite queen of Rameses II, was buried in the Valley of the Queens in one of the finest tombs created. 520 square meters of wall paintings show her journey to become an *akh*. The *akh* is the form that the justified deceased assume and is the result of the union of the *ba* and the *ka*. There are seven cows and Nefertari is shown greeting each cow. They all have different coloured hides and different inscriptions which refer to spell 148 of the *Book of the Dead*. The cows have the power to provide the spirit of Nefertari with food offerings. Below the cows are oars, intended to help the deceased manoeuvre through the stars. A corridor descends from the tomb chamber its crookedness is thought to reflect the *"crookedness of the beyond"*. One of the walls shows Maat, Serket (the scorpion goddess who was important in the afterlife) and, on a larger scale, an enthroned Hathor. She wears a vulture headdress and a cow horn sun disc. Her dress is green and Serket wears a red dress. Hathor is called *"she who is chief in Thebes"*.[364] In the sarcophagus chamber Hathor is portrayed wearing a red dress. The choice of colour for the dress was significant adding yet another layer of meaning. Green is associated with life and renewal, red is also seen as life-giving as well as being associated with death. After scenes showing the gates the deceased has passed through a large relief shows Nefertari paying homage to enthroned Anubis, Osiris and Hathor, who is wearing the symbol for *"the west"* as a crown. In one of the annexes Nefertari is shown adoring Hathor who is depicted as the Hathor Cow, the *"Mistress of the West"*. At the end we see Nefertari being welcomed by Isis (three depictions), Hathor (two depictions) and Anubis.[365]

Hathoric Rites for the Deceased

Tomb illustrations show various Hathoric rites for the deceased. These would have been carried out when the body was first laid in the

---

[363] *Two Monuments of the Tias*, Malek, 1974:161-167
[364] *House of Eternity: The Tomb of Nefertari*, McDonald, 1996:82-85
[365] *House of Eternity: The Tomb of Nefertari*, McDonald, 1996:101

tomb and at regular intervals afterwards. In the tomb of Pepyankhheryib at Meir there are scenes of musicians. Above a woman playing a harp is an inscription to his daughter Peshernefert, along with his prayers to Hathor that she greet his daughter and guide her into the afterlife. Funerary dances were common (see chapter 9). The Red Chapel of Hatshepsut has an illustration of these. Women sing and shake *sistra* accompanied by a male harpist and three men designated as *"the choir"*. Another troupe of women are performing acrobatic dancing.

It was important that the deceased could eat and drink so there were many food offerings. Beer and wine were particularly appreciated. *"I will offer you a loaf at the offering table...I will offer you a libation of sweet beer and a mdz-receptacle (of) dates...I will bring you wine from the oasis."*[366] An earthenware offering bowl from the 1st Intermediate Period has an inscription *"giving thee bread and beer at the side of Hathor, the Lady of the horizon"*.[367] Sometimes it wasn't necessary to offer the actual items. A letter from the 1st Intermediate Period is from a mother to her deceased son, she says *"May Osiris...provide for you...by giving you bread and beer in the presence of Hathor, lady of the horizon"*.[368]

Two Middle Kingdom graves at Meir contain offerings presented to the deceased during festivals for the dead under the patronage of Hathor. Reliefs show three dancers who wave their *menat* and *sistrum*. The inscription reads *"For your vitality, the neck-ornaments of Hathor. May she lengthen your life to (the number of) years that you desire"*. This seems a strange request for someone who is dead. Perhaps it relates to the concept of eternally renewing life. A man offers the deceased bread *"for your vitality, the snw-bread of Hathor: may she be favourably inclined towards you"*.[369]

The Dendera calendar tells of the procession of Hathor from her sanctuary to the cemetery. These occurred on the 10th *Thoth*, 30th

---

[366] *The Liturgy of Opening the Mouth for Breathing*, Smith, 1993:31
[367] *A Letter to the Dead on a Bowl in the Louvre*, Piankoff & Clere, 1934:157-169
[368] *Letters from Ancient Egypt*, Wente, 1990:214
[369] *Egyptian Festivals*, Bleeker, 1967:133

Phaophi and 20th *Tybi*. The ritual was called the *"Aspersion of the Dead"* and reflects Hathor giving water to the deceased.[370]

The *Beautiful Feast of the Valley* was the Theban equivalent of the popular Hathor festival celebrated throughout Egypt since at least the Old Kingdom. People wore *w3h*-collars, garlands of fragrant flowers which symbolised regeneration and rebirth. It was believed that the ancestor's *kas* could be revived by the strong scent of the flowers. Families held all-night vigils on their ancestor's tombs. It has been suggested that some experienced ecstatic states brought on by the drink and music and dance with its hypnotic rhythms. The sounds would have called the ancestors' spirits and a person in a trance state could have journeyed into the afterworld to visit them. This does have shamanic overtones which is not normally considered part of Egyptian religion. As New Year's Day dawned a lighted torch was extinguished in a bowl of cow's milk, itself a symbol of rebirth, to signify the dead returning once more to Hathor. It would have been unwise to encourage the deceased to remain with the living. The families then presented bouquets and offerings to the deceased with the phrase *"to your ka"*.[371]

Entering the Afterlife

The relatives had carried out all the rituals for the deceased and placed them in a symbolically rich coffin and tomb. All they could then do was make regular offerings and pray for their departed loved ones. The deceased were now in the hands of the deities. They are promised that *"the doors of the sky are opened to your beauty: may you go forth to see Hathor"*.[372] There are many spells in the *Coffin Texts* for sending the soul into the realm of the dead. *"I indeed have prepared a path to the place where Re is, to the place where Hathor is."*[373] The compassionate Mistress of the West welcomes the deceased as she does the setting sun. *"May the west give her hands to him."*[374]

---

[370] *Men and Gods on the Roman Nile*, Lindsay, 1968:278

[371] *Temples of Ancient Egypt*, Shafer, 2005:137

[372] *Hieroglyphs & the Afterlife in Ancient Egypt*, Foreman & Quirke, 1996:87

[373] *The Ancient Egyptian Coffin Texts Volume II*, Faulkner, 2007:136. Spell 496

[374] *Ancient Egyptian Autobiographies*, Lichtcheim, 1988:48

There are a number of ways to cross into the afterlife. As in many other ancient religions the first task of the deceased is to cross a river. For the Egyptians this was the *Winding Waterway*, which was the Milky Way, a heavenly reflection of the Nile. This is done with the sometimes reluctant aid of a ferryman. An alternate option is to ascend into the sky. In one *Coffin Text* spell for *"joining the river-banks"* the deceased states *"my sandals are Hathor, I will cross the sky, I will traverse the earth"*.[375] Here the deceased asks Hathor's help in ascending into the afterlife. *"I have grown on incense, I have climbed up on the sunbeams; O Hathor, give me your hand."*[376]

The Greco-Roman Period introduces the concept of Hathor holding the keys to the afterlife. This may have come from the funerary beliefs of the conquerors where Hades is portrayed holding the keys to his realm. Smith says some translate the word as the feather of Maat but he believes that it refers to an object like a key which opens the ways to the afterlife.[377] Hathor becomes the *"doorkeeper of the house of life...she in whose hand are the keys to the West, to whom the portal(?) has been assigned, without whom they do not close, nor do they open without her knowing"*.[378] The early funerary texts do refer to gatekeepers so this concept may have a partly Egyptian basis and the *Coffin Texts* refer to the doors of the sky.

Nourishment in the Afterlife

Cattle were important in the funerary cult. A vignette for a spell from the *Book of the Dead* shows a bull and a number of cows which will provide nourishment for the deceased. The bier on which the deceased was placed was often in the shape of a cow. There are many reliefs of cattle in tombs and tomb-chapels showing scenes such as calves suckling, cattle fording rivers and men milking.

The concern over what the deceased would eat and drink in the afterlife was present since the earliest times. In part this is a reflection of the ever present threat of famine and drought and also the fear that the deceased would have to rely on offerings from the living which

---

[375] *The Ancient Egyptian Coffin Texts Volume I*, Faulkner, 2007:145. Spell 169
[376] *The Ancient Egyptian Coffin Texts Volume I*, Faulkner, 2007:221. Spell 300
[377] *Traversing Eternity*, Smith, 2009:446
[378] *Traversing Eternity*, Smith, 2009:297

could not be guaranteed for any length of time. Hathor was known since the early Old Kingdom as the tree goddess who gave nourishment to the deceased. It is in this form that the *"mistress of the West"* is shown welcoming the deceased to the afterlife with purifying and refreshing waters.[379] As she receives and revives the weary setting sun so she will receive and revive the deceased. Hathor as the tree goddess offered the deceased shade and nourishment, essential should the offerings from the living cease. The deceased says *"I thrive as I eat it beneath the (foliage and) branches of the im3-tree of Hathor my Mistress, who has provided food offerings, who has provided bread and beer (in Busiris) and bounty in Heliopolis"*.[380]

A great fear for the deceased was eating faeces and drinking urine in the afterlife. Strange as this fear is to us it was very real to the Egyptians. It again reflects a concern as to what the deceased will eat in the afterlife and a suspicion that everything was reversed and confused. The deceased need to be able to guarantee the purity of the food and drink they consume. Purity, important in life, was essential in the afterlife and Hathor was one of the deities who would assist the deceased in their purification.

Rebirth

It isn't clear when the deceased are reborn. Is it when they enter the afterworld or is it after they have reached the Judgement Hall and been found to be vindicated? Do you have to be reborn to be able to travel to the Judgement Hall? I am taking the former view which shows Hathor in her midwife role. She brings the deceased into the afterlife and sets them on their path just as she delivers the child into this world. *"She will give him life in the West...like Re, daily."*[381] As mother of the sun god Hathor gives life to the rising sun each morning so she is inextricably linked with all resurrection and rebirth. *"N's soul and shade are made to appear by Hathor."*[382]

---

[379] *The Complete Gods and Goddesses of Ancient Egypt*, Wilkinson, 2003:143
[380] *The Book of the Dead or Going Forth by Day*, Allen, 1974:71. Spell 82
[381] *Hathor and Thoth: Two Key Figures of the Ancient Egyptian Religion*, Bleeker, 1973:42
[382] *The Ancient Egyptian Coffin Texts Volume II*, Faulkner, 2007:235-236. Spell 663

An illustration from the tomb of Sety I (now in the Louvre Museum, Paris) shows Hathor welcoming Sety to the afterlife. She is shown as a woman holding out her *menat* necklace, a symbol of rebirth, to the king. Many of the royal tombs have illustrations of Hathor on the pillars around the burial chamber. She is depicted embracing the king and holding out an *ankh*, the symbol of the new life that awaits him. In the burial chamber of Amenhotep II there are more depictions of Hathor than there are of the afterlife gods Osiris and Anubis. In the tomb of Irynefer and in a number of funerary papyrus the Divine Cow illustrates spell 71, the *Coming Forth by Day*. Here the deceased comes forth into the afterlife following the example of Mehet-Weret who came forth from the primeval waters when there was no life. The sun god is reborn each morning and the Egyptians might have believed that the deceased were continuously reborn as well. "*You will rise up…diurnally in exaltation each day.*"[383]

There are references in the funerary texts to "*Your impediment will be removed by Hathor*".[384] It is assumed that "*impediment*" is a discreet way of referring to lifelessness although it could also refer to any major injury such as loss of limb that occurred to the deceased in life, or indeed to the corpse. Many cultures refer obliquely to death and corpses as a way of skirting around an unpleasant and distressing subject. To the Egyptians, with their respect for the power of words, saying something made it so therefore stating plainly that someone was dead might have hampered their chances of rebirth.

The Journey Through the Afterlife

Hathor plays a role in the deceased's journey through the afterlife but she isn't a guide of souls as such, a psychopomp, in the true sense of the word. This task falls to Anubis and Thoth. Hathor is considered to receive the setting sun and protect it until the morning and so the deceased desire her protection in the "*following of Hathor*".[385] Hathor will do all she can to ensure that the worthy deceased survive the

---

[383] *The Liturgy of Opening the Mouth for Breathing*, Smith, 1993:30
[384] *The Ancient Egyptian Coffin Texts Volume I*, Faulkner, 2007:36. Spell 44
[385] *The British Museum Dictionary of Ancient Egypt*, Shaw & Nicholson, 2008:136

afterlife. In one spell the deceased says "*I am one of your sacred cattle*".[386] Look after me as you do your beloved cattle.

At certain times the deceased associate parts of their body with deities to give themselves extra power and protection and in the hope of intimidating any demons they meet. In one spell the deceased states that their eyes are Hathor, who is an appropriate protector given her role as the Eye of Ra and one of the restorers of the Eyes of Horus. In a spell for "*warding off the harm*" from the Book of the Dead the deceased associate various body parts with protective deities. "*My eyes are (those of) Hathor...My belly and my backbone are (those of) Sekhmet.*"[387] Is this reinforcing courage comparable with our saying of 'not having the stomach for a fight' or 'spineless'? Or is it just a part of the body that needs protection? Sometimes the deceased associated themselves with a deity. This was used in healing and protection spells in life. The deceased align themselves with the energy and power of a deity to help them overcome the obstacles.

Like some of the other afterlife deities Hathor possesses magical clothing which will protect the deceased. "*Hathor has provided clothing for you.*"[388] In the Coffin Texts there are many references to the various garments of Hathor. "*I don the dress of Hathor.*"[389] By wearing her clothes the deceased can assume the persona of Hathor. "*I have put on the cloak of the Great Lady, and I am the Great Lady.*"[390] One spell is titled "*Weaving the dress for Hathor*". This is a reflection of textile offerings which were a very popular offering to Hathor particularly by women. As the deceased has gifted Hathor with clothes so Hathor will reciprocate and provide magical, protective clothing for the deceased. "*I have woven the dress for Hathor...and she has woven the dress for me.*"[391] Funerary and afterlife clothing were very important and a guarantee that Hathor herself would provide your afterlife garments would have been very comforting. One garment referenced in the funerary texts is the *sndw.t*. This is a very ancient garment, a linen

---

[386] *The Ancient Egyptian Coffin Texts Volume II*, Faulkner, 2007:159. Spell 542
[387] *The Book of the Dead or Going Forth by Day*, Allen, 1974:48. Spell 42
[388] *The Ancient Egyptian Coffin Texts Volume I*, Faulkner, 2007:37. Spell 44
[389] *The Ancient Egyptian Coffin Texts Volume II*, Faulkner, 2007:128. Spell 484
[390] *The Ancient Egyptian Coffin Texts Volume II*, Faulkner, 2007:130. Spell 485
[391] *The Ancient Egyptian Coffin Texts Volume II*, Faulkner, 2007:130-131. Spell 486

apron worn by the king as a mark of dignity and rank. By claiming that Hathor has woven the apron the deceased identifies with a deceased king who is hoping to become a god. A *Pyramid Text* spell states that "*his apron is upon him as that of Hathor...He ascendeth into the sky*".[392]

Some of the spells allude to the dressing of the cult statue. "*They see me as the Sole One with the secret seal. I don the dress, I wear(?) the robe, I receive the wand(?), I adorn the Great Lady in her dignity.*"[393] There is also reference to the deceased fastening the *tstn* of Hathor. This will permit safe passage particularly through the Island of Fire. The determinative of this word suggests that it is some kind of breast or neck ornament which was knotted at the back. The deceased also associate their funerary garments with Hathor herself, in a similar way in which they associated parts of their body. An ascension text refers to "*my kilt which is on me is Hathor*".[394]

Knotting and weaving are symbolic acts which is also why the deceased refer to them. They reflect the divine powers which create order out of chaos and something out of nothing and illustrate the web of life. They are also magical acts for the same reason, spells are woven and knotting played an important part in magic.

Hathor is also there to provide general help and protection as the deceased travel through the dangers of the afterworld. One such spell is illustrated by the deceased offering incense to the Hathor Cow who tells them "*I will assure your protection every day*".[395] The deceased can also use her name to threaten the demons. "*As for any god who shall oppose [himself] to me...he shall not go up to Hathor who is in the sky.*"[396]

One of the many dangers the deceased face on their journey is the fishing net. It is illustrated in the *Book of the Dead* with baboons catching souls, represented as fishes, in the net. The purpose of the net is not clear but the fear it generated is. Hathor is one of the deities invoked for help in avoiding this dangerous obstacle. "*I know the name of the two fingers that grasp it (i.e. the cleat); they are two fingers on the*

---

[392] *Ancient Egyptian Poetry and Prose*, Erman, 1995:2-3
[393] *The Ancient Egyptian Coffin Texts Volume II*, Faulkner, 2007:129. Spell 484
[394] *The Ancient Egyptian Pyramid Texts*, Faulkner, 2007:108. Utterance 335
[395] *Traversing Eternity*, Smith, 2009:478
[396] *The Ancient Egyptian Coffin Texts Volume II*, Faulkner, 2007:300. Spell 769

hand of Re (and finger)nails on the hand of Hathor."[397] Knowing the names of objects and being able to align them to deities was an important way of gaining control. One *Coffin Text* spell refers to offerings of fish in a spell against the net and fish trap. The spell refers to cooking fish which is then brought to the offering table. The deceased are in effect saying 'here is fish for you to eat, now there is no need to try and catch me'.

As well as asking for help the deceased re-enact the myths. They would have done this during life as part of festivals and healing ceremonies. By doing what the deities do they align themselves with their power and work with the natural flow of events rather than against them. The deceased hope to take part in the daily activities of the deities. *"I have tied the knot for Hathor...I have taken my oars so that I may convey Hathor to the horizon."*[398] The knot refers to the mooring rope of the bark of Ra.

Judgement

Having survived the perils of the journey through the afterworld the deceased are judged before the deities. Their heart is weighed against the feather of Maat and only those whose heart is not heavy with sin will receive eternal life. *"May you ascend and see Hathor, may your complaint be removed, may your sin be erased by those who weigh in the balance on the day of reckoning characters."*[399] Hathor is sometimes depicted in the illustrations of the deceased in the Judgement Hall at the *Weighing of the Heart* ceremony. In the *Book of the Dead of Ani* Hathor and the other occupants of the solar barque are present acting as witnesses to the judgement. Even if she is not present she does take an interest in the proceedings. *"Hathor will hear all that he says in the Tribunal of the Two Gods."*[400]

---

[397] *The Book of the Dead or Going Forth by Day*, Allen, 1974:152. Spell 153
[398] *The Ancient Egyptian Coffin Texts Volume II*, Faulkner, 2007:287. Spell 753
[399] *The Ancient Egyptian Coffin Texts Volume I*, Faulkner, 2007:35. Spell 44
[400] *The Ancient Egyptian Coffin Texts Volume III*, Faulkner, 2007:59. Spell 908

Heaven

"*My soul shall follow Hathor.*"[401] Ideas about heaven were vague and often contradictory. One thing is certain the deceased had a say in where they went just as they could chose which deities to worship on earth. Some of the hopes for the afterlife are expressed in the *Anastasi* papyrus. "*May you see the sun in the sky when it initiates the year...may Neper give you bread and Hathor give you beer...May you drive your opponents away.*"[402]

The deceased desire to be in the retinue of Hathor and to be of service to her. One stele from the 22nd Dynasty shows the deceased, depicted as her son Ihy, standing before Hathor. There are many spells for joining Hathor in her solar barque. Some spells detail the tasks that the deceased will perform on board. "*I am he who has charge of the rigging.*"[403]

Several *Coffin Text* spells are to be the scribe of Hathor. "*I am the scribe of Hathor, the writing materials of Thoth are opened for me.*"[404] Being a scribe was a high status occupation, many high ranking officials portrayed themselves as scribes. The king's scribes in particular would have held a lot of prestige, power and responsibility and this is what the scribe of Hathor would also have. "*Hathor lays her hands on me, for I am a scribe whom she loves and who daily does what she wishes...the face of Hathor is bright for me, Hathor lays her hands on me.*"[405]

Conclusion

Hathor's own words provide the best summary of her afterlife role.

> "*I am the one who guides the great ones who are lost and exhausted on the roads of the reborn...Who guides those who are lost in the underworld,*
> *I am Hathor, Queen of the northern sky, Who watches over the reborn,*

---

[401] *Senenu, High Priest of Amun at Deir el-Bahri*, Brovarski, 1976:57-73
[402] *Ancient Egyptian Tombs*, Snape, 2011:226
[403] *The Ancient Egyptian Coffin Texts Volume II*, Faulkner, 2007:287. Spell 752
[404] *The Ancient Egyptian Coffin Texts Volume II*, Faulkner, 2007:158. Spell 540
[405] *The Ancient Egyptian Coffin Texts Volume II*, Faulkner, 2007:155. Spell 533

I am a haven of tranquillity for the just, A ferry for the chosen."[406]

---

[406] *The Living Wisdom of Ancient Egypt*, Jacq, 1999:147

CHAPTER 18

THE SEVEN HATHORS

"Hear me, you seven Hathors who weave fate with a scarlet thread."[407]

Introduction

Seven is a very significant number in Egyptian magic as it is the sum of three (representing plurality) and four (representing totality). It suggests wholeness and perfection. Both Hathor and Sekhmet have a seven-fold form which sometimes appears to be showing seven aspects of their personality. They appear to be the only deities who have this seven-fold aspect. (For the technically minded a group of seven is a hebdomad.)

---

[407] *Ancient Egyptian Literature*, Foster, 2001:90

Foretellers of Fate

The Seven Hathors were the goddesses who pronounced the fate of the new born child and they can foretell the time and manner of a person's death. In the *Tale of the Two Brothers* when the wife of Bata was created by the god Khnum "*the seven Hathors came to see her and said with one mouth: 'She will die a violent death'*".[408] In the *Tale of the Doomed Prince* the Seven Hathors appear at the prince's birth. "*Presently the Hathors came to determine a fate for him.*"[409] His death was to be by crocodile, snake or dog. They don't decree fate just foretell it. This means that fate can be averted by planning, magic, bravery or luck.

The word for fate was derived from the word to ordain or fix. The Egyptian concept of fate was similar in some ways to the Norse belief of *wyrd*, a force which existed alongside the deities which they were also subject to. The Seven Hathors are associated with this force as are some other deities such as Thoth, Meskhenet and Renenutet. Meskhenet presided over the birth and was personified as the birthing bricks used by the mother. She could decide the child's fate at the time of birth. In his role as regulator of time Thoth was also responsible for the destiny and lifespan of individuals. In later periods the cobra goddess Renenutet was associated with destiny having the power to look into the future and determine the length of life. These deities seem to have had the power to determine fate rather than just foretell it.

As a lot of magic is to avoid or alter a person's fate the magician sometimes had to act against the Seven Hathors who had foretold a particular fate for a person.

Magic

The Seven Hathors have a strong magical aspect. They were appealed to in love charms and their red hair ribbons were used to bind dangerous spirits. Red is associated with Hathor and it is a powerful colour symbolising life and death, and the heat and power of the sun. The colour is used as a warning to predators in the natural world and by extension to the predators of the supernatural world. The

---

[408] *Ancient Egyptian Poetry and Prose*, Erman, 1995:156

[409] *The Literature of Ancient Egypt*, Simpson et al, 2003:76

ribbons that the Seven Hathors had worn would be infused with their power making them very effective magical tools. Knotting was used for magical purposes. A knot could bind, bring together or release when the knot was untied. One cure for a scorpion sting invokes the Seven Daughters of Ra, namely the Seven Hathors, to make seven knots. *"Hi you scorpion who came forth from under the tree with its sting erect, the one who has stung the herdsman in the night when (he) was lying down!...the seven children of Pre stood lamenting; they made seven knots in their seven bands and they hit the one who was bitten (with them)."*[410] The knots might have acted as a barrier to the poison.

A spell for *"Bringing a Medicine"* calls upon the Seven Hathors. *"Hail to you, club of willow-wood that protects the body, whose knob is (made) of the pure acacia. The seven Hathors – they will take care of the protection over the body until the body is sound...like the rising of Re over the land. Protection is at my hand!"*[411] A love spell to make a named individual *"come after me"* starts *"Hail to you, O ye Seven Hathors, who are adorned with strings of red thread"*.[412] They were also invoked for protection as in this conjuration against a demon. *"The Hathor-goddesses will learn that your heart has left."*[413]

Afterlife

In the afterlife the Seven Hathors can provide eternal life for the deceased who suckle from the *"seven cows in the realm of the dead"*.[414] These cows are illustrated both in the *Book of the Dead* and in tombs such as that of the 19th Dynasty queen Nefertari. Here each Hathor Cow has a name:

> *"Mansion of kas."*
> *"Silent One."*
> *"She of Chemnis."*
> *"Much Beloved."*
> *"She who protects."*
> *"She whose name has power."*

---

[410] *Ancient Egyptian Magical Texts*, Borghouts, 1978:77-78
[411] *Ancient Egyptian Magical Texts*, Borghouts, 1978:46
[412] *The Song of Songs and the Egyptian Love Songs*, Fox, 1985:233
[413] *Ancient Egyptian Magical Texts*, Borghouts, 1978:21
[414] *An Ancient Egyptian Book of Hours*, Faulkner, 1958:10

"*Storm in the sky.*"[415]

The Seven Hathor Cows are accompanied by four rudders which may represent the cardinal points.

Handmaidens

The Seven Hathors can also be seen as Hathor's handmaidens. This is one of their hymns to her.

> "We gladden Thy Majesty daily
> And Thy heart rejoices when Thou hearest our songs;
> We rejoice when we behold Thee,
> Every day, every day.
> Our hearts are uplifted by the sight of Thy Majesty,
> For Thou art the possessor of the garland of flowers,
> The leader of the choral dance,
> The bestower of inebriety that knows no end."[416]

Conclusion

The Seven Hathors seem to posses a magical power which Hathor does not have, particularly in relation to fate. Perhaps their seven-fold aspect magnifies their *heka*. The power of seven in relation to Hathor is also seen in a *Coffin Text* spell to *Become Hathor*. It refers to the "*company of seven cobras*" and the swallowing, or incorporation, of the "*seven uraei*".[417] In their afterlife roles the Seven Hathors perform the same role as Hathor in protecting and nourishing the deceased.

---

[415] *The Complete Gods and Goddesses of Ancient Egypt*, Wilkinson, 2003:77

[416] *Hathor and Thoth: Two Key Figures of the Ancient Egyptian Religion*, Bleeker, 1973:1

[417] *The Ancient Egyptian Coffin Texts Volume II*, Faulkner, 2007:199, spell 612

CHAPTER 19

SEKHMET

"Hail to you, Sakhmet among the great ones, Lady of the sky, mistress of the Two Lands; what you wish is what you do among the gods who are in their shrines. All men are possessed with the awe of you."[418]

Introduction

One question that has to be asked about Sekhmet is this. Is she an alter-ego of Hathor or is she an independent goddess? She can certainly be viewed as an independent goddess but at other times she is clearly an alter-ego of Hathor who contains the destructive elements of the solar goddess. When Hathor is angry she is Sekhmet and it is possible to understand Hathor more by taking this approach.

---

[418] *The Ancient Egyptian Coffin Texts Volume II*, Faulkner, 2007:225. Spell 651

Goddesses are never straightforward though and it is equally valid to see Hathor and Sekhmet as separate deities. It is no use asking what the Egyptians believed as they were quite happy to take both views as equally valid and the goddesses' names are substituted freely. An inscription on a statue of a High Priest of Memphis refers to "*An offering the king gives to Ptah...Sekhmet the great, who protects her father, and Hathor Neb(et)-hetepet*".[419] In this particular dedication Hathor and Sekhmet are referred to as different goddesses whilst in others they are "*Sekhmet-Hathor*" the one Goddess.

In most chapters I have viewed Sekhmet as an aspect of Hathor the same way I have viewed, for example, the Hathor Cow as a form of Hathor. There are important aspects of Sekhmet that haven't been covered by this strategy and this chapter deals with Sekhmet where she appears more as an individual goddess in her own right. The Goddess alone knows who she is so I make no apologies for my interpretation.

Names and Epithets

The name Sekhmet (Sakhmet in some texts) means "*the powerful one*"[420] or "*the mighty one*" which is an excellent description of her.[421] Sekhmet personifies the aggressive aspect of the solar goddess and the destructive power of the sun. As described in chapter 5 she is a daughter of Ra and most closely linked with the royal and divine *uraeus* and fire breathing Eye of Ra. Her epithets reflect her aspects and many of them she shares with Hathor, and some other goddesses.

> "*Lady of bright red linen.*"
> "*Lady of the Acacia.*"
> "*Mistress of Ankhtawy.*"[422]
> "*Mistress of Egypt.*"[423]
> "*Mistress of fear.*"[424]

---

[419] *A Battered Statue of Shedsunefertem, High Priest of Memphis*, Leahy, 2006:169-184

[420] *The Wisdom of Ancient Egypt*, Kaster, 1993:66

[421] *Conceptions of God in Ancient Egypt*, Hornung, 1996:66

[422] *The Routledge Dictionary of Egyptian Gods and Goddesses*, Hart, 2005:138-139

[423] *Echoes of Egyptian Voices*, Foster, 1992:65

"Mistress of the desert."[425]
"Right Eye of Re."[426]
"Serpent who is upon her father."[427]
"The fiery one."[428]

Epithets such as the "*Lady of life*"[429] may be a euphemism to placate her and to avoid acknowledging her destructive power. It could also be a reference to her ability to cure or prevent the plague.

Iconography

Sekhmet can be depicted as either a lioness or as a lioness-headed woman, the latter being the most common. As a lioness-headed woman she usually has a long, tripartite wig and wears the sun disc as a crown. This sometimes has a protective *uraeus* draped over it. Her long dress is normally red, the colour most associated with her as it is the colour of warfare and disease. In some depictions her dress has a rosette pattern over the nipples which is said to reflect the patterns found on the shoulder hair of lions. Wilkinson suggests that this pattern might represent the shoulder star in the constellation of Leo.[430] Some depictions of Sekhmet show her with the double crown of Egypt which represents Sekhmet combined with Mut. (See below for her association with Mut.) Standing statues of Sekhmet frequently depict her holding the papyrus sceptre in her left hand. Hathor is not portrayed as a lioness because she would be in her Sekhmet aspect if she was. Sekhmet is nothing but a lioness goddess, indeed she is the pre-eminent one.

---

[424] *The Quest for Immortality: Treasures of Ancient Egypt*, Hornung & Bryan, 2002:168
[425] *Traversing Eternity*, Smith, 2009:148
[426] *Echoes of Egyptian Voices*, Foster, 1992:65
[427] *Egyptian Mythology*, Pinch, 2002:188
[428] *Hymns to Isis in Her Temple at Philae*, Zabkar, 1988:69
[429] *The Ancient Egyptian Coffin Texts Volume II*, Faulkner, 2007:225. Spell 651
[430] *The Complete Gods and Goddesses of Ancient Egypt*, Wilkinson, 2003:182

Lions in General

Most Egyptian leonine deities are female. Many of the goddesses viewed as the Eye of Ra were depicted as lionesses, or later cats. The lion is dangerous especially when hungry, the lioness more so when she has cubs to protect. Aelian said that "*to encounter a Lion when famished is dangerous but when he has eaten his fill he is extremely gentle*".[431] The lion evoked the solar aspects of the sky and was viewed as an appropriate animal to mark the horizon. Aelian reports "*The Lion is a very fiery animal, and this is why the Egyptians connect him with Hephaestus, but, they say, he dislikes and shuns the fire from without because of the great fire within himself. And since he is of a very fiery nature, they say the Lion is the house of the sun, and when the sun is at its hottest and at the height of summer, they say it is approaching the Lion.*" (The lion being zodiac sign of Leo.) He says that in Heliopolis there are "*Lions in the entrance to the temples of the god*" and that "*they appear in dreams to those whom the god regards with favour and utter prophecies, and those who have committed perjury they punish...for the god inspires them with a righteous indignation*".[432]

Lions were common in Egypt in the Pre-dynastic Period and were present in the Nile Valley until the Late Period. The lion was an important royal symbol. The species that occurred in Egypt were the African lion (*Panthero leo*), the Berber lion (*Leo barbarous*) and the Persian lion (*Leo persicus*). Hunting lions was a royal prerogative and draws on sacred and kingship matters rather than mere hunting skills. Lions were shown in one of two forms in hieroglyphs; either reclining or striding.

Lioness Goddess

The earliest depiction of a lioness is on a limestone fragment from a 3rd Dynasty monument of Djoser at Saqqara. It has reliefs on three sides and depicts snakes, jackals and lionesses within a ceremonial gateway. Despite having a mane it is assumed that the animal is a lioness due to her tail. In Egyptian art the lioness is always depicted with a non-tufted, erect tail. Lionesses were the more popular even

---

[431] *On the Characteristics of Animals Volume I*, Aelian & Scholfield, 1957:251

[432] *On the Characteristics of Animals Volume III*, Aelian & Scholfield, 1957:21

though a lion is stronger and more magnificent. It was felt that the lioness would protect the king, or whoever she was looking after, as effectively as she protected her cubs.[433] This form of Sekhmet was inspired by sightings of lionesses. They are majestic as well as fear inspiring so very suggestive of a goddess and they could appear silently as if by magic. Cults and sanctuaries to lioness goddesses were often close to wadis as they were the places at the edge of the desert where lions would come down from the desert to drink and to prey on cattle.

Lioness goddesses were said to hold the untamed aspects of the female principle. One could ask what happened to the untamed male principle, the dark side of gods is conveniently forgotten. Ra decides to kill humanity but in the end it is the lioness goddess who takes the blame. *"Its punishment is heavier than the punishment of Sakhmet when she rages."*[434] Through Sekhmet's association with the Hathor as sky goddess the lioness could be seen as the guardian of the sky. *"I am Sekhmet-Uta who sits at the starboard side of the sky."*[435]

The Aspects of Sekhmet

While Hathor is also a sky, cow and tree goddess Sekhmet is purely a solar goddess. Her solar aspect could hardly be missed in this description from Philae. *"Mistress of the burning flame, mistress of the House of Flame, who burns him-whose-character-is-evil with her flaming eye, the great flaming goddess, who scorches the rebels."*[436] The scorching hot desert winds were said to be her breath. Sekhmet has two main aspects; she was an aggressive and protective goddess but also a healing one. Because of these powers she was often invoked in magic for both healing and protection.

Healing and the Pestilence of Sekhmet

With her great healing power Sekhmet embodies the ambivalences of life. As part of her aggressive aspect Sekhmet controls the demons who cause diseases, especially plagues, and therefore she can heal

---

[433] *A Fragmentary Monument of Djoser from Saqqara*, Hawass, 1994:45-56
[434] *Ancient Egyptian Literature Volume III*, Lichtheim, 2006:212
[435] *The Book of the Dead or Going Forth by Day*, Allen, 1974:36. Spell 23
[436] *The Evil Eye of Apophis*, Borghouts, 1973:114-150

them. Her priests were famed for their medical knowledge and powers of healing for both humans and animals. They were able to propitiate Sekhmet and negate the illness which she sent. The *Edwin Smith* surgical papyrus describes medical practitioners as *"any priest of (the goddess) Sekhmet"*.[437] Healing and preventative rituals could be carried out on a very large scale. Pinch suggests that the huge numbers of Sekhmet statues in the temple of Mut at Karnak were the relics of such a ritual.[438] Texts such as the surgical papyrus show that the Egyptians had a considerable amount of medical knowledge and rational practice but the underlying belief was that illness was sent by Sekhmet, or was the result of a malevolent spirit or the evil eye. Many doctors may have believed that exorcising the demons was the most important part of the healing process.

Fevers and plagues were common before the inundation and were often referred to as the *"Carnage of the Year"*. At this time the river was at it lowest and the temperature at its highest. The run up to the new year was a worrying time, as well as disease being rife there was the fear that the inundation would be too high or too low. Once the inundation arrived it was said that *"Egypt flourishes with life. Sekhmet does not launch her pest"*.[439] The epagomenal days, the five days between the end of the old and the beginning of the new year, were considered a period of transition and hence a dangerous time when some deities, especially Sekhmet, released demonic powers. The dark equivalents of the Seven Hathors are the *"seven arrows of Sakhmet"*.[440] These always brought evil fortune, mainly in the form of infectious diseases. There are also the *"slaughterers of Sekhmet"* seven knife-wielding demon messengers of the goddess who were particularly prevalent at the end of the year. On New Year's day people exchanged presents, often in the form of amulets of Sekhmet or Bastet, which were intended to pacify Sekhmet.

Strong spells were needed to save the people from disease and pestilence. Incantations were recited and amulets and statuettes dedicated to Sekhmet to propitiate her. During the Greco-Roman period reciting litanies and addressing her by her many names were

---

[437] *A Note on the Edwin Smith Surgical Papyrus*, Wilson, 1952: 76-80
[438] *Magic in Ancient Egypt*, Pinch, 2006:53
[439] *Men and Gods on the Roman Nile*, Lindsay, 1968:87
[440] *Hymns to Isis in Her Temple at Philae*, Zabkar, 1988:121

considered effective. It was also a time of purification when the physical and moral contamination of the old year had to be driven away from the individual. *"The evils of the past year that had adhered to him have been driven off...he has presented propitiatary offerings on account of them, and his face is turned to the Lady."*[441] The inventory in the temple of Edfu shows a book entitled *"the book of appeasing Sakhmet"*.[442]

This is from one of many spells from the *Book of the Last Day of the Year*. *"Hail to [you] gods there, murderers who stand in waiting upon Sakhmet...Be on your way, [be distant] from me!...You shall not [surrender] me to any bad misfortune this year. For I am Re, who appears in his eye! I have arisen as Sakhmet...I will not fall for your slaughtering."*[443] Those words were to be said over a piece of fine linen. Images of Sekhmet and Ra were then drawn on the linen which was knotted twelve times. After an offering of bread and beer and the burning of incense the linen strip was tied around the throat.

The plague was described as an evil wind, the breath of the emissaries of Sekhmet. While some diseases are airborne this was probably just a lucky guess as the doctors did not understand about infectious diseases. It has been suggested that plagues and epidemics were more common during the mid 2nd millennium BCE due to increased contact with neighbouring states. Was this the reason for Amenhotep III's statues of Sekhmet? A pair for each day of the year to try and contain the power of Sekhmet and to transmute it into protection for king and country.[444]

"Don't you take this heart of mine away, this breast of mine for Sakhmet!"[445] These words are to be said over drawings, done in myrrh, of Sekhmet, Bastet, Osiris and Nehebkau (a protective snake god) and then applied to the throat. Myrrh was used as a medicine and it does have antiseptic and fungicidal properties so it might have had some protective value in reducing or preventing infection.

A new born child was very vulnerable and a protective amulet was usually placed around the baby's neck. Often this was a short text, in

---

[441] *Hymns to Isis in Her Temple at Philae*, Zabkar, 1988:119
[442] *The Priests of Ancient Egypt*, Sauneron, 2000:135
[443] *Ancient Egyptian Magical Texts*, Borghouts, 1978:12-13
[444] *Magic in Ancient Egypt*, Pinch, 2006:143
[445] *Ancient Egyptian Magical Texts*, Borghouts, 1978:16

effect a promise of protection from a deity, written on papyrus and inserted into a tube. One from the god Khonsu for a baby girl, Buirharkhons, claims to "*save her from Sekhmet and her son*" as well as other misfortunes such as falling walls, leprosy, blindness, the evil eye and meteorites.[446]

Other Types of Healing

Sekhmet is also associated with the healing of wounds and fractures possibly because of her association with warfare.

Veterinary Skills

Cattle were very important to the Egyptians and like people, they needed protecting and healing. Many reliefs show cattle husbandry such as feeding by hand and assisting a cow to give birth. Herdsmen are shown making magical gestures of protection. There were also veterinary surgeons and we even have the veterinary papyrus of *Kahun*. Dating to the Middle Kingdom it is the only known papyrus dealing with animals. Treatments include parasites, eye infections and the more deadly diseases one of which might be Rinderpest. A 12th Dynasty inscription refers to Aha-nakt, a *wab*-priest of Sekhmet, who is described as a *rekh kau* "*one who knows oxen*". In an Old Kingdom relief three priests of Sekhmet are supervising the butchery of sacrificial cattle. An inscription from the Ptolemaic tomb of Petosiris says "*your herds are numerous in the stable, thanks to the science of the priest of Sekhmet*".[447]

Magic

Much of the magical power invoked in Sekhmet's name was for healing magic, though her ferocity added a much welcome power to protective spells. Some of the spells from the *Leyden* papyrus are for divination, for "*inquiry of the lamp*". They invoke "*The fury of Sekhmet*

---

[446] *Ancient Egyptian Religion*, Quirke, 1992:112
[447] *How Now Sick Cow?* Lord, 2010:20-24

thy mother and of Heke thy father is cast at thee".[448] Heka (Heke) is the god personifying magical energy. A very useful invocation against a crocodile invoked Sekhmet. "*Oh you water-dwellers: your mouths are closed by Re, your throats are stopped up by Sakhmet.*"[449] She was invoked in a 22nd – 25th Dynasty hieratic document regarding some kind of settlement. "*As for one who shall disregard it, he shall (fall to) the sword of Amon-Re, he shall (fall to) the blaze of Sakhmet.*"[450]

As the arrows of Sekhmet were so dangerous they made powerful weapons for the competent magician. One spell uses them against the Evil Eye and turns the arrow of Sekhmet against the perpetrator. "*Sakhmet's arrow is in you.*"[451]

Like Hathor, Sekhmet has power over an individual's fate and she can determine good or bad luck. She is associated with the fortune of passing time, in particularly her ability to determine a good or bad year for the country. She was said to be able to guarantee the coming of good years with high floods and good harvests.

Protector

Sekhmet was well known for being dangerous and destructive. In the *Tale of the Eloquent Peasant* the unhappy complainant says to the Chief Steward "*you exceed (even) the Lady of Pestilence!*"[452] Her destructive aspects are put to good use in warfare and the punishment of enemies of state and of the deities.

Protector of the King and State

Given Sekhmet's power and ferocity it was inevitable that kings and warriors associated themselves with her. They could be inspired by her war-like actions and she would be their protector. In the *Story of Sinhue* it was said of the king "*The fear of whom was throughout the*

---

[448] *The Leyden Papyrus*, Griffith & Thompson, 1974:57
[449] *Ancient Egyptian Magical Texts*, Borghouts, 1978:86
[450] *The Smaller Dakhla Stela (Ashmolean Museum No. 1894. 107b)*, Janssen, 1968:165-172
[451] *Ancient Egyptian Magical Texts*, Borghouts, 1978:2
[452] *The Literature of Ancient Egypt*, Simpson et al, 2003:32

lands like that of Sekhmet in a year of plague".[453] A hymn to Senusret III (12th Dynasty) calls him *"he that shooteth the arrow as doth Sekhmet"* and *"like Sekhmet unto foes that overstep his boundaries"*.[454] The nomarch (a nome governor) Nehri I, from the 1st Intermediate Period, said of himself *"I was a fortress to which all folk (clung), one at whom the people trembled, the terror of whom was in (the hearts of men) like Sakhmet in the day of battle"*.[455]

As a war goddess Sekhmet accompanies the king into battle. Her weapons are arrows *"with which she pierces hearts"*. A fiery glow emanated from her body and the hot desert winds were her breath.[456] In a text from the temple of Horus at Edfu the king asks for protection against his enemies. *"Let a slaughter be made of them like as when thou didst prevail over the enemies of Re in the primordial age in that thy name of Sakhmet...O Sekhmet, shoot thine arrow at all enemies of the Living Falcon. O Bastet mayest thou draw out their hearts...(Mine) arrow shall not miss them. I am Sakhmet who prevaileth over a million."* Another part of the text refers to *"the papyrus-wand of Sakhmet is about the flesh of the Living Falcon"*.[457]

Sekhmet was also acknowledged as the divine mother of the king. Thutmose III was described as *"the fierce-eyed lion, the son of Sekhmet"*.[458] Sety I (19th Dynasty) was taking no chances. He calls himself *"son of Bastet, foster-child of Sekhmet, Lady of Heaven...born of Pakhet; reared by the Sorceress...brought up by Edjo"*.[459] (Edjo is Wadjet.)

Protector in the Afterlife

Like many deities Sekhmet is invoked during mummification. *"She will bring you clothing within the sanctuary, the precious vestment of the*

---

[453] *Ancient Egyptian Poetry and Prose*, Erman, 1995:18
[454] *Ancient Egyptian Poetry and Prose*, Erman, 1995:134-136
[455] *The Rebellion in the Hare Nome*, Faulkner, 1944:61-63
[456] *The Gods and Symbols of Ancient Egypt*, Lurker, 1986:106
[457] *The King of Egypt's Grace Before Meat*, Blackman:57-73
[458] *Ancient Egyptian Poetry and Prose*, Erman, 1995:168
[459] *Texts of Hatshepsut and Sethos I Inside Speos Artemidos*, Fairman & Grdseloff, 1947:12-33

lady of the uraeus. She will give you her roll of cloth."[460] Funerary linen brought by the goddess herself was particularly protective.

The afterworld was a dangerous place and Sekhmet made a very useful protector and she is present in all the funerary texts. The deceased need not worry. *"Does Seth extend a hand against you? Sekhmet will scorch him with the flame of her mouth."*[461] They associate themselves with her great power either by declaring that they are Sekhmet or by aligning specific parts of their body with her. In the *Book of the Dead* spell 42 puts the stomach and the spine under Sekhmet's protection. One spell to pass by the divine guards of the afterworld says *"I have power over you in this my name of Sakhmet"*.[462] Similarly *"to go out into the day...My striking-power is Sakhmet the divine"*.[463] With Sekhmet as their protector the deceased need not fear demons. *"The mansion of Sekhmet beats out a rhythm for your ka...Sekhmet the chieftainess of the Libyans will keep you safe. She will assure you protection, the mistress of the desert."*[464]

Sekhmet also appears as a guardian of the doorways of the afterworld. The first portal is *"vigil of fire. It is its flame which repels from it. Fifty cubits along its side is its fire, and the front of its flame traverses the earth from this sky...It is charwood. It came from the arms of Sekhmet."*[465] Similarly, the third portal is compared to the *"fiery blast of the mouth of Sakhmet"*.[466]

In the *Book of Gates* it is Sekhmet who protects the souls of *"Asiatics, Negroes and Libyans"* in other words all non-Egyptians.[467] This is another link to Hathor who presides over foreign countries and foreigners.

---

[460] *Traversing Eternity*, Smith, 2009:234
[461] *Traversing Eternity*, Smith, 2009:86
[462] *The Ancient Egyptian Coffin Texts Volume II*, Faulkner, 2007:224. Spell 648
[463] *The Ancient Egyptian Coffin Texts Volume II*, Faulkner, 2007:269. Spell 711
[464] *Traversing Eternity*, Smith, 2009:148
[465] *Hieroglyphs & the Afterlife in Ancient Egypt*, Foreman & Quirke, 1996:88
[466] *The Ancient Egyptian Coffin Texts Volume I*, Faulkner, 2007:269-270. Spell 336
[467] *Egyptian Religion*, Morenz, 1992:51

Protector of Ra

First and foremost Sekhmet is the protector of Ra. As stated in a relief at Philae she is the "*the primeval snake, the noble lady who stands up while smashing and sending out her heat against the rebels of her father*".[468] A statue of Sekhmet describes her as "*Sakhmet the great, the Eye of Re...who subdues the rebels*".[469] The enemies of Ra included rebellious humans and demons but the most deadly of all was Apophis the Chaos Serpent who constantly threatened not only the existence of Ra but all of creation. Other deities helped in the fight against Apophis but the two most formidable deities were Seth and Sekhmet.

The *Book of Overthrowing Apep*, in the *Bremner-Rhind papyrus*, tells of the fate of Apophis from the wrath of Sekhmet. "*He is put on the fire, and it has power over him in its name of Sekhmet...His head is severed from his neck, Sekhmet cuts out his heart, she puts him in the flame on her finger...she sunders his soul from his body and she has power over him in this her name of Sekhmet.*" One spell used against the general enemies of Ra is "*thou commandest them to the execution block of Sekhmet the great, Lady of Ishru...they burn upon the altar of Sekhmet*"[470] and "*[I] cast thee on thy back and thine intestines shall be cut out, for the executioners of Sekhmet slay thee*".[471] Sekhmet is present in the *Book of the Amduat* where her aggressive nature makes her the perfect protector of Ra on his journey through the underworld during the twelve hours of darkness. Along with Thoth she heals the wounded solar eye.

Protector of Horus

Sekhmet, like many of the other deities, was involved in protecting Horus the son of Isis and Osiris. From the *Triumph of Horus* it was said of Horus "*Sakhmet abideth in front of him and Thoth protecteth him*" with "*Sakhmet prevailing over him that is rebellious towards thee*".[472]

---

[468] *The Evil Eye of Apophis*, Borghouts, 1973:114-150

[469] *The God Nehebkau*, Shorter, 1935:41-48

[470] *The Bremner-Rhind Papyrus: III: D. The Book of Overthrowing Apep*, Faulkner, 1937:166-185

[471] *The Bremner-Rhind Papyrus: IV*, Faulkner, 1938:41-53

[472] *The Myth of Horus at Edfu: II. C. The Triumph of Horus Over His Enemies. A Sacred Drama (Concluded)*, Blackman & Fairman, 1944:5-22

The *Sallier* papyrus tells how on the night of the 25th *Thoth* "*Sakhmet went to the Eastern Mountains to strike the companions of Seth*".[473] Horus is quick to compare himself with his powerful allies once he had triumphed over Seth. "*Come and see [Horus] who has pierced the Lower-Egyptian Bull...He maketh the river to flow blood-stained, like Sakhmet in a blighted year.*"[474]

Protector of Osiris

One temple ritual tells of the body of Osiris being guarded by four lioness goddesses; Sekhmet, Shesmetet, Bastet and Wadjet.[475]

Relationships

Triads, a grouping of three deities, became popular during the New Kingdom and the Memphis triad of Ptah, Sekhmet and Nefertem was formed at this time. This triad is alluded to in the Ptah chapel of Sety I at Abydos. The king carries a double *djed*-pillar, which is the characteristic sceptre of Ptah, as well as a lion-headed sceptre with a sun disc suggesting Sekhmet.[476] There is an illustration of Rameses III with the Memphis triad on a papyrus. Sekhmet's lion head is tinged green and she wears a tripartite wig and a large sun disc over which is draped the protective *uraeus* cobra. She holds an *ankh* and a sceptre which is in the form of a stylised papyrus stem. The papyrus has connotations of flourishing life, happiness, satisfaction and support. This alludes to Sekhmet's softer, more nurturing side and her sustaining aspect equating her to Hathor. A love song emphasises this nurturing aspect. "*The river is wine, Ptah is its reeds, Sekhmet is its lotus leaf...Nefertem is its lotus flower.*"[477]

---

[473] *Men and Gods on the Roman Nile*, Lindsay, 1968:404

[474] *The Myth of Horus at Edfu: II. C. The Triumph of Horus Over His Enemies. A Sacred Drama (Concluded)*, Blackman & Fairman, 1944:5-22

[475] *Egyptian Mythology*, Pinch, 2002:134

[476] *A Memphite Triad*, Kakosy, 1980:48-53

[477] *The Literature of Ancient Egypt*, Simpson et al, 2003:310

Ptah

Ptah is considered Sekhmet's partner especially at his cult centre of Memphis. "*Sakhmet, the beloved of Ptah.*"[478] He was the creator god of Memphis from the 1st Dynasty. Ptah was worshipped throughout Egypt and was considered the patron of craftsmen. There is no obvious link to Sekhmet but the Egyptians saw one. "*Sekhmet, great of love, heart of Ptah.*"[479]

Nefertem

Nefertem is the god of the primeval lotus blossom and his name suggests the concept of perfection. He is the blue lotus from which the sun rises and in the *Pyramid Texts* he is the lotus blossom in front of Ra's nose. Nefertem can be depicted as a man with a headdress in the shape of a lotus plant but he is sometimes shown with a lion's head to show his association with Sekhmet. In Memphis Sekhmet is considered the mother of Nefertem and Ptah. In Buto he is considered to be the son of Wadjet but Bastet can also be his mother.

The Worship of Sekhmet

Who worshipped Sekhmet? As with all major deities Sekhmet would have been appealed to by a wide range of people at certain times in their lives for healing and protection. People who lived in her cult city of Memphis would have worshipped her because she was their local goddess. It is unlikely that she was as popular as Isis and Hathor who were more benevolent and less dangerous but that did not mean she was without devotees. "*You will hear the voices of the crowds of the nomadic tribeswomen on the day of acclaiming Sekhmet.*"[480]

The following is from a tomb in Thebes.

> "*Hail to thee, Lady of fragrance,*
> *Great Sekhmet, Sovereign Lady*
> *Worshipped one,*

---

[478] *Ancient Egyptian Literature Volume II*, Lichtheim, 2006:101
[479] *Excavations at Armant, 1929-31*, Myers & Fairman, 1931:223-232
[480] *Traversing Eternity*, Smith, 2009:424

> *Serpent who is upon her father...*
> *Your rays illuminate the Two Lands."*[481]

Sekhmet would protect her worshippers from non-physical dangers as well. Samut, *"the accountant in charge of the cattle of Amun"*, had this to say about Sekhmet. *"The matter is in the hands of Sekhmet the Great. The scope of her actions cannot be measured. No servant of hers can ever fall victim to chicanery."*[482] (Chicanery is the use of trickery to achieve objectives.)

Amulets of Sekhmet were most common during the 3rd Intermediate Period while engravings of Sekhmet on scarabs favoured during the New Kingdom. Moulds used for making figurines and amulets have been found in the temple of Ptah at Memphis dating to the 19th Dynasty.

Most of the information we have about offerings comes from temples and tombs and reflects offerings from the kings and priests. Wine offerings were very much appreciated by Sekhmet. *"How sweet is its taste to the nose of the Leader of the gods, Sekhmet."*[483] Meat offerings would have been common and are referenced in the funerary texts. *"You will smell the odour of fat from goats and pigs when Sekhmet is appeased."*[484] An offering text for an ox says that *"its heart belongs to Sakhmet the Great"*.[485]

Sekhmet Temples

Temples and their functions are covered in detail in chapters 23 and 24.

---

[481] *The Tomb of Antefoker*, Davies, 1915:24
[482] *The Gods of Ancient Egypt*, Vernus, 1998:184
[483] *Wine and Wine Offering in the Religion of Ancient Egypt*, Poo, 1995:121
[484] *Traversing Eternity*, Smith, 2009:416
[485] *The Ancient Egyptian Pyramid Texts*, Faulkner, 2007:235. Utterance 580

Abusir

Sahura (5th Dynasty) built a temple to Sekhmet of Memphis in his funerary temple at Abusir. Here she is called "*Sekhmet of Sahure*".[486] As in all major temples there are many statues of various deities. One statue of Sekhmet became an object of popular devotion in the New Kingdom when the corridor was roofed over and used as a public shrine for her. A gold plated, jewel encrusted frame was attached to the stone around her statue.[487] A number of votive stelae were found in small niches in the temple walls. These were inscribed with prayers and pictures of human ears; these symbolised the ears of the Goddess as the petitioners hoped she would listen to their prayers and respond to them. A reflection of this practice can be seen today in some Roman Catholic churches which have altars and statues dedicated to various saints. The more effective the saint the more candles and flowers they get.

Karnak

In the temple of Amun there is a small temple to Ptah which consists of five gateways leading to a columned hall containing three chapels. Two are dedicated to Ptah and one to Hathor, which contains a slightly larger than life-size black granite statue of Sekhmet. The statue is in a dark sanctuary lit only by light from a small hole in the roof. It is a sight that impresses and inspires may of today's visitors and pilgrims. Sekhmet stands and holds a papyrus sceptre and at certain times sunlight and moonlight filter onto her statue. Although atmospheric it is purely a modern phenomenon. It is somewhat disappointing to learn that the lighting of this statue was not part of the original temple. Legrain excavated the site at the beginning of the 20th century and he removed the slabs to create light-openings. The ancient openings were just inside the entrance door to provide light for the priest or priestess to perform the daily rituals.[488]

Statues of Sekhmet lined the processional highway between the precinct of Mut and the temple of Amun. Mut was the consort of Amun.

---

[486] *Ancient Egyptian Religion*, Cerny 1952:70
[487] *The Gods of Ancient Egypt*, Vernus, 1998:168
[488] *The Temple of Ptah at Karnak*, Thiers & Zignani, 2011:20-24

It is here that Amenhotep III placed the famous black granodiorite statues of Sekhmet. It is estimated that there were originally 730 statues, one seated one and one standing for each day of the year.

Many of these statues are in excellent condition as they were preserved when the precinct was covered by sand dunes which protected them from erosion. They are of the finest workmanship. The whiskers are shaped like daisy petals with little drilled dots near the point of each whisker and there are talon shaped hooks below the inside corners of each eye.[489] In the seated statues Sekhmet wears a tight fitting gown, with wide straps, and a broad collar. The best carved statues have a daisy over each breast. Judging from other depictions of costume this is an old fashioned style of dress, old being good in Egyptian eyes. Her right hand rests flat on her thigh and she holds an *ankh* in her left. She wears a typical woman's wig and a sun disc and *uraeus*. Around her face is a ruff of hair. Remains of paint have been found on some statues suggesting that they were painted. The eyes of some Sekhmet statues were red. As well as emphasising her raging aspect this would underline her close association with the fiery Eye of Ra.[490] These Sekhmet statues were taken from the precinct by later rulers to other locations and today there are dozens of her statues in museums around the world.

Kom el-Hisin

There is the outline of a rectangular enclosure from the temple of Sekhmet-Hathor. It was identified by inscribed statues of Rameses II and Amenemhat III.[491]

Letopolis

There was a principle temple of Sekhmet at Letopolis.[492]

---

[489] *Egypt's Dazzling Sun: Amenhotep III and his World*, Kozloff & Bryan, 1992:226

[490] *The Quest for Immortality: Treasures of Ancient Egypt*, Hornung & Bryan, 2002:169

[491] *The Complete Temples of Ancient Egypt*, Wilkinson, 2000:108

[492] *The Complete Temples of Ancient Egypt*, Wilkinson, 2000:83

Luxor

Excavations at Kom el-Hettan in the Amenhotep III temple recently discovered over 80 statues of Sekhmet in black granite.[493]

Memphis

Sekhmet's principal cult was in Memphis. A city in the Memphis region is also known as Ankh Tawy, the *"Life of the Two Lands"*, and Sekhmet is called *"Mistress of Ankh Tawy"*.[494]

Associations and Other Lioness Goddesses

Sekhmet was equated with Mut of Thebes and Pakhet. There are a number of other lioness goddesses whom Sekhmet can be aligned with, particularly as the Eye of Ra or the *uraeus*.

Mut

Mut's name has the same root as the word for mother and she was another one of the king's divine mothers. She is usually portrayed as a slim woman with a vulture shaped headdress surmounted by the crowns of Egypt. By the New Kingdom she was called *"Queen of the gods"*.[495] Mut is a daughter of Ra and is frequently depicted as a lioness-headed goddess, providing an obvious association with Sekhmet. The New Kingdom saw the rise to power of the Theban rulers so the Theban triad became more powerful and absorbed other deities. Sekhmet was included as the aggressive manifestation of Mut, *"the Flame of Mut"*.[496]

---

[493] *News From Egypt*, Taher, 2010:9-16
[494] *Understanding Hieroglyphics: a Quick and Simple Guide*, Wilson, 1993:79
[495] *Egyptian Mythology*, Pinch, 2002:168
[496] *Egypt's Dazzling Sun: Amenhotep III and his World*, Kozloff & Bryan, 1992:225

Pakhet

Pakhet *"She who scratches"* was the local lioness-headed goddess of Beni Hasan.[497] She was very much a lioness goddess *"whose eyes are keen (?) and whose claws are sharp, the lioness who sees and catches by night"*.[498] Her epithets were *"goddess of the mouth of the wadi"* and *"she who opens the ways of the stormy rains"*.[499] Lion claw amulets were worn by royal women to evoke Pakhet's protective powers. Some illustrations show the lioness-headed barque of Pakhet escorting the solar barque. Like the other lioness goddesses she can take the form of the uraeus. A rock cut temple was dedicated to Pakhet near Beni Hassan by Hatshepsut and Thutmose III. It consists of a vestibule with eight Hathor Headed columns connected to an inner chamber where the cult image once stood.[500] The Greeks associated her with Artemis, the goddess of the hunt, and the chapel became known as Speos Artemidas, the Cave of Artemis.

Bastet

Bastet is sometimes considered the more sympathetic form of Sekhmet. The king is *"Bastet who guards the Two Lands, he who worships him is sheltered by his arm. He is Sakhmet to him who defies his command, he whom he hates will bear distress."*[501] (Bastet is covered in more detail in chapter 21.)

Mestjet

An illustration on a 21st Dynasty stele from Abydos shows a woman and her daughter offering to a lioness-headed goddess called Mestjet the *"Eye of Ra"*.[502]

---

[497] *Gods of Ancient Egypt*, Watterson, 2003:167
[498] *The Ancient Egyptian Coffin Texts Volume II*, Faulkner, 2007:105. Spell 470
[499] *Gods of Ancient Egypt*, Watterson, 2003:167
[500] *The British Museum Dictionary of Ancient Egypt*, Shaw & Nicholson, 2008:311
[501] *Ancient Egyptian Literature Volume I*, Lichtheim, 2006:128
[502] *The Cult of Ra*, Quirke, 2001:32

Shesmetet

Shesmetet is a lioness goddess and was considered a manifestation of Sekhmet. She may have been a foreign goddess as one epithet is *"Lady of Punt"*.[503]

Wadjet

"I am Sakhmet-Wadjet who dwells in the west of heaven."[504] Wadjet is a cobra goddess of the Delta region who presided over Lower Egypt. She was identified with the fire-spiting *uraeus* and as the Eye of Ra could be depicted as a lioness, hence the link with Sekhmet. A 26th Dynasty wooden statue of Wadjet depicts her as lioness-headed. She is called the *"Green One"* in reference both to the colour of the snake and the papyrus swamps of the Delta. In some myths it is Wadjet who nurses and protects the Horus child in the marshes of Khemmis.

A purification formula from a Greco-Roman temple invokes *"Sekhmet of yesterday, Wadjet of today...protect the king with that papyrus of life which is in your hand, in this your name of Wadjet."*[505]

Conclusion

Having studied Sekhmet in more detail it is clear that she is just as much a goddess in her own right as she is an alter-ego of Hathor. Perhaps this might also have been true of the other aspects of Hathor. The Egyptians might have known individual goddesses behind Hathor the tree goddess or the sky goddess. One thing is clear, the *"great flaming goddess"* Sekhmet was not prepared to be overlooked in this way.

---

[503] *The Routledge Dictionary of Egyptian Gods and Goddesses*, Hart, 2005:146

[504] *Ancient Egyptian Literature Volume II*, Lichtheim, 2006:120

[505] *A Wooden Figure of Wadjet with Two Painted Representations of Amasis*, James, 1982:156-165

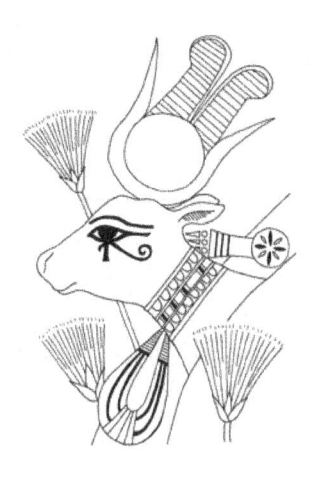

CHAPTER 20

RELATIONSHIPS WITH OTHER DEITIES

"The gods are joyful at meeting you."[506]

Family Relationships

Hathor is a very independent goddess but she does have family relationships, she is both a wife and a mother. Unlike with Isis this role is not her major aspect, she is Hathor first and foremost and her relationships are secondary aspects whereas Isis is one hundred percent committed to and entangled with the fate of both Osiris and Horus. Some of Hathor's relationships may well be symbolic rather than actual and in the early periods there is no evidence of any

---

[506] *The Ancient Egyptian Pyramid Texts*, Faulkner, 2007:144, Utterance 437

partners. Hathor's relationships with Ra and Amun have been covered previously (chapter 5) so will not be discussed here.

Like many deities Hathor is sometimes part of a family grouping called a triad which consists of a god, goddess and child. At Edfu and Dendera Hathor is partnered with Horus and their son Ihy or Harsomtus. At Kom Ombo she is partnered with Sobek and their son Khonsu. The family triad was a convenient means of linking formerly independent deities. It was mostly done in the New Kingdom. Triads can be deities of the same sex though these are rarer, family groups were the most popular. The family was of great importance to the Egyptians so this is not surprising. They didn't see a person as an individual but as a member of society and of a small family unit. Family was also important as it was the context where new life was generated. The triad helps to answer the problem of divine plurality and unity. To the Egyptians the number three wasn't just a number, three signified the infinite plural. To indicate plural in hieroglyphs it is either shown as the hieroglyph repeated three times or three strokes placed after the hieroglyph.

Horus of Edfu

Horus of Edfu was Horus the Elder. He was an ancient god, probably Pre-dynastic, and is depicted as a falcon. From earliest times the falcon represented the cosmic powers and his eyes formed the sun and moon. He was closely associated with kingship. Originally a sky god, Horus was later venerated as a solar god both of which closely align him with the sky and solar aspects of Hathor. During later periods he was joined with Ra to become Ra-Horakhti.

The annual visit of Hathor to the temple at Edfu was a major event celebrating their *"beautiful union"*. Scenes carved on the temple walls show the barques of Hathor and Horus moored together and the king offering them wine. This festival is covered in further detail in chapter 22. The solar god reunites with the sky goddess to renew creation. Their relationship is symbolic rather than being a personal love match as with Isis and Osiris.

Ptah

Ptah is one of the earliest gods, a creator god who formed all living things on his potter's wheel, but his influence was concentrated around his cult centre of Memphis. Here he has Sekhmet as his consort (see chapter 19). Ptah created the world through speaking and later fragments of this myth say that Hathor assisted him. "*The mistress of the sycamore was with him.*"[507] In some of the traditions Hathor is believed to be the daughter of Ptah. There is a festival where Ptah leaves his temple in Edfu to pay a visit to his daughter at Dendera. This is replicated in Lower Egypt by the visit of Ptah of Memphis to Hathor of the Southern Sycamore. Why Hathor is considered his daughter is not clear as Ptah is a chthonic god with no solar links. Hathor had a strong cultic presence in both these cities so maybe they became partners as a consequence of that rather than through any shared aspects. Hathor and Ptah were jointly worshipped at Medinet Habu and in the Sinai but their association there was not a close one.

Sobek

At Kom Ombo Hathor is partnered with Sobek and their child is the moon god Khonsu. This is seen as a rather forced grouping as Khonsu is normally associated with the Theban gods and is the son of Amun and Mut. Horus is worshipped at Kom Ombo but not as the husband of Hathor. Sobek is a powerful crocodile-headed god, his name simply meaning crocodile. He was linked with fertility, both of vegetation and of humans, and was associated with kings. For some reason he was combined with the sun god as Sobek-Ra. He often wears the sun disc and cow horn crown with tall plumes.

Hathor is linked with the Nile inundation and also with the north wind. It was this wind that helped boats sail upstream for part of their journey. In her Wild Cow aspect Hathor has strong ties to the marshy lands of the Delta and adjacent to the Nile which is also a prime habitat for crocodiles. Whether any of this is a factor in trying to explain her partnership with Sobek is unclear. It is more likely that it was Sobek's association with Ra which was the deciding factor.

---

[507] *Hathor and Thoth: Two Key Figures of the Ancient Egyptian Religion*, Bleeker, 1973:66

Sons

Texts at Dendera refer to two sons of Hathor and Horus of Edfu, Ihy and Harsomtus. Her sons are in her retinue at times but Hathor is not the ever present mother like Isis. They also remain as child gods unlike Horus son of Isis who grows to adulthood. Hathor's motherhood may signify something different and less personal, the spontaneous birth of gods as part of the triumph and power of her life giving powers. Child gods became important during the later periods, particularly the Greco-Roman Period.

Ihy is the divine musician and is part of Hathor's retinue but is seldom depicted anywhere but the temple of Dendera. There are references to him in the *Coffin Texts* and the *Book of the Dead* as "*lord of bread...in charge of beer*".[508] His name means "*sistrum player*". He is usually depicted as a naked young boy with a side-lock of hair and his finger in his mouth (a sign of youth). Sometimes he carries a *menat* and *sistrum*. The *mammisi* at Dendera celebrated the mystery of the conception and birth of Ihy. He can also be the son of Isis, Nephthys or Sekhmet.

Harsomtus was conceived on the fourth day of the festival which celebrated the marriage of Hathor and Horus of Edfu. His name means "*Horus the Uniter of the Two Lands*".[509] The unification of Upper and Lower Egypt was of paramount importance to the Egyptians and Harsomtus personifies that which is restored and complete. Like Ihy he is part of Hathor's retinue. At Dendera he is shown sitting on a lotus flower that has risen above the water and can be depicted as a child, a man or a serpent. This is the primeval lotus out of which the sun child emerges.

Horus the Younger

There are references in the funerary texts to "*Horus the son of Hathor*"[510] and mention of Hathor protecting and nursing the Horus child in the marshes of Khemmis. "*I have wandered through the*

---

[508] *The Routledge Dictionary of Egyptian Gods and Goddesses*, Hart, 2005:77
[509] *Understanding Hieroglyphics: a Quick and Simple Guide*, Wilson, 1993:84
[510] *The Book of the Dead or Going Forth by Day*, Allen, 1974:162. Spell 166

northern marshes, when I stopped at Khebt, protecting my Horus."[511] The Horus referenced is the same one who is the son of Isis and Osiris. This Horus is never the husband of Hathor. References to Horus as the partner of Hathor always refer to Horus the Elder. However the texts are confusing and the two Horus get merged a lot of the time. The king is both the sky god Horus the Elder and at the same time Horus the son of Osiris.

Hathor also gets involved in helping the adult Horus defeat Seth in the *Triumph of Horus*. All the major deities appear to have been drafted in. "*The net which belongs to Min, which was woven for thee and spun for thee by Hathor, mistress of the Coriander.*" Seth is defeated and all celebrate. "*Triumphant over their enemies are Hathor, Mistress of Dendera, and Thoth twice great, Lord of Hermopolis.*"[512]

Other Relationships

– Bes

Bes is a very ancient god who may have originally come from the Sudan. He is a dwarf with a large head, lion's mane, flat nose and bow legs. His ugliness made people laugh and it scared away the demons. He sometimes has a female counterpart Beset. Bes was always viewed as a friendly and benevolent god. He was a protector of women and children and for some reason he was closely associated with childbirth and his images adorn the Greco-Roman *mammisi*. A Greek inscription calls him "*greatest god of the maternity of women*".[513] He also protected against snakes and demons. In later periods Bes acquired a reputation as the god of dreams and his image was carved on beds and headrests to protect the sleeper from bad dreams. As an effective and protective deity Bes was welcomed by all levels of society but he never had any temples. He was a household god, a god of the people rather than of the king and state and was particularly popular amongst the poorer people.

Bes was a favourite of Hathor and of the Hathor cults. In the Greco-Roman temples Bes is depicted playing music to pacify the returning Distant Goddess. The Hathor temple of Dendera was a

---

[511] *The Great Goddesses of Egypt*, Lesko, 1999:109
[512] *The Triumph of Horus*, Fairman, 1974:102&116
[513] *Religion in Roman Egypt*, Frankfurter, 1998:125

regional centre of Bes veneration and a festival of Bes was celebrated here. His presence and his popularity continued into the Christian period. The Christians felt threatened by the power he held for the local people. Consequently they denounced him as evil and mutilated his images in the *mammisi*. They left depictions of Hathor and Ihy-Harsomtus intact probably because they reminded them of the Virgin and Child.

Bes seems to have functioned in the same way as an archangel or saint in that he mediates between humans and Hathor. An obstetrical spell from the 19th Dynasty appeals to Bes to fetch an amulet from Hathor (see chapter 13). It has been suggested that the verb *bes* means *"to usher in"* or *"enter"* and that when used in religious passages it signifies initiation. Bes might have been involved in initiation possibly reflecting his birthing role.[514]

That Hathor was close to Bes is obvious but how did this alliance come about? Was Bes connected with childbirth just because Hathor was? This seems unlikely but it is unusual to have a god with such a strong connection to childbirth. Like Hathor, Bes was associated with alcohol and music. He is often depicted playing instruments. Classical writers mention that when Hathor travelled in western Asia she was accompanied by musically talented monkeys and dwarves. Bes is ugly but Hathor does not discriminate on the basis of physical appearance. They are both compassionate deities with enough similar interests to maintain a friendship.

– Maat

Maat is also a daughter of Ra but with a very different personality to her solar sister Hathor. Both are shown in the solar barque protecting their father. Maat is harmony, truth and justice at all levels from creation down to the individual. *"The Mistress of the universe, who lives by truth."*[515] She is integral to the existence of Ra and in the Middle Kingdom is described as being the air he breathes. She came

---

[514] *Egypt's Dazzling Sun: Amenhotep III and his World*, Kozloff & Bryan, 1992:356

[515] *Hathor and Thoth: Two Key Figures of the Ancient Egyptian Religion*, Bleeker, 1973:20

into being at the moment of creation for without order and harmony there could be no stable creation.

Despite her destructive aspects as Sekhmet and all the drinking and partying Hathor remains faithful to the cosmic order. She is on the side of *maat* not of chaos, *isfet*. She is loyal to her father Ra and protects him from the Chaos Serpent Apophis. As the Eye of the Sun she punishes the rebellious and as the *uraeus* she protects Ra and the king, whose primary duty is towards *maat*. Hathor and Maat are often shown together in temples. Like Hathor, Maat is called "*mistress of the north wind*". She "*opens the nostrils of the living and gives wind to the god in his ship*".[516] In the *Book of Breathing* of Karasher there is an illustration of *the Weighing of the Heart*. The vindicated Karasher offers to an enthroned Osiris and a goddess called "*Maat-Hathor who resides in the West*".[517] As well as the solar crown she wears the ostrich feather of Maat.

Hathor and Maat do have opposite characters but sisters don't have to be identical. In fact they are ideally paired, Maat guides while Hathor empowers both individuals and creation. Hathor is the motivating force of life whilst Maat is truth, justice and order. These controlling and tempering forces are needed if life is to flourish. In some of the Dendera inscriptions Hathor is addressed as Maat on occasions.

– Thoth

Thoth is the god of wisdom and knowledge and, as with the goddess Maat, he is a counterbalance to Hathor. It is he who pacifies the Angry Eye and persuades the Distant Goddess to return. His cool wisdom and kindness balances her exuberant and volatile personality. It is Thoth's duty to calm Hathor down each day. For this reason he is responsible for the wine offering to Hathor. Thoth is also a protector of Ra and is frequently portrayed in the solar barque. At Hermopolis Thoth is partnered with the goddess Nehmataway "*she who saves the*

---

[516] *Hathor and Thoth: Two Key Figures of the Ancient Egyptian Religion*, Bleeker, 1973:69

[517] *Journey Through the Afterlife: Ancient Egyptian Book of the Dead*, Taylor, 2010:225

unfortunate".[518] Nehmataway wears a *sistrum* headdress and is associated with a local version of Hathor.

As Thoth is the Moon God it is fitting that he is aligned with the Eye of the Sun. This pairing of day and night is seen in the tomb of queen Tausert and king Sethnakhte (20th Dynasty) in the Valley of the Kings. The pillars of the sarcophagus hall are decorated with Thoth who protects them at night and Hathor who protects them by day.[519] The dominant themes in Egyptian religion are creation, the maintenance of order, procreation and eternal life. Although both Thoth and Hathor are viewed as creators and have afterlife aspects they have a major role to play in this life where Hathor is responsible for the continuation of life and Thoth ensures that life's energy is regulated so it doesn't burn out of control.

---

[518] *Hathor and Thoth: Two Key Figures of the Ancient Egyptian Religion*, Bleeker, 1973:67

[519] *Valley of the Kings*, Weeks, 2010:227

CHAPTER 21

ALTER EGOS & ASSIMILATIONS

"I arise as She-the-Scratcher, the Great One, with burning eyes."[520]

Merging and Identification

Regardless of their popularity and power the destiny of the Egyptian deities was influenced by political change. Egyptian religion began with the local deities of tribal clans. Over time areas coalesced, through unification or conquest, until Egypt became one country. As cities became prominent their deities became more important and widespread. In order to preserve their favourite deities the local priesthood would declare them to be just aspects of the national deity. Very popular ones would be found a place in an existing pantheon others just faded away. The tendency was for the local deities to

---

[520] *The Wandering of the Soul*, Piankoff, 1972:7

become syncretised, fused into a single cult. This ensured their survival as well as enhancing the power and aspects of the national deity.

There is mention of 18, 42 and 362 forms of Hathor.[521] This is due to the large number of local goddesses who Hathor assimilated, or was equated to, but it is also a way of emphasising the greatness of Hathor. As Hathor was a universal goddess she was often regarded as the form of the indigenous goddess in areas where she had no cult. Thus at Thebes she was identified with Mut, at Buto with Wadjet and at Elephantine with Sothis. Cow goddesses associated with Hathor have been discussed in chapter 3 and are not listed here. Hathor herself was absorbed by Isis and this is covered separately in chapter 25.

Anat

This goddess was introduced to Egypt from the Near East and was first attested to in the Middle Kingdom. She was primarily a war goddess but like Hathor had the epithets *"Mother of all the gods"* and *"Mistress of the Sky"* and a strong sexual aspect.[522] She was similar to the warrior goddess Astarte from Canaan and Syria. The Egyptians considered her to be a daughter of Ra and so sometimes equated her with Hathor. She was favoured by the Hyksos rulers and became a fairly important goddess in the Delta region during the 3rd Intermediate Period. The texts use the names Anat and Astarte interchangeably but they had different cults even in Egypt.[523]

Anukis (Anuket)

Anukis was a goddess from the south, with a cult centre in the Aswan region, and was considered a daughter of Ra. Her name means *"embracer"* which is ambiguous; it could mean a loving embrace or a strangling one. She was associated with Hathor of Thebes and viewed as the mother of the king. These two goddesses shared many attributes and epithets particularly in the 18th Dynasty. Both goddesses are

---

[521] *Hathor and Thoth: Two Key Figures of the Ancient Egyptian Religion*, Bleeker, 1973:72

[522] *The Routledge Dictionary of Egyptian Gods and Goddesses*, Hart, 2005:22

[523] *The British Museum Dictionary of Ancient Egypt*, Shaw & Nicholson, 2008:33-34

present at the jubilee festival of Amenhotep III rather than just Hathor as occurred in other jubilee festivals.

During the New Kingdom gazelles and ibex became closely associated with Anukis of Sehet Island (near Aswan) and hence with Hathor. Late Period literature refers to a *Lake of the Gazelle* which is believed to be in the Delta near Tell-Muqdon a site considered sacred to Hathor.[524] In the *Book of Traversing Eternity* one spell refers to the deceased encountering Hathor who is seated on a couch surrounded by a herd of antelope, gazelles and deer who regard her as their mother. The gazelle symbolised grace and elegance but their desert habitat also associated them with Seth.

Aphrodite

The Greeks associated Hathor with their goddess Aphrodite the goddess of love. She embodies natural sexuality as well as all the arts associated with love and passion. As Aphrodite Urania she represents the more mystical aspects of love and the soul. Hathor's sensual aspects align her well with Aphrodite although she lacks the cruel side of Aphrodite who will punish those who neglect or cross her.

Baalat

Baalat was a goddess from the Canaanite and Semitic lands, she is a female counterpart of the god Baal. At Hathor's temple at Serabit el-Khadim in Sinai a statue is dedicated to Hathor (inscribed in hieroglyphs) and to Baalat (inscribed in Semitic script). She was associated with trading and mining hence her identification with Hathor but unlike Anat she wasn't adopted by the Egyptians and she remained in the outlying regions. She was the original "*Mistress of Byblos*"[525] who protected the cedar-wood trade between Babylon and Egypt, a role later taken over by Hathor.

---

[524] *Egypt's Dazzling Sun: Amenhotep III and his World*, Kozloff & Bryan, 1992:351

[525] *The Routledge Dictionary of Egyptian Gods and Goddesses*, Hart, 2005:44

Bastet

The cat-headed goddess Bastet (Bast) is another Solar Eye goddess and daughter of Ra. *"The first-born daughter of the Lord of All, she is your protection until day dawns, until you go down to the realm of the dead."*[526] She is an ancient goddess, first attested to in the 2nd Dynasty, but was originally an aggressive lioness-headed goddess. Like Sekhmet, Bastet was associated with the dangers of the last few days of the year and cat amulets were popular New Year gifts. By the New Kingdom she had become more benign and was associated with the cat. She can be shown either as a cat or a cat-headed woman. Bastet is often portrayed holding the *sistrum* and many *sistra* are decorated with cats or kittens.

As well as being a more approachable version of the lion some have suggested that the cat was chosen as a religious symbol due to its aloofness. Cats were considered solar animals, although today we are more likely to associate them with the moon, and many depictions of cats show them with the sun disc and *uraeus*. Cats are both fertile and destructive; they have many kittens but also kill many creatures so represent both the renewal and the destruction of life. The cat is associated with Mut, Hathor, Neith, Tefnut and Pakhet as well as Bastet. Bastet was not always the friendly house cat, one *Book of the Dead* spell (135) refers to her fiery rage. An inscription on one of Rameses II's war scenes, from the Great Hypostyle Hall at Karnak, describes the king as *"his [bow] being with him like Bastet"*.[527]

Bastet's main cult centre was at Bubastis in the Delta region. The festival of Bastet was described by Herodotus in the 5th century BCE. *"The Egyptians meet in solemn assembly…on a number of occasions, the most important and best attended being the festival of Artemis at Bubastis…they come in barges, men and women together, a great number in each boat…the women keep up a continual clatter with castanets and some of the men play flutes, while the rest, both men and women, sing and clap their hands. Wherever they pass a town on the river-bank…some of the women…shout abuse at the women of the place, or start dancing, or stand up and pull up their skirts. When they reach*

---

[526] *The Ancient Egyptian Coffin Texts Volume I*, Faulkner, 2007:55. Spell 60
[527] *Minor War Scenes of Ramses II at Karnak*, Gaballa, 1969:82-88

Bubastis they celebrate the festival with elaborate sacrifices, and more wine is consumed than during all the rest of the year."[528]

Bastet was considered a divine nurse and protector of the king. At his *ka* chapel at Tell Basta Pepy I is shown receiving an *ankh* from a lioness-headed Bastet. *"Bastet. Giving all life."*[529] The use of epithet *"son of Bastet"* in royal names occurs in the Theban 23rd and late 22nd Dynasty but it is seldom used at any other time.[530] Bastet was considered the mother of Nefertem and of the *"savage faced"* lion god Miysis, the *"lord of slaughter"*.[531]

Bastet doesn't have the same relationship with Hathor that Sekhmet does though they have some similar aspects. They may have been seen as complimentary at times. This duality is seen in the Djoser complex and at the 4th Dynasty temple of Khafra where the north is represented by Bastet and the south by Hathor. At the temple of Philae Hathor is described as *"she rages like Sekhmet and she is friendly like Bastet"*.[532]

Mati

On the tomb of Nebib and his wife at Deir el-Gebrawi there is mention of *"Mati, mistress of Iatkemt"*. She was a lioness-headed goddess of the region, little is known about her but she was still worshipped in the locality in Greco-Roman times as she appears on the temple lists of the period. At Dendera she was considered a form of Hathor.[533]

Mut

As Mut is more closely associated with Sekhmet this is covered in chapter 19.

---

[528] *The Histories*, Herodotus & Selincourt, 2003:119

[529] *Texts From the Pyramid Age*, Strudwick, 2005:92

[530] *Partisan Royal Epithets in the Late Third Intermediate Period and the Dynastic Affiliations of Pedubast I and Iuput II*, Muhs, 1998:220-223

[531] *The Gods and Symbols of Ancient Egypt*, Lurker, 1986:32

[532] *The Cat in Ancient Egypt*, Malek, 1993:95

[533] *Texts From the Pyramid Age*, Strudwick, 2005: 366

Qadesh

Qadesh was a Syrian goddess who was introduced to Egypt in the New Kingdom. Her name means *"holy"*. She was the goddess of sexual pleasure and so was aligned with Hathor as well as Anat and Astarte. Qadesh is portrayed naked and facing forward which is unusual in Egyptian art. It is normally only Bes and Hathor Heads which are depicted in this manner. A 19th Dynasty stele from Deir el-Medina shows Qadesh with Hathor symbolism. Her hair is the Hathor style and she holds lotus flowers and either snakes or papyrus stems. She is standing on a lion. Qadesh is usually in a triad with Min and the Near Eastern god Reshep. She was particularly popular in the 19th Dynasty especially amongst the ordinary people.

Satis (Satet)

Satis was a protective goddess of the frontier with Nubia and any cross-border incursions were *"driven off by Satis, Lady of Elephantine, who will shoot at them with her arrows"*.[534] At Elephantine Satis is associated with the inundation and is considered a daughter of Ra. She is identified with Hathor in the Eye myths and is also considered the *"mistress of heaven"*.[535] In some variations of the Distant Goddess myths a pair of goddesses are worshipped as the aggressive and pacified forms of the Eye; at Aswan it is Satis and Anukis.[536]

Sekhmet

See chapter 19.

Seshat

Seshat, whose name means *"female scribe"*, is the goddess of all forms of writing and notation including accountancy, surveying and census. She is sometimes considered the wife of Thoth. An ancient goddess Seshat was more widely worshipped during the Old Kingdom.

---

[534] *The Ancient Egyptian Coffin Texts Volume I,* Faulkner, 2007:234. Spell 313
[535] *On the Position of Women in the Egyptian Hierarchy,* Blackman, 1921:8-30
[536] *Egyptian Mythology,* Pinch, 2002:130

She is primarily a goddess for the king rather than the people but she does have afterlife aspects. At Dendera Hathor is called *"queen of writing, mistress of the book, the one who commands the written word"*[537] and at Edfu she is *"Lady of writing, the mistress of the library"*.[538] These epithets are all closely connected to those of Seshat. Has Hathor assimilated Seshat or taken over her writing aspect? There is little to connect Seshat to Hathor. As a Great Goddess was Hathor assumed to be literate? Most of the Egyptian deities made use of Thoth as their scribe. Or does it refer to the act of writing as an art, a creative expression? Whatever the reasons writing and Hathor have a long association, one Book of the Dead spell says of Hathor *"She is wont to proceed to Heliopolis bearing the (hiero)glyphic writings, the roll of Thoth"*.[539]

Sothis

See chapter 4.

---

[537] *Hathor and Thoth: Two Key Figures of the Ancient Egyptian Religion*, Bleeker, 1973:69
[538] *The Evil Eye of Apophis*, Borghouts, 1973:114-150
[539] *The Book of the Dead or Going Forth by Day*, Allen, 1974:62. Spell 68

CHAPTER 22

THE WORSHIP OF HATHOR

"How happy is he who contemplates Hathor."[540]

Introduction

Hathor was the most widely worshipped goddess in dynastic Egypt and was viewed as kindly and protective. There were many temples dedicated to her throughout Egypt but the Egyptians also detected her presence in nature; in the rustling of papyrus in the swamps, in the breeze through sycamore leaves and in places in the desert where there were conspicuous outcrops of rock. We have found no detailed doctrine about Hathor, maybe there never was one, and so to understand what the Egyptians felt about Hathor we have to work from funerary texts, hymns, prayers and songs as well as the Greco-Roman information

---

[540] *Hathor and Thoth: Two Key Figures of the Ancient Egyptian Religion*, Bleeker, 1973:82

about festivals and rituals. Religious truths tended to be depicted as symbols and in myths rather than being described directly.

The Egyptian Concept of Religion

For the Egyptians communication with the divine was very important. A Middle Kingdom proverb says *"there is no life for the one who ignores god"*.[541] Their religion was the basis of their civilization and their culture and society had been shaped by the power of their religious beliefs. Art and literature had an important function in magic and in the cults, they were only secularised in later periods. Science too had a religious basis the priests were doctors and they studied astronomy, natural history and geography.

Duality was a core concept running through Egyptian religion and probably arose through the geography of Egypt with features such as the clear divide between the desert and the irrigated land and the way the south-north flowing Nile bisected the land. It also gave a negative undercurrent to their theology. Constantly aware of the ease of their own annihilation should the inundation fail the Egyptians perceived creation as a fragile state of being which existed precariously in the hostile and chaotic *Nun*. Here life was not only exposed to the risk of death but also to the ultimate annihilation and the return of everything to the *Nun*. Order, in the form of *maat*, had to be constantly affirmed and imposed on all levels of creation and society because order is intrinsically predisposed to decay into disorder. The deities, most of them anyway, controlled the principles governing order at a cosmic level and humans were meant to do the same on earth. This could be one way of looking at the dual nature of Hathor, her benign life affirming aspect constantly threatened by the potential for destruction and death in her aspect of Sekhmet.

Modern religions were created by the preaching of those who had received a message from God or those who discovered a divine truth. The Egyptian religion by comparison grew out of the life of the early inhabitants. Knowledge of the divine came from their observations of nature and the cosmos rather than through a revelation to a chosen few. Their concept of the deity was different. Although Hathor may be viewed as a cow goddess, a sky goddess or a tree goddess she is not the

---

[541] *A Newly Identified Stela from Wadi el-Hudi*, Espinel, 2005:55-70

personification of natural phenomena. Like all deities she is an independent spiritual being who is closely tied to the natural world. To the Egyptians the deities were not merely visitors to this world they belonged to the world and were of the world. Concealed at night they appeared in the morning as the sunlight illuminated the earth. Egypt was considered the centre of the world and every temple or sanctuary was a reflection of the primeval mound and heaven and every day a reflection of the first day of creation. It has been suggested that the earliest conception of deities was as natural phenomenon then they were conceived in ever more concrete terms, becoming more recognizable and less transcendent. The Egyptian deities possessed human characteristics; they spoke, thought, laughed, got angry, travelled by boat, drank and in Osiris' case died.

In a polytheistic society everyone could find a deity that seemed most relevant to them. Some deities were considered more powerful, being part of the state religion and worshipped by royals, but at an individual level the worship of one particular deity wasn't seen as morally superior to the worship of another. In addition the Egyptians were very practical when it came to deities. They selected the one most likely to help them with a particular problem at a specific time. As the deities were seen as active players in life appealing to them was a practical way of resolving problems. Letters of the New Kingdom always started with a standard form of greeting *"I call upon Amun, Mut, Khonsu, Sekhmet, and any god by whom I pass"*.[542] There was no such thing as too many gods or indeed worrying about worshipping the 'wrong gods' but some people did devote themselves to one deity.

Propitiation

Life in Egypt was hard and hazardous. People had to constantly contend with dangerous animals, crime and warfare, the risk of flood and famine, the loss of livestock and crops and infertility. Infant mortality was high, child-birth hazardous and illness common and inexplicable. Myths were used to try and explain personal and national calamities. Rituals were used to help solve everyday problems and to maintain stability and well being. The Egyptians believed that by performing rituals and presenting themselves respectfully before their

---

[542] *Religion and Ritual in Ancient Egypt*, Teeter, 2011:102

deity they increased the benevolent presence of the deity whilst keeping their dangerous aspects at bay. There was always a violent or dangerous side to deities that had to be propitiated by appropriate rituals and offerings. It wasn't unreasonable to attribute the bewildering problems of life to the displeasure of the deities. How else could sudden swings in fortune be explained, how one person could die for no apparent reason whilst another survived a major disaster or disease? If all the deities were all-loving and all-powerful then how could misfortune and suffering be explained?

Hathor and Royals

Hathor was always a goddess favoured by royalty. A cylinder seal of Menkaura (4th Dynasty) calls the king *"beloved of Hathor, beloved of the gods"*.[543] Hathor was very popular amongst the royals in the New Kingdom which resulted in temple building programmes by kings such as Rameses II and Hatshepsut. When the Ptolemies were on the throne they seemed equally enamoured of her. From the Old Kingdom, and possibly earlier, Hathor was considered to be the mother of the king. In later periods she was seen as the mother of all the people. The bull embodied the personality of the king, strong and virile, while the cow represented Hathor's protective and nurturing aspects. The king was often referred to as a bull and son of the Divine Cow.

Pepy I calls himself the *"son of Hathor"* in preference to the usual *"son of Re"*.[544] A 20th Dynasty letter refers to *"Hathor, the goodly mother of Pharaoh"*.[545] In the *Pyramid Texts* the king states that he is the eldest son of Hathor, namely Horus, and that he wishes to be reunited with *"his mother...the Great Wild Cow"*.[546] Horus son of Hathor was the embodiment of the cosmos (encompassing sky, sun, moon and winds) and was the origin of the king's divinity and destiny. The king was seen as a reincarnation of Horus. Both Pepy I and Mentuhotep II (11th Dynasty) state that they are the *"son of Hathor of Dendera"* and they were active in promoting the Hathor cult. Hathor nurses the royal baby

---

[543] *The Egyptian Collection in the Museum of Art at Cleveland, Ohio*, Williams, 1918:166-178
[544] *Kingship and the Gods*, Frankfort, 1948:44
[545] *Letters from Ancient Egypt*, Wente, 1990:50
[546] *Kingship and the Gods*, Frankfort, 1948:174

who is made the true future king by the divine milk he feeds on. This was a common depiction in the *mammisi* (see chapter 23). A relief at Luxor depicts the birth of Amenhotep III. The ram-headed Khnum forms the prince and his double (or shadow) on his potter's wheel while Hathor sits opposite and holds out an *ankh* giving life to the inert body.[547]

The king's divine conception is depicted in the chapel of Mentuhotep II. Hathor shakes a *sistrum* at Mentuhotep's father who sits on a bed. On the left Hathor is shown carrying the infant king. In another relief the king is identified with Hathor's son Harsomtus whom Hathor is nursing. In Hatshepsut's mortuary temple at Deir el-Bahri the Hathor Cow is depicted licking Hatshepsut's hand, this can be interpreted either as a mark of favour or that Hathor acknowledges the queen and bestows power upon her. Hatshepsut is also shown being suckled by the Hathor Cow. Hatshepsut said she built the shrine of Hathor in her mortuary temple for *"her mother Hathor, Chieftainess of Thebes"*.[548] At the Hathor shrine at Djeser-djeseru the suckling king is clearly equated with Horus in the marshes of Khemmis. *"I inhabited Chemmis as the protection of my Horus...I am your mother, sweet of milk."* In another scene Hathor says *"I have endowed your person with life and power, as I did for Horus in the nest of Chemmis"*.[549]

Even when Isis was merged with Hathor they had distinct functions as regards their royal duties. When the emphasis was on the king's divinity he was the son of Hathor and suckled by the Divine Cow *Sekhat-Hor "She who remembers Horus"*. If the line of succession was of importance the king's mother was Isis as it was she who granted him the legal authority to rule.[550] Hart suggests that Horus was originally the son of Hathor and the king claimed his divinity by aligning himself with Hathor. As Isis and Osiris gained in popularity the king had to be the son of Isis to claim the throne.[551]

The Libyan king Osorkon I wanted to show that the deities supported his right to rule. An inscription at Karnak tells how he was *"given life by Khnum and suckled by Hathor"*. Hathor is depicted saying

---

[547] *The Gods and Symbols of Ancient Egypt*, Lurker, 1986:74

[548] *Senenu, High Priest of Amun at Deir el-Bahri*, Brovarski, 1976:57-73

[549] *Votive Offerings to Hathor*, Pinch, 1993:176

[550] *Kingship and the Gods*, Frankfort, 1948:44

[551] *The Routledge Dictionary of Egyptian Gods and Goddesses*, Hart, 2005:62

"O son of my body...I created you specifically to be the great ruler of Egypt".[552]

Hathor watches over the king all of his life. As the goddess of regeneration and renewal she has the ability to keep him young and continually endow him with her power. An illustration to one *Pyramid Text* spell shows the king wearing a ceremonial apron decorated with Hathor Heads. This is a symbol of magical protection and shows the king's loyalty to Hathor. The apron was a very ancient item of clothing, the 1st Dynasty king Narmer is shown wearing one. Drinking the milk of the sacred cows kept by the Hathor temples was part of the coronation ceremony and if done regularly was said to bestow life, dominion and power on the king. Reliefs at Kheruef's tomb show Hathor attending the king's *heb-sed* festival. This was carried out after 30 years of his reign and renewed the king's fitness and vitality and empowered him to rule for a further period. Here the king is shown raising the *djed*-pillar while Hathor stands behind him with her hand on his shoulder as she protects him with her power. This ceremony symbolised the resurrection of Osiris and the stability of the monarchy. The *heb-sed* festival for Amenhotep III shows the king in the solar barque with Hathor. He is depicted as a young man to show that he had been rejuvenated and reborn.[553]

In the *Pyramid Texts* "*it is Unas who pulled up papyrus*", that is he performed rituals in honour of Hathor.[554] The role of Hathor underwrites much of the court rituals. In the Hathor temple at Dendera the king is shown offering a mirror, made by Ptah and Sokar, to Hathor. Ptah is the patron god of metalworkers and Sokar is a divine craftsman as well as being the god of death as transformation. They are often combined to form the tripartite god Ptah-Sokaris-Osiris. A mirror is a fitting gift to Hathor as the mirror represents the sun, especially the sun disc, which is given to the Eye of the Sun by the king who is, ideologically speaking, the son of the sun god. The fact that it was made by Ptah and Sokar suggests it has rebirth associations, perhaps reflecting the role of Hathor and the Eye of the Sun in this process. In one hymn from the temple of Ptolemy II the king recites "*it is to fasten*

---

[552] *The Libyan Anarchy: Inscriptions from Egypt's Third Intermediate Period*, Ritner, 2009:231

[553] *The Great Goddesses of Egypt*, Lesko, 1999:118

[554] *Kingship and the Gods*, Frankfort, 1948:177

for you the wsh-collar to your neck that the Son of Re Ptolemy has come to you, O Hathor, mistress of Biggeh". The relief illustrating the scene shows Hathor and calls her *"the Great, mistress of Biggeh, Eye of Re, lady of heaven, mistress of all the gods"*.[555]

One very important ritual carried out by the king, or the High Priest on his behalf, was the presentation of offerings to the deities. In the temple of Dendera a scene shows the king offering a wine jug to an enthroned Hathor. As well as physical offerings the kings offered *maat*. They offered a statuette of the goddess Maat to the deity to show that they were following her laws. From the temple at Dendera Hathor offers *maat* back to the king, who was probably in greater need of it than she was. *"I [Hathor] give thee maat so that thou mayest live from it, so that thou mayest unite closely with it and so that thy heart may rejoice."*[556] It was essential for all of Egypt that the king was imbued with *maat* so that he would rule wisely and fairly and uphold law and order.

Hathor was the goddess most associated with queenship. She was seen as the wife of the king from a very early period. In Menkaura's 4th Dynasty mortuary temple at Giza Hathor is depicted standing next to the king, showing her role as his wife, and also seated by him as his mother. By this time the king's principal wife acted as the High Priestess of Hathor and may have been viewed as an earthly manifestation of Hathor in the same way that the king was a manifestation of Horus. Queens often had the title *"Priestess of Hathor, Mistress of the Sycamore Tree"*.[557] The royal women related to the king as Hathor relates to Ra in both their titles and their iconography. In later periods this role was taken by Isis.

During the New Kingdom the purposeful blurring of queens with Hathor was more prevalent than ever before. During this period the king's legitimacy and creative power were very dependent upon his union with Hathor. In particular the 17th and 18th Dynasty queens were firmly associated with Hathor as divine consort and mother of the king. Amenhotep III commissioned a very large number of statues of various deities, either he was very pious or wanted to stress his association and identification with them. It is interesting to see that he

---

[555] *Adaption of Ancient Egyptian Texts to the Temple Ritual at Philae*, Zabkar, 1980:127-136

[556] *Egyptian Religion*, Morenz, 1992:121

[557] *Revealing the Secrets of Dendera*, Taher, 2011:22-31

sometimes had himself portrayed with lunar attributes (the Egyptians had lunar gods such as Thoth and Khonsu) whilst his principal wife, Tiy, had solar attributes and was closely identified with Hathor. Queen Tiy was the first queen to be shown wearing cow horns and a sun disc in her headdress. At Amenhotep's *heb-sed* festival she is depicted standing behind the king who is seated next to Hathor.

The Worship of Hathor by Non-royals

Hathor was a goddess who crossed all social boundaries. She was a goddess for women, craftsmen, labourers and the poor as well as for queens and kings. The major theme of Hathor's cult was optimistic joy particularly during her festivals. Egypt was not a paradise on earth especially for the poorer people. Infant mortality was high, life expectancy low and childbirth a major cause of death amongst women and there was a constant threat of famine and drought. Despite this the Egyptians, to judge by their literature, were not a pessimistic people. A series of songs named the Harper's songs tell people to celebrate this life and take pleasure whenever they can. "*Heap up your happiness, and let not your heart become weary.*"[558]

This did not mean that you could participate lightly in Hathor's service. An inscription over the doorway at Edfu would apply equally well to Hathor. "*Everyone who enters this gateway, beware of entering in impurity...come not in sin, enter not in impurity, speak no lie in his house.*"[559]

At Amarna

The heretic king Akhenaten accepted only the god Aten and held that he was the only human who could communicate with that god. The rest of the population, in theory, had to worship via the king. He downgraded the status of all other cults and in particular made a concerted effort to suppress the Theban deities Amun, Mut, Khonsu and Montu. It is not possible to establish how hard his officials worked at this suppression. It is likely that they were more lenient towards the

---

[558] *Hymns, Prayers and Songs*, Foster, 1995: 155

[559] *Hathor and Thoth: Two Key Figures of the Ancient Egyptian Religion*, Bleeker, 1973:84

other solar cults and to the less threatening domestic deities. At the Theban mortuary temple of Amenhotep III depictions of Hathor, Osiris and Thoth were not vandalised. The cults of Hathor, Sekhmet and Maat were very popular amongst the royal women and this may have allowed these cults to continue at an official level.[560]

Artefacts found at Amarna show Hathor's presence was still felt and needed. These include: fifty-seven Hathor Head faience pendants, a rare example of a Hathor image on a scarab, a few Hathor rings and a bronze *menat* decorated with a Hathor Head, a figure of the goddess and the Hathor Cow in a boat and twenty-two pottery fragments decorated with Hathor Heads. There were four pendants with a lioness-headed goddess, probably Sekhmet, and a few figurines of the same goddess.[561] A wooden Hathor Head was found in the workers' village and it is thought to have come from a Hathor shrine.

Hathor the Women's Goddess

Hathor influenced how women were viewed but society's view of women influenced how the Egyptians perceived Hathor. She was a sexual goddess and because women's sexuality is both celebrated and feared this attribute is reflected in the dual nature of Hathor-Sekhmet. Hathor's worship centred upon feminine values which would have been an empowering aspect for Egyptian women who lived, like all women, in a society focused towards the masculine. Women in Egypt were the most liberated of the ancient cultures but they were still disadvantaged compared to the men of their social class. They were expected to marry young, bear many children and generally played a minor role in public life.

Hathor is celebrated as the goddess of pleasure, love and sexuality. This gave her particular appeal to women as they were able to celebrate their feminine essence and natural impulses rather than be ashamed of them as many other religions and deities demanded. Women were particularly active in the cult of Hathor because she was associated with the areas of life that were important to them; love, fertility and childbirth. She was an important protective deity for women and during the New Kingdom she was particularly associated with women and

---

[560] *Private Religion at Amarna: the Material Evidence* Stevens, A : 2007:6
[561] *Private Religion at Amarna: the Material Evidence* Stevens, A : 2007:34-38

their well being. In an 11th Dynasty letter a daughter writes to her mother "*may Hathor gladden you*".[562]

Fish amulets were exclusively female and were an emblem of Hathor. They tended to be worn by young girls, either as a pendant on a necklace or in their hair, because Hathor looked after the interests of unmarried girls. The fish was an ambiguous animal for the Egyptians sometimes sacred at other times abominated. The Nile tilapia and Abydos fish acted as pilots for Ra's solar barque during its journey through the underworld. Being protectors of Ra gave these fish a direct link to Hathor as does the fact they were an emblem of rebirth. The tilapia is a mouth-brooder and the sight of her spitting out her young was symbolic of Ra spitting out his first-born children Shu and Tefnut. It also echoed the sun being swallowed by the sky goddess and born again at dawn.

Did Egyptian women prefer to worship goddesses? This is almost impossible to answer and might well be the wrong question to ask. The Egyptians worshipped many deities and will have been personally attracted towards specific ones for a number of reasons. They were free to worship who they wanted. Many men, including kings, were devoted to Hathor so she wasn't exclusively a women's goddess. Her attributes and her association with issues important to women make it inevitable that women would have been attracted to her and felt comfortable in her presence. There is some evidence that women had a degree of control over domestic worship, there is a high percentage of female-related religious items found in homes. The domestic cult of Deir el-Medina shows a bias towards goddess worship with Hathor, Taweret (the hippopotamus goddess and a protector of women in childbirth) and Meretseger (the cobra goddess of the Theban area) being the dominant deities. Does this suggest that the women preferred goddesses? Certainly Deir el-Medina is unusual in that the men spent more time away from home than in more traditional settlements which might have led to a greater emphasis on the female cults.[563]

---

[562] *Letters from Ancient Egypt*, Wente, 1990:63
[563] *Dancing for Hathor: Women in Ancient Egypt*, Graves-Brown, 2010:46

Hathor's Help to Mortals

A number of the deities were described as *"hearing"* that is they were seen to listen to the supplicant's requests and to respond to them. One epithet of Hathor is *"the Beautiful One hears"*.[564] Ra, Horus, Thoth and Amun are also described as hearing deities. One petitioner of Hathor says *"I beseech thee to hear me, O Golden Majesty"* another *"I pray that thou wilt turn thy heart to me"*.[565] From a Late New Kingdom Hathor shrine at Deir el-Bahri comes a votive offering in the form of an ear. There is no inscription but its message is clearly 'please hear my prayer'. A small stele from Serabit el-Khadim in Sinai is dedicated to Hathor who is shown as a young woman in front of an offering table. The inscription reads *"Hathor, Lady of Turquoise, [may she give g]ood life, praise and love to..."*. The donor has an appropriate Asiatic name meaning *"Shalim hears"*, Shalim is the Ugarit god of the setting sun.[566]

The help that Hathor gave to people has been discussed throughout the book and much of this help relates to her particular aspects; be they finding a partner, childbirth or the passage through the afterlife. She also gave blessings to her followers. The biography of the nomarch Khety I of Siut tells of his successful life. *"I filled the pastures with dappled cattle...Cows gave birth to twins; byres were full of calves. I was favoured by Sekhat-Hor."*[567]

Encountering Hathor

State religion was there to serve the state and the king not the people. Despite this the Egyptians were very religious but they conducted their worship privately at home or at small shrines which became the focus for popular religion. Hatshepsut and Thutmose III built special shrines at which ordinary people could come and pray to either Amun or the Hathor Cow.

Evidence of domestic worship comes from personal items such as amulets and jewellery and also from cultic objects and statues found in

---

[564] *A God Who Hears*, Giveon, 1982: 40

[565] *Hathor and Thoth: Two Key Figures of the Ancient Egyptian Religion*, Bleeker, 1973:20

[566] *A God Who Hears*, Giveon, 1982: 38

[567] *Ancient Egyptian Autobiographies*, Lichtcheim, 1988:28

Hathor

houses. Amulets are worn to protect the wearer and the words used for amulets reflect their purpose. S*a*, *meket* and *nehet* all derive from verbs meaning to guard or to protect.[568] Hathor was a popular form for amulets as were Bes, Taweret, the scarab and the *wedjat* Eye. This is one example of how Hathor crossed all social boundaries. Bes and Taweret were household deities of the workers whereas Hathor was the goddess favoured by royalty. Vessels with Hathor images on have been found in domestic contexts from the Pre-dynastic through to the Greco-Roman Periods.

At night the barriers between the worlds became thinner and so this was conducive to encountering the divine presence. Dreams were taken very seriously by the Egyptians and a number of dream interpretation manuals have been found. Ipuy fell asleep during the day, whilst celebrating, and had a vision of Hathor. *"My heart spent the day in her festival when I saw the Lady of the Two Lands in a dream, and she placed joy in my heart. Then I was refreshed with her sustenance."*[569] The stele of Djehutiemhab, an overseer of the fields of the temple of Amun in Karnak, had an encounter with Hathor in a dream. *"At dawn, my heart was delighted, I was rejoicing and I gave myself over to the West in order to do as she said. For you are a goddess who does what she says, a noble lady to whom one owes obedience...Place your face in order to let me bow down to it. Reward (with) your beauty."*[570] Qenherkhospshef gives praise to Hathor and includes a description of his visit to the Valley of the Queens which tells how he spent the night in the forecourt of the temple. *"I ate offering cakes during feast days beside the great spirits...I spent the night in your parvis; I drank water and broke the vessels on the curbstone in the parvis of Menet. I had my body spend the night, graced by the shadow of your presence; it was in your temple that I spent the night."*[571] (A *parvis* is the forecourt of the temple, Menet is a cave in the Valley of the Queens.)

Intercessory statues became popular during the New Kingdom. They relayed prayers to the deities in a similar way as do saints in Christian churches. In the temple of Thutmose at Deir el-Bahri is a

---

[568] *Ancient Egypt*, Oakes & Gahlin, 2004:454
[569] *Biographical Texts from Ramessid Egypt*, Frood & Baines, 2007:232
[570] *Behind Closed Eyes*, Szpakowska, 2003:139
[571] *The Gods of Ancient Egypt*, Vernus, 1998:173

statue of Amuneminet a 19th Dynasty priest. The inscription says he will pass on requests to Hathor in exchange for offerings. *"I am the is-priest of the goddess [Hathor], the messenger of his mistress."*[572]

Praising Hathor

There are two main ways of asking for assistance and praising and thanking deities, through hymns and prayers or by making offerings.

Hymns and Prayers

We do have a few examples of hymns and prayers to Hathor. This one is from the stele of Ipuy.

> *"May I pray to her*
> *for the greatness of her name,*
> *for the strength of her striking power.*
> *Love of her is in the hearts of the people.*
> *Her beauty is with the gods.*
> *The Ennead shall come to her bowing down*
> *for the greatness of her eminence."*[573]

The *Chester Beatty* papyrus contains a number of songs to Hathor.

> *"I shall laud the Golden One,*
> *extol her Majesty.*
> *I shall exalt the Mistress of Heaven,*
> *give homage to Hathor,*
> *thanks to (my) lady."*[574]

From the temple of Dendera we have:

> *"O perfect, O luminous, O venerable!*
> *O great sorceress!*
> *O luminous mistress,*
> *O gold of the gods."*[575]

---

[572] *Religion and Ritual in Ancient Egypt*, Teeter, 2011:96
[573] *Behind Closed Eyes*, Szpakowska, 2003:135
[574] *The Song of Songs and the Egyptian Love Songs*, Fox, 1985:54

A man who was in Nubia fighting "*the rebels*" sent a letter to his son, who was an administrator in Thebes. He asked his son to pray to the Theban deities (Amun, Mut and Khonsu) and Hathor to "*bring him back in good health*".[576] From the 18th Dynasty tomb of Amunemhet at Thebes comes this advice. "*Tell your requests to the Cow of Gold, the Lady of Happiness...may she give us excellent children, happiness and a good husband.*" There was nothing to fear from Hathor. "*If cakes are placed before her, she will not be angry.*"[577]

The deceased continued to worship Hathor and this is depicted in their tombs. "*I have come before you, O lady of the Two Lands, Hathor great of love...I kiss the ground for your ka.*" They were careful to remind Hathor of their devotion and obedience to her during their life:

> "*I was your true servant, loyal to your command. I did not spurn the words of your mouth, I was not ignorant of your teaching. I was upon the path which you yourself set, upon the road which you made.*"[578]

Offerings

Offerings are made to deities for a number of reasons which all echo the reasons we give gifts to other people. They are made almost as an obligation because it is customary to do so, to show love without expecting anything in return, as part of a request or to say thank you for something done. The most common form of offering is a gift saying 'please do this for me'. An advance payment to the deity looking at it in cynical terms. On a more spiritual level something from the material world is being given to the divine world so that divine energy can flow back to complete the cycle. Another reason for offering is out of fear or guilt, to propitiate a deity that seems to have been offended by something done or not done.

---

[575] *Gods and Men in Egypt 3000 BCE to 395 CE*, Dunand & Zivie-Coche, 2004:22
[576] *Ancient Egyptian Religion*, Quirke, 1992:134
[577] *The Great Goddesses of Egypt*, Lesko, 1999:114
[578] *Ancient Egyptian Tombs*, Snape, 2011:229

Food Offerings

The stele of Horrure has the following advice. *"Offer, offer, to the Lady of Heaven! May you propitiate Hathor! May you do this, it is good for you! Increase this, it will be well for you!"*[579] A relief shows butchers preparing meat offerings with the inscription *"move your arm for the consecrated gift to the lord of eternity and to Hathor"*.[580] Bread was an important offering and once blessed by the priests was sacred. Presenting offerings brought a person into direct contact with their deity. *"Lay cakes before me that I may speak to Hathor."*[581] In a letter from 20th Dynasty Deir el-Medina the scribe writes to the deputy of the crew Hay *"Come that you may receive offering bread for Hathor"*.[582]

Votive Offerings

There are huge quantities of votive offerings to Hathor especially from the 2nd Intermediate Period and the New Kingdom. These cover a variety of objects donated to Hathor by ordinary people, either as a request for assistance or in gratitude for her help. Some were found in huge quantities which suggest they were deposited as part of a group ritual during a festival or procession. Others were left by individuals. The shape of the votive object often reflected the nature of the request such as ears to encourage her to listen or figurines for healing and fertility. Other objects found are model phalluses, beads, amulets, cows and Hathor Heads. They are usually simply made, mostly are in clay though a few are of faience. Many seem to have been mass produced using a mould, testifying to their popularity. A large number of votive objects were manufactured at the Dendera temple and these would have been sold as votive offerings or as amulets to be taken home.

The nature of the votive offerings varied depending upon the location of the temple and the aspect of Hathor the donor wanted to appeal to. Votive objects with cow form and decoration were in the majority at Deir el-Bahri and Faras whereas at Gebel el-Zeit the most

---

[579] *Ancient Egypt*, Oakes & Gahlin, 2004:179

[580] *Hathor and Thoth: Two Key Figures of the Ancient Egyptian Religion*, Bleeker, 1973:44

[581] *The Gods and Symbols of Ancient Egypt*, Lurker, 1986:35

[582] *Letters from Ancient Egypt*, Wente, 1990:139

characteristic offering was pottery fertility figurines until the New Kingdom when jewellery items predominate.

Female Figurines

Female figurines have been found from the Badrian Period (Predynastic) onwards and have caused controversy as to their function. The figurines are made in clay, wood, ivory and stone and are highly stylised, they are usually naked and their sexual features are often emphasised. One unusual characteristic is that the legs have been truncated, it is suggested that this is to stop them 'walking away'. There are about six main types based on appearance and workmanship. They can wear amuletic jewellery such as a cowrie shell girdle or a crescent moon pendant. A few wear patterned dresses which are similar to those worn during Hathoric dances. They often have a wig in the style of Hathor; luxurious tresses with the ends curling over. It has been suggested that hair is a symbol of rebirth due to its ability to grow despite being shaven off. Sometimes the figures are shown nursing or lying in bed beside a baby boy or girl.

These figurines have been found in tombs, temples and houses. During the Middle to New Kingdoms they were popular as votive offerings in Hathor temples, during later periods they occur in Isis temples. They are found in the tombs of men, women and children. Various theories as to their purpose have been suggested. At one time they were dismissively called 'dolls' without asking why adults would have toys in their tomb. Another suggestion was that they were for the 'posthumous gratification of the deceased' again without questioning why so many women had them in their tombs.

The current belief is that they were to symbolise and reinforce the sexual aspects of rebirth and regeneration and to emphasis the female creative principle. This does tie in with the fact that many were left as votive offerings in Hathor temples. As fertility amulets placing them in temples near the power of Hathor would have charged them with her energy and made them more effective. In funerary contexts it has been suggested that they acted to increase the deceased's powers of regeneration. The deceased were frequently called upon to aid the living so figurines in some tombs might be fertility charms where a deceased relative was asked to help with conception. One letter addressed to a deceased relative asks *"cause that there be born to me a healthy male child*".[583] Contents from the tomb of a 13th Dynasty doctor-magician suggest that some may have been used in protective rites for mothers and children. One box contained papyri some of which were spells connected with pregnancy, childbirth and the protection of babies and young children. Around the box were wands and female figurines. It is thought that the doctor imbued the figurines with magical power and gave them to the patient.[584]

Textiles

Linen was the main textile in Egypt. Textile production was the second industry after agriculture and one which women were heavily involved in both at a domestic level and as an organised industry attached to temples and elite households. In the Old Kingdom women acted as overseers and the job appears to have been well paid. By the Middle Kingdom the overseers tended to be male, following a general trend in society of a reduction of opportunities for women. Reliefs in New Kingdom tombs depict male weavers, it is likely that the larger workshops were dominated by men but domestic production was still the role of women. Some goddesses, but not Hathor, are associated with weaving; the main ones are Neith (despite being a goddess of warfare and hunting) and Tayet (responsible for mortuary and afterlife linen).

Textiles were viewed as a suitable offering to Hathor, particularly by women, due to their involvement with their production and the fact that they were highly valuable objects because they were so labour intensive to produce. Textiles were sometimes taken by tomb robbers in preference to metal artefacts. As well as being used for clothing, textiles were used in temples for funerary rites and sometimes as a medium of exchange. Large numbers of textile offerings have been found mostly from the 18th and 19th Dynasties. They are particularly prolific at the Hathor temple of Deir el-Bahri.

There are plain cloths, often with bead fringes, which were used to wrap votive offerings in. Other cloths were decorated. Some had images drawn in black ink, others were highly decorated. The quality of the artwork varies considerably. All show Hathor in one of her various

---

[583] *Votive Offerings to Hathor*, Pinch, 1993:218
[584] *Votive Offerings to Hathor*, Pinch, 1993:217

forms; as a woman, a Hathor Cow in the Western Mountains, a Hathor Cow in a papyrus thicket or as a statue of a cow. Some of the cloths may have been to drape over shrines or statues. Peg holes have been found on the walls of temples suggesting that the cloths were hung as decoration either permanently or just brought out at specific times. Some of the cloths are of such good preservation that they were probably never removed from their storage chest. Shirts were also popular, these range in size from baby to adult and are decorated in a similar way to the cloths. These are not funerary items, they are made of coarse to medium linen rather than the fine weave reserved for funerary garments and are made in the same way as normal clothes. Some of the shirts may have been used to dress cult statues.

Given women's association with textiles and clothes it is unsurprising to find that the majority of donors were female. Textiles were an expensive item and many were given by multiple donors, either by a family or an artisan group. Why were the textiles donated? Some were a general offering. One was inscribed "*Hail to you, who shines as Gold, the Horus Eye upon the head of Re, may you give life, prosperity, health, skill, favour and love for the ka of the Mistress of a Household, Mutemwiya*".[585] Baby clothes might have been dedicated to Hathor in request, or thanks, for a safe delivery or by infertile women wishing to conceive. The inscriptions do not give any clues. Did the shirts represent the body of the donor hence putting themselves under the protection of Hathor?

Cow Figurines, Plaques and Pendants

Cow figurines were popular offerings at Deir el-Bahri. They range from faience models only 3cm in length to a limestone carving 25cm in length, an unusually large size for a votive offering. Others are made of pottery or wood. As usual they vary greatly in quality and the detail of the decoration. One is inscribed on the flank "*Hathor, Lady of Heaven*".[586] Many of the other votive objects were domestic items but plaques are only found in temples or tombs and were specially made for the purpose. Plaques and pendants of cows made of bronze or copper were popular items. They were also made in clay, glass and

---

[585] *Votive Offerings to Hathor*, Pinch, 1993:126
[586] *Votive Offerings to Hathor*, Pinch, 1993:162

faience. Some of the cows are unadorned others wear the sun disc between their horns and or a lotus collar. One is decorated with a *wedjat* eye above the collar. Pendants are of flat openwork and were probably strung with beads to make a votive necklace.

Bowls, Chalices and Goblets

Bowls found in the tombs at Thebes suggest a possible connection to the cult of Hathor due to their decoration. They show the primeval swamp and thus the fecundity of Hathor as the cosmic goddess responsible for creation. Some were drinking cups for use in cultic rituals, in particular for the offering of milk or wine to the Hathor Cow. Many bowls found as offerings in Hathor temples have water and lotus motifs. The marshland imagery of lotus and papyrus allude to fertility and the Hathor Cow. They are decorated with the Hathor symbols of *sistra* and *menat* and have inscribed dedications to Hathor. The Carnarvon chalice, dating to the 3rd Intermediate Period, is decorated with scenes of swamps in which calves stand on papyrus skiffs.

There are chalices, made of bronze or glass, which have very detailed relief decoration dating from 18th – 22nd Dynasty. These seem to be for offerings in funerary rituals. The 19th Dynasty tomb of Ameneminet shows the Hathor Cow greeting the deceased as he approaches the mountain gates of the West. Her head emerges from a papyrus thicket and in front of her is a chalice filled with vegetable offerings. A similar depiction is found on an 18th Dynasty votive cloth from Deir el-Bahri. One relief chalice has scenes of cattle around the border including one where a man holds one hand to the mouth of a Hathor Cow and the other to a calf running towards its mother. Other scenes show men herding and caring for cattle. In the background are papyrus plants.

Jewellery and Amulets

Amulets were popular offerings and come in a variety of forms. As to be expected those with symbolism pertinent to Hathor predominate; lotus, bunches of grapes, baboons, ducks, tilapia fish and *uraei*. Bes and Taweret amulets were also common. Pregnant women wore

Taweret amulets so they were considered a suitable offering to Hathor in her childbirth and fertility aspects.

Hollow ball beads, made to be worn around the neck as a necklace or plaited into the hair, were also given as votive offerings. Several examples come from the Hathor temple at Faras which is between the 1st and 2nd cataracts in Nubia. This temple is dedicated to the "*Lady of Ibshek*". These beads form a significant percentage of the votive offerings to Hathor at this site.[587] Faience bracelets were given as votive offerings, a lot don't appear to have been worn so may have been made solely for that purpose. Away from coastal areas cowrie shells were scarce objects so were considered a suitable offering as was their shape which suggested female sexuality and fertility.

Throw-sticks or Wands

Throw-sticks were used for hunting and are similar in appearance to the boomerang. In the *Coffin Texts* there is reference to them being used in self-defence by the deceased. By the Middle Kingdom some magic wands had a similar appearance. These were largely apotropaic, that is they were designed to repel malevolent forces. In the New Kingdom they were linked to the Solar Eye. It is not clear if these votive objects are throw-sticks or wands. Most are made of faience and are about 25-50cm in length. They have similar features to Middle Kingdom wands and have the *wedjat* eye inscribed on them. One wooden throw-stick has an inscription to Weret-Hekau, the cobra goddess who personified magical power especially in regard to the *uraeus*.

In scenes of hunting in the marshes a man is shown killing birds with a throw-stick and there are often cats collecting the fallen birds. One suggestion is that this scene is a metaphor for the king destroying his enemies, mirroring the way that Hathor destroys the chaotic enemies of Ra. Water birds are linked to the forces of chaos probably because of the visual and aural impact of large flocks wheeling around the wetlands. The cat is linked to Hathor as a solar animal and to the Solar Cat (a form of Ra) who fights Apophis under the *ished*-tree.

---

[587] *Gifts of the Nile: Ancient Egyptian Faience*, Friedman, 1998:212

Beds

A 22nd - 24th Dynasty votive bed was found at Medinet Habu. It is decorated with images of women on a boat picking papyrus and the god Bes stands on either side of the bed. It was probably used in fertility rituals. A stele of Petiesi, a soldier and priest of Isis at Philae, describes the donations he made to the temple. One item was *"a bed of ebony for the house-of-appeal of Hathor"*. Ebony was the most expensive wood available.[588]

Stelae

At Deir el-Medina several craftsmen set up stele to Hathor. Nefersenut and his sons kneel before Hathor, depicted as a woman, and he holds a brazier containing an offering. Ramose set up two stelae in the shrine of Hathor pleading for a son. His prayers were not answered on this occasion for we know that he later adopted a son. Perhaps he already had plenty of unappreciated daughters.[589]

Greco-Roman Objects

A Greek amulet from about 100 CE (now in the British Museum, London) has an inscription which forms the text to an image of three deities; a falcon-headed Bait, a frog-headed Hathor and a winged serpent Akori. The text reads *"One is Bait, one is Hathor, one is Akori – to these belongs one power. Be greeted, father of the world, be greeted, God in three forms."* Bait is the Greek derivation of the Egyptian word *bik*, falcon, so it is assumed that this means Horus. A frog-headed Hathor is very unusual, it may refer to her as a primordial or a fertility goddess.[590]

Some columns in the Greco-Roman temples have deep grooves in them, made by people scraping off particles. These magically charged particles would have been drunk in water or incorporated in amulets.

---

[588] *A Pious Soldier: Stele Aswan 1057,* Ray, 1987:169-180
[589] *Ancient Egypt,* Oakes & Gahlin, 2004:177
[590] *Egyptian Religion,* Morenz, 1992:255

Festivals

Public festivals were the one time that the ordinary people could view the cult statue and participate in rituals. During the major festivals no one worked unless they had to and everyone seems to have enjoyed some serious eating and drinking. Animals given as offerings were cooked in the temple kitchens and served to the general public. For many it would have been one of the few times that they tasted meat. It is likely that some of those who attended the festivals were transported into a state of elation or ecstasy and it is this experience which is the root purpose of the festival. It is unlikely that we could experience the same responses as far too often we are overstimulated, easily bored and too cynical.

At a basic level festivals break the monotony of daily life, especially when it consists of never-ending work. They allow people to escape and to experience something sacred. A religious festival will bring a particular myth 'down to earth' allowing everybody to participate in it. The numerous festivals will have been an important part of being Egyptian as well as forming the highlights of personal and community life. They lasted anywhere between one and fifteen days. Major rites of passage, particularly death, would also have been dealt with at festivals. Most of the festivals we have information about are from the Greco-Roman Period and it has to be remembered that these may well have been very different from those of earlier periods.

Festivals were usually celebrated in or around the temples and consisted either of rituals in the sanctuary or a procession of the statue, or both. Often they were very local in character. Even the country wide festivals would have local variations and were often celebrated at slightly different times. At these public festivals the ordinary people were fully involved and could participate and celebrate as much as they wanted. It seemed to be a personal choice. The work registers from the Valley of the Kings show periods of absence and different individuals take time off work for different festivals.

Hathor Festivals

It should come as no surprise that Hathor was a goddess of feasts and festivals. At the Hathor temple at Philae scenes on columns show Bes dancing at the return of the "*Lady of favours, mistress of the dance...lady of drunkenness with many festivals*".[591] At all major festivals Hathor's presence is indispensable as her lively character will light up and enhance all gatherings. *"Fortunate the ones who have taken part in the festival of Hathor."*[592] As a pre-eminent goddess she was present in most major festivals. Hathor festivals originated in the Pre-Dynastic Period but most of the details about them come from the Greco-Roman Period. A number of Hathor's festivals are described below. Appendix I gives a summary of Hathor festivals from two of the temple calendars.

The Egyptians believed that Hathor imbued her sacred statues with her energy so viewing the statue was the nearest a person could get to being in the presence of the Goddess. The procession wasn't just the display of a statue it was Hathor descending to earth to appear before her followers. Travelling by boat was ingrained in the Egyptian psyche. Reflecting the importance of boats for transport the Egyptian deities travelled in boats. From the Pre-dynastic Period divine emblems and statues were carried by boat whether they were on water or not. The temple boats evolved into small-scale gilded replicas of actual boats which the priests carried mounted on poles. The models were the same shape as the Nile boats but they had an *aegis* (a shield or figure) of the deity at the prow and stern. The cabin was replaced by a *naos* which contained the cult image. The boat was kept in the inner sanctuary of the temple either on a plinth in front of the *naos* or in a special shrine. When the procession went by water very ornate boats were used to transport the deity in their boat.

A journey by boat had religious significance. The boat used by the deity was a sacred object and was considered divine as it represented the essence of the deity as well as carrying the statue which held the deity's essence and power. The water the boat sailed on had a dual symbolism being both life-giving and life-taking. It represented chaos and death both as the primeval waters of the *Nun* and the mundane but ever present risk of flooding and drowning in rivers and lakes. By sailing on the water Hathor expressed her authority over chaos and death as well as her life-giving and nurturing aspects.

---

[591] *Dancing for Hathor: Women in Ancient Egypt*, Graves-Brown, 2010:168

[592] *Hathor and Thoth: Two Key Figures of the Ancient Egyptian Religion*, Bleeker, 1973:82

The Inundation

"*On that beautiful day of the start of Inundation, you shall hear jubilation in the temple of Khmun, when the Golden one appears to show her love.*"[593] The inundation took a while to travel north and each major temple along its route celebrated when it arrived. From the Late Period comes a green glazed flask, 13cm high. It was used to hold water taken from the rising Nile and is decorated with a cow goddess.

The Feast of the Valley

This was first attested to in the 11th Dynasty and was held on the new moon of the 2nd month of *Shonu*. It lasted for two days. The 18th Dynasty tombs of Thebes often contain a banquet scene which relates to the *Beautiful Feast of the Valley*. Images of Amun were carried in sacred boats from Thebes to visit various Hathor sanctuaries at the necropolis of Deir el-Bahri. There are temple inscriptions referring to this festival, one at Hatshepsut's mortuary temple shows soldiers and standard bearers taking part in the procession.

This was an important local festival for everybody. Relatives of the deceased gathered around their tombs to watch the statue of Amun process to the temple of Hathor from across the river. A flotilla of smaller vessels will have followed Amun's ship which contained the statue of Amun on his sacred barque. The barque was put on a sledge to be pulled overland. As they passed through the necropolis the musicians and onlookers made a lot of noise so that the deceased could hear them. By the late afternoon the procession had reached Deir el-Bahri. This bay in the cliffs was associated with the entrance to the afterworld and Hathor resided there in her aspect of Goddess of the West. The statue of Amun rested overnight at the sanctuary temple whilst Amun and Hathor celebrated their wedding. That night, in the company of their deceased ancestors, the relatives partied and drank.

The belief was that this broke down the barriers between humans and the deities and reunited the living with the dead. Hathor was considered to be present during the feasting. Offerings were burnt and myrrh scented oils were poured over them so that the thick, fragrant smoke would establish a link to the afterworld. In one tomb a man is

---

[593] *Ancient Egyptian Literature Volume III*, Lichtheim, 2006:53-54

shown offering four loaves of bread to the deceased *"for your vitality, the snw-bread of Hathor: may she be favourably inclined towards you"*.[594]

Various graves have depictions of offerings to Hathor during this festival. On one a group of singers offer a fan to *"Hathor, queen of the heavens"* another says it will *"dedicate all beautiful and good things"* to Hathor.[595] The sanctuary where Amun and Hathor spent the night became a place of pilgrimage for those seeking fertility charms and cures. Huge numbers of clay figurines of women and of Hathor were found here.

The Festival of the Beautiful Union

At this festival the cult statue of Hathor left her temple at Dendera and sailed 152km south to spend two weeks with Horus of Edfu. The procession was timed to arrive at Edfu on the new moon in the month of *Epiphi (Epep)*. Hathor had her own special ship called the *"mistress of love"*. The flotilla, composed of both official's and individual's vessels, increased in size at every city it passed and all the major temples sent a representative to be present at the ritual of the Sacred Marriage. The journey took four days.

On the first day the Hathor statue visited Mut in the temple of Isrw at Thebes. On the second day the flotilla reached the sanctuary of the goddess Anukis. Hathor was associated with both these goddesses so visiting their temples strengthened her ties to them as well as providing a relevant stop for the flotilla. By the third day the flotilla arrived at Hierakonpolis, here Hathor greeted the local Horus who accompanied her on the rest of the voyage. The cult statue of Horus of Edfu set out to meet Hathor at the quayside of *Wst.t Hr* on the fourth day.

Before they left *Wst.t Hr* offerings were made and rituals carried out to determine the most propitious time for their departure. The barques then set sail to the Hill of Geb where great offerings were made. Towards evening on this day of the new moon the flotilla landed at the quay of the Temple of Horus where they were met by cheering crowds. The two statues were carried into the sanctuary in the temple at Edfu for the wedding ceremony. Texts from the temple at Edfu describe one

---

[594] *Egyptian Festivals*, Bleeker, 1967:133

[595] *Hathor and Thoth: Two Key Figures of the Ancient Egyptian Religion*, Bleeker, 1973:43-44

of the doors. *"The Door of the Golden One, the Mistress of Dendera, and it is her perfect way to enter her house to unite with her image in the Sanctuary, and (also the way) to proceed to her barge to make her way (in procession) to Behdet at the appropriate time."*[596]

The temples provided food and drink for the festival and the city celebrated. *"Its youths are drunk, its citizens are glad...rejoicing is all around...There is no sleep to be had in it until dawn."*[597] The following day the statues were taken up the mountain of Behdet to a high sanctuary. One of the rituals carried out was to the *"godly souls"*. On the second day they processed to the summit of the mountain. Further rituals were carried out on the third and forth days, there is no mention of what these were other than they were held *"within the holy places"* so they would have been secret rather than public rituals. Hathor then left for Dendera marking the end of the festival.[598]

Hathor and Horus reunited for their wedding night might have promoted or generated fertility. The marriage festival could also be taken as a ritual renewing the deities or as reinforcing the foundation of kingship. It was probably a mixture of all elements, comparable to our treatment of the Christmas period which is simultaneously religious, be it Christian or pagan, social and commercial.

Some texts infer that Hathor comes to Edfu as the returning Sun Eye to be reunited with her father. On her arrival Ra-Horus cries out with joy and embraces her. This turns the myth away from a marriage towards a reuniting of father and daughter. The Upper Egyptian tradition views Hathor as the daughter of Ptah so in their version Ptah leaves his temple in Edfu to pay a visit to his daughter at Dendera. This is replicated in Lower Egypt by the visit of Ptah of Memphis to Hathor of the Sycamore.

The Festival of Drunkenness

Tekh, which means the *"time of drunkenness"*, was an alternate name for the month of *Thoth (Djehuti)*. It was derived from the most important feast of the month, the *Festival of Drunkenness*, held on the

---

[596] *The Temple of Edfu*, Kurth, 2004:66
[597] *Gods of Ancient Egypt*, Watterson, 2003:125
[598] *Hathor and Thoth: Two Key Figures of the Ancient Egyptian Religion*, Bleeker, 1973:94

20th at which Hathor was propitiated with offerings of wine and beer.[599] As humanity was saved when Sekhmet got drunk on beer, and forgot about slaughtering them, getting very drunk was a major feature of these festivals. This may be part of the reason why one calendar of lucky and unlucky days warns against traveling on the day of this festival.

The New Year

A scene from the tomb-chapel of Amenemhet shows the New Year Hathor festival. During this festival there were special celebrations in the temple then a procession through the town stopping at houses to bestow the blessings of Hathor on the residents. As they danced and sang the priestesses held out the emblems of Hathor, the *sistra* and *menet*, towards the audience. Did the onlookers try and touch them or was the gesture just to project the energy towards the people? One scene shows a performance in a private house by the musician-priestesses of Amun of Karnak and of Hathor of Dendera and the *ihwey*-priests of Dendera. It must have been considered worthwhile, or important, for the staff of the Dendera temple to travel the 50km to Thebes for this festival.[600]

Texts from the Dendera calendar describe how Hathor is carried in her ship to the roof of her temple to be reunited with her father. This ritual was performed alongside the public festivals but was done in secret. It was carried out at sunrise on the 1st of *Thoth*. The statue of Hathor was carried in procession onto the roof of the temple and into the *Chapel of the Union with the Sun's Disc*. The rays of the first sunrise of the New Year shone on the statue of Hathor reuniting her with her father Ra and reinvigorating the statue. The walls of the stairways she used are covered in carved scenes depicting this ritual. One inscription describes how she "*raises herself...at the head of her retinue and takes her place in her boat, she illuminates her temple on New Year's Day, and she unites (her) rays with (those) of her father in the horizon*".[601] The two deities reinforce each other and are reunited in an echo of the return of

---

[599] *Traversing Eternity*, Smith, 2009:152
[600] *On the Position of Women in the Egyptian Hierarchy*, Blackman, 1921:8-30
[601] *Hathor and Thoth: Two Key Figures of the Ancient Egyptian Religion*, Bleeker, 1973:89

the Wandering Eye. The text tells how all the other deities celebrate because of the harmony in heaven through the unity between Hathor and Ra. The reliefs on the staircase walls show the procession ascending one staircase and descending another.

A similar festival occurred at Edfu on the day of the New Year when Horus-Ra "*is accompanied by his great Uraeus-snake, the Mistress of Dendera*".[602]

Pulling Papyrus

The festival of *Plucking the Papyrus for Hathor* was specific to the Delta region. Scenes of the deceased "*pulling the papyrus for Hathor*" date back to the 4th Dynasty. It is mentioned in the *Pyramid Texts*, "*I have torn out the papyrus-plant...I have joined my mother the Great Wild Cow*"[603] and there are many tomb reliefs showing the event. In the tomb of Meresankh at Giza there is an illustration of her and her mother pulling papyrus where they "*view every perfect thing in the marsh*". As well as referring to the festival of that name, it also alludes to the marshes and swamps of the afterworld and is a metaphor for creation and rebirth. The tomb of Fetekta at Abusir shows two boats one of which has the inscription "*travelling downstream to pull papyrus for Hathor*". The other inscription refers to the return journey "*having pulled papyrus for Hathor*".[604]

The ceremony was called *sss w3d.w* and it is suggested that this phrase is derived from the sound of rustling papyrus rather than the word for picking. The verb *sss* means to rustle and is closely connected to *sss.t*, the *sistrum*.[605] The shaking of the papyrus would produce a rustling sound which was soothing to the Goddess, reminding her of her home in the papyrus swamps of the Delta. This ritual was also performed to bless fishermen, herders and farmers who worked in these swampy areas and were at constant risk from the unpredictable and dangerous animals that lived there, to say nothing of mosquitoes and other small but unpleasant or deadly creatures. This was a multi-

---

[602] *The Temple of Edfu*, Kurth, 2004:63
[603] *The Ancient Egyptian Pyramid Texts*, Faulkner, 2007:79. Utterance 271
[604] *Texts From the Pyramid Age*, Strudwick, 2005:420
[605] *Hathor and Thoth: Two Key Figures of the Ancient Egyptian Religion*, Bleeker, 1973:88

purpose festival, a festive custom with a religious undertone. Families could have a pleasant trip through the papyrus groves where they would pick papyrus to present to loved ones, the rustling of the papyrus forming a gentle musical accompaniment to the voyage. This developed into a more solemn ritual where picking the papyrus becomes an act of homage and worship of Hathor.

The Voyages of Hathor

Attendance lists from Middle Kingdom Lahun mention the "*Sailing of Hathor*" during the fourth month of the Inundation. In winter there is the "*Sailing of Hathor lady of Hutnennesut*". It is believed that the latter festival involved taking Hathor's statue from Lahun to Herakleopolis.[606] At Beni Hasan there is mention of a voyage of Hathor to the temple of the Seven Hathors. This took place on the 21st to the 30th of *Mechir*.[607] Ritual voyages are also mentioned as taking place on 1st *Hathyr* but there is no note of this in the calendars.

Return of the Wandering Goddess or the Distant Goddess

Many temple festivals celebrate the return of the Wandering Eye Goddess. Graffiti and rock inscriptions show that people went into the desert to help bring her home, just as Thoth and Shu did in the myths.[608]

Hathor's festivals tended to be joyous ones and at times her cult has an ecstatic character. This is in contrast to Isis whose major festival was the mourning of the death of her husband Osiris. During the celebration of Hathor as the pacified Angry Eye anything that might cause her to connect to her angry and destructive aspect was forbidden, in particular any activity or behaviour connected with death. This was referred to as *bwt*, which equates to our concept of taboo. There was a *bwt* about hunger and thirst which could ultimately result in death. "*The goddess of this day is Nebetuu (Hathor), for whom hunger*

---

[606] *Daily Life in Ancient Egypt*, Szpakowska, 2008:143

[607] *Hathor and Thoth: Two Key Figures of the Ancient Egyptian Religion*, Bleeker, 1973:91

[608] *Egyptian Myth: A Very Short Introduction*, Pinch, 2004:109

and thirst is bwt." A hymn from the temple at Dendera explains what is taboo during festivals. *"What is bwt for him is (your) hunger and (your) thirst, what is bwt for him is the st3 of the sun goddess."* The word st3 is similar in concept to mourning. The wretchedness associated with bereavement is incompatible with the feast of Hathor at which there is joy and rejoicing. The king makes an offering to Hathor to remove any sorrow that she may feel. *"It is a dancing presentation to my mistress, a deliverance from sorrow for your ka. The st3 of the sun goddess is my bwt."*[609]

Another festival referring to the myth of the Distant Goddess occurred on the 19th to 20th *Tybi* which *"was inaugurated for the goddess by her father; it was celebrated for her when she returned from Bwgm"*.[610] The site of the Hathor temple at Philae was said to mark the place where the Goddess arrived from her self-imposed exile. This would have been a boisterous and noisy festival of celebration.

Conclusion

For such a universal and well loved goddess there are surprisingly few hymns and prayers to Hathor compared to some of the other deities. There are, by contrast, huge volumes of votive offerings. Random chance and differing survival rates will have produced a bias towards artefacts over the written word but it would appear that Hathor was seen as a goddess who appreciated votive offerings. Was this because she was very much of this life, a physical goddess? She certainly had a connection to specific objects, such as *sistra* and mirrors, which is missing in the other deities. In view of her character Hathor might have been regarded as a goddess who appreciated presents and parties rather than hymns and prayers. Just because we don't have many examples of hymns and prayers, it doesn't mean that they weren't an important part of her worship, just that they weren't written down or haven't survived. What we do know for certain was

---

[609] *On Fear of Death and the Three Bwts connected with Hathor*, Frandsen, 1999:131-135

[610] *Hathor and Thoth: Two Key Figures of the Ancient Egyptian Religion*, Bleeker, 1973:91

that she was extremely well loved. *"It is the kind one, being kind to the one who looks at her."*[611]

---

[611] *The Evil Eye of Apophis,* Borghouts, 1973:114-150

CHAPTER 23

HATHOR'S TEMPLES

"This perfect house is surrounded on all four sides by an Enclosure wall, its kingdom is the kingdom of Ra. Its perfect façade shines to the south. There is nothing on earth that can compare with it."[612]

TEMPLES IN EGYPT

The Egyptian temples were not the cathedrals of their day open to anyone to visit or observe or join in the rituals. They were the earthly residence of the deity and hence were sacred and segregated areas that only royalty and temple staff were allowed to enter. Some areas were so sacred that only the High Priest and the king could enter. The hidden nature of the temple was emphasised by high encircling walls, semi-

---

[612] *The Temple of Edfu*, Kurth, 2004:67

darkness in lesser rooms and the total darkness of the sanctuary. Outer courtyards were open to the public on certain occasions and for the making of offerings. The Offering Court at the temple of Edfu was described as where "*the multitudes*" can enter.[613] Public religion was primarily for the benefit of the king and the state. Personal piety was very much encouraged but was considered a private affair. The only time the public were involved in religious ceremonies was during the feasts and festivals of which there were many. Although the Egyptians were tolerant their religion was exclusive in some ways, non-Egyptians may have been prohibited from participating at times. There is an instruction from the temple of Khnum regarding the festival of Opet which states "*do not permit any Asiatic to enter the temple*".[614]

Temples could be considered portals into the realm of the divine through which there was a two way flow of energy. Human prayers and offerings flowed in and divine grace and power flowed out. As such they were highly charged magical foci and needed to be hidden from the material mundane world to stop their power being abused and for the protection of the people.

The major temples were vast structures with forests of columns which dwarfed the human observer, they were designed to show the majesty and power of the deity. They filled the onlooker with awe and gave an illustration of how insignificant they were in comparison to the mighty deities although they were not intentionally designed to make humans feel unworthy. The remaining architecture of some of the temples is awe inspiring but they are mere shadows of the temples in use. The darkness of the temple and the golden statues of the deities were brought alive by rituals infused with light and colour.

Temples as Centres of Power

The main temples held considerable amounts of land. Some of these will have been used by the temple staff for their livelihood whilst others were farmed commercially. There is a Greek papyrus from Pathyris regarding the bequest of Tathotis to her daughter Kabahetesis. The location of the plots are described, one being bounded in the south and east by the "*sacred land of Aphrodite*". Another similar text

---

[613] *The Temple of Edfu*, Kurth, 2004:66
[614] *Egyptian Religion*, Morenz, 1992:53

mentions land in the same area near the river and the desert as *"vacant lands of Hathor"*. The name Hathor and Aphrodite are used interchangeably in the documents. It could be that the plots owned by the temple before the Greek conquest were referred to as Hathor's and those acquired afterwards as Aphrodite's.[615] One of the ways that temples acquired land was by donation. On his stele Washtihat says he *"donates 5 arouras of field to the estate of Hathor, the Lady of Turquoise"*.[616]

The high ranking staff of the major temples will have wielded considerable economic and political power, which is probably why kings controlled appointments to such positions. The temples were also centres of learning and the focus of intellectual and social life and formed the heart of a large community.

Notes on Architecture

Temples started as small mud-brick shrines with stone entrance ways and ended up as vast towering complexes constructed out of sandstone or limestone. Temples tended to follow a standard pattern. There is more variety of style in the smaller village temples as, being less important, they had more freedom to adapt to new styles. Some were built of mud-brick and decorated with painted plaster. Whatever its architectural style the temple was a replica of creation and heaven as well as being the earthly home of the deity.

The normal pattern was an open courtyard beyond which was the *hypostyle*, a colonnaded hall. This was broader than it was deep and filled with columns around a central processional way which formed the main axis of the temple. Beyond this hall were smaller halls and sanctuaries. The *naos*, or main sanctuary, was the most sacred and secret part of the temple. It was an oblong room without natural light and kept locked, it symbolised the mysterious and unapproachable nature of the deity. By the New Kingdom the temples of the major deities had increasingly become the focus of the area's religious and social life and they reflected both the wealth and piety of their patrons.

---

[615] *A Greek Testament from Pathyris*, Pestman, 1969:129-160
[616] *The Libyan Anarchy: Inscriptions from Egypt's Third Intermediate Period*, Ritner, 2009:409

6 - A Hathor Head column from the Hathor temple in Hatshepsut's mortuary temple.

During the reign of Amenhotep III there was an increasing emphasis on solar cults and the introduction of large open sun courts.

Mammisi, temples which celebrated the mysteries of the birth of the child gods, began to appear for the first time in the New Kingdom. Some were also dedicated to the divine conception and birth of kings. The *mammisi* were independent structures in the main temple complex. By the Greco-Roman Period they were present in all the major temples. The Ptolemies were particularly keen on them as the birth of the king could be linked to the birth of the child gods and this helped to support their right to rule Egypt.

The larger temples had a sacred lake, or pool, alluding to the time of creation when the land rose out of the *Nun*. This was echoed annually, on a larger scale, when the fertile soil rose out of the receding inundation. The lake was used by the temple staff for purification and also for acting out ceremonies. Water was essential for the temple. Stone basins, used for libation and purification rituals, have been found in Hathor temples at Faras and Deir el-Bahri. They are decorated with ritual scenes. A rough stone tank was found outside the northern entrance to the Hathor shrine at Serabit el-Khadim and several stone basins were found within.

There were gardens attached to temples which provided flowers and foliage for decoration and offerings as well as some of the ingredients needed for the manufacture of perfumes and incense. The *Anastasi III* papyrus describes the Delta house of Rameses and refers to "*greenery from House-of-Hathor*".[617]

The Greco-Roman Period brought huge changes in culture to Egyptian society and consequently Egyptian religion. There was a widespread programme of temple building which shows a distinct style whilst incorporating many ancient elements. No doubt many traditionalists were unimpressed. This period of temple building spanned about 600 years, about 1/6th of all temple building time in Egypt so it is a considerable legacy and a sign of just how inspired the Greeks and Romans were by the Egyptian religion.[618] All this temple building by the Ptolemies wasn't purely a reflection of personal piety, it was a very effective way of demonstrating their power, but by building

---

[617] *The Delta Residence of the Ramessides*, Gardiner, 1918:179-200
[618] *Temples of Ancient Egypt*, Shafer, 2005:186

temples to Egyptian rather than Greek deities they acknowledged the importance of the Egyptian religion which would have greatly helped their acceptance as rulers by the general population.

The normal approach to the Greco-Roman temple was along a processional way, usually lined with statues. This led to a gate, or *pylon*, and into an open air colonnaded courtyard. This was open to the general public. Behind were the *hypostyle* and the sanctuaries which were closed to all but priests and priestesses. Some temples had shrines for the general public and openings for the submission and receipt of oracles. The later temples were enclosed by a massive outer wall and details of the daily cult rituals were recorded on the temple walls, providing us with a wonderful source of detailed information. Gold was used extensively in the decoration of temples and it is thought that the images on the walls of the sanctuaries were gilded.

Like those of their predecessors the Greco-Roman temples were often centres of industry such as textile production or animal husbandry. They were also used as convenient places for drawing up legal documents and for adjudicating disputes. A lawsuit dating to around 117 BCE refers to judges "*sitting in the judgement house*" which was in the Hathor temple at Sharuna.[619]

Hathor Head Columns

The papyrus columns in temples represent the papyrus and lotus which grew on the primeval mound and which represented Upper and Lower Egypt. A number of the columns have capitals with religious iconography. The Hathor Headed ones are particularly striking but there are other forms such as *sistrum*, lioness, serpent, papyrus flower or sycamore.

The Hathor Head on a column is a fusion of human and bovine features. The capital of the pillar forms a human face but it has a slightly triangular shape with hair curls and cow ears. This does give an other-worldly appearance which encouraged one modern myth of Hathor as one of a group of aliens who established contact with the Ancient Egyptians. Hathor was called the "*female soul with two faces*" and one of her original cult symbols may have been two cow heads

---

[619] *Egyptian Law Courts in Pharaonic and Hellenistic Times*, Allam, 1991:109-127

Hathor

surmounted on a pole which eventual morphed into the Hathor Head columns. Hathor Heads were carried on poles and displayed during festivals. A plaque from Serabit shows one which may have been carried as a sacred standard during mining expeditions.[620]

Hathor Head capitals were used from the Old Kingdom, the earliest one found is in the palace of Djoser. It consists of a Hathor mask fixed over the top of fluted columns. The style evolved and by the Middle Kingdom the capitals consisted of two opposing faces with the hair curling upwards and outwards. A second form appeared in the New Kingdom where the hair hung vertically. Hathor Heads from the Greco-Roman Period often have four faces and the hair style varies.[621]

The two faces of Hathor on the columns may illustrate her dual roles as goddess of life and death, midwife of birth and rebirth and her liminal position on the boundary between the worlds of the living and the dead. Equally it could allude to her dual nature of benevolent and dangerous. Prayers to Hathor often contain the phrase "*may your merciful face be towards me*".[622] The *sistrum* is used to pacify the deities, Hathor in particular, so did the Hathor Head columns have the same function? The use of four faces raises more questions. Most four faced columns are from the Greco-Roman Period but the earliest one comes from the 18th Dynasty. Did this arise from a desire for further symmetry and pattern with the east-west alignment representing life and the afterlife and the north-south one representing the unification of Egypt? It could allude to the ever watchful Eye of Ra which looks in all directions for the enemies of Ra or to Hathor as the "*Mistress of the Four Quarters of Heaven*".[623] The sky is supported by four columns and there are four legs of the Celestial Cow. There is an inscription in the temple of Edfu "*rejoice in the four faces of Re*"[624] which may refer to the four faces of the Hathor columns. As the Eye of Ra or the Sun Disc Hathor is in effect the visible part of the sun god.

Hathor Head columns, not surprisingly, are found in buildings associated with Hathor. Examples occur throughout Egypt, such as in the temple of Hatshepsut at Deir el-Bahri and the temple of Nefertari at

---

[620] *Votive Offerings to Hathor*, Pinch, 1993:155
[621] *A New Temple for Hathor*, el-Sayed, 1978:5
[622] *Hathor Rising*, Roberts, 2001:57
[623] *Votive Offerings to Hathor*, Pinch, 1993:158
[624] *Wine and Wine Offering in the Religion of Ancient Egypt*, Poo, 1995:129

Abu Simbel. The most famous are to be found in the Ptolemaic temple of Hathor at Dendera. Here there are twenty-four columns decorated with Hathor faces on all four sides. Hathor Head columns are only found in religious buildings and on religious furniture. It is unlikely that they were viewed as a representation of Hathor in the same way that way her cult statue was, because Hathor's statue could be infused with her power. Despite this there is evidence that they were the focus of unofficial cults. A giant Hathor face on the outside rear wall of her temple at Dendera was an object of popular devotion. Inscriptions do show worshippers adoring, or offering to, a Hathor Head column but this might just be a way of representing the worship of Hathor.[625]

Some authors have suggested that the Hathor Head column is a *'tree of life'* linked to the *djed* pillar which represented the resurrection of Osiris and symbolised the fertility of the soil and the annual regeneration of vegetation. Hathor Head columns are usually associated with marsh vegetation which shows very little seasonal change but it still could symbolise the ever present fertility generated wherever Hathor resides. Votive plaques and stelae do show Hathor Head columns flanked by lotus buds and they can have blue lotus capitals. In some the Hathor face replaces the open lotus flower which is commonly shown between two buds. This symbolises the primal lotus from which the infant sun god emerged and emphasises Hathor's role as mother of Ra. A votive Hathor Head column from Deir el-Bahri sits on a double-stair base. This sign is used to refer to the primeval mound which arose from the *Nun* and links Hathor with the emergence of creation.

Objects in the Temple

The *ba* of the deity was believed to manifest in all of their temples and statues. It could be thought of as their energy actively focused onto many places at the same time. The *ba* is the deity's divine substance and vitality. The living sacred animals were sometimes called the *ba* of the deity.

---

[625] *Votive Offerings to Hathor*, Pinch, 1993:155

Statues

Statues housed the divine essence of the deity they portrayed. The Egyptians did not see any problem in reattributing symbols and images. As long as the deity recognised the statue that was all that really mattered. Once a statue had been completed rituals were performed on it in the workshop which was called the *House of Gold*. The ceremony of the *Opening of the Mouth* made the statue 'come alive' in preparation for being inhabited by the deity. An inscription in the sun temple of Niuserre lists works carried out "*fashioning and opening the mouth in the House of Gold of (statues of) Re and Hathor*".[626] The statue was considered to be inanimate but the ritual gave it vitality allowing it to be a temporary residence for the deity. The *ba* of the deity could then descend and enter the image. The following inscriptions from the temple at Dendera explain how Hathor's divine power enters the cult statues: "*She flies from heaven...to enter the horizon of her ka upon earth, she flies upon her body, she coalesces with her form...She coalesces with her form, which is engraved in her sanctuary...She settles upon her form, which is engraved upon the wall.*"[627] As well as cult statues there were numerous statues made for private worship. It is possible that a similar ritual was carried out either by the priests or priestess or by their owners.

The Sacred Barque

Boats were deeply embedded in the Egyptian psyche. Virtually everyone lived close to a river. Given the importance of boats in everyday life it is inevitable that the deities travelled in boats. At first impression it seems odd that there is a solar barque to transport Ra but then we refer to space-ships. Even when travelling over dry land the deities used a boat. In the dry land of the underworld Ra is still in his barque and it is towed along. When the Nile ran low navigation was difficult and many times the crew would have had to drag the boat off sandbanks and through too shallow water. It would have been a familiar sight to the Egyptians. Statues of deities were always carried in boats and every temple had a gilded and decorated barque for use in processions. The statue was housed in a central cabin, sometimes

---

[626] *Texts From the Pyramid Age*, Strudwick, 2005:90
[627] *Egyptian Religion*, Morenz, 1992:152

hidden by a linen veil. Just as a statue could hold the power of the deity so could their barque. At Dendera Hathor's barques were named *"mistress of love"* and *"the one who illuminates the two lands"*[628] and they were considered an expression of Hathor.

HATHOR'S TEMPLES

There were more temples and shrines throughout Egypt to Hathor than to any other goddess. Her most important temples were at Gebelein, Cusae, Deir el-Medina and Dendera, which was her greatest cult centre. She was also the primary goddess in the Horus temple at Edfu and the Ptah temple at Memphis. Even though a temple might be dedicated to a specific deity many other deities were present and worshipped there. Hathor is no exception, she was welcomed in all temples. A Greco-Roman text refers to Hathor as one who *"makes great the Mansion of Life"*. That is, her presence in the temple increases its importance and power.[629]

Dendera

Dendera was the ancient capital of the 6th nome of Upper Egypt and the cult centre of Hathor from the 4th Dynasty. Due to its location it was an important centre and had a necropolis from the earliest dynasties. It is located at the edge of the western desert on the left bank of the Nile, 60km north of Luxor, and close to the mouth of the Wadi Hammamat route to the Red Sea. It is sited on the great bend of the Nile which resulted in the temple being orientated north-south rather than the normal east-west. During the Late Period the epithet Ta-neteret, meaning *"of the goddess"*, was added to its name and the Greeks called it Tentyrus.[630] The temple is one of the best preserved and most complete of the Greco-Roman temples and is continually being studied. Here Hathor's solar aspect is emphasised. On the rear wall of the *naos*, marking its axis, Hathor's face rests on the hieroglyph sign for gold (an ornamental collar above three granules) and the sun

---

[628] *Hathor and Thoth: Two Key Figures of the Ancient Egyptian Religion*, Bleeker, 1973:60

[629] *The Mansion of Life and the Master of the King's Largess*, Gardiner, 1938.1:83-91

[630] *Gods of Ancient Egypt*, Watterson, 2003:122

rests on her head. The rain spouts on the roofs are decorated with lion-headed gargoyles. As well as having a cultic relationship with the temple of Horus at Edfu the temple of Dendera also has an architectural one. The same workforce built and decorated the pylons and the main temple buildings are very similar in design.[631]

History of the Hathor Temple at Dendera

It is believed that the earliest shrine was to "*She of the Pillar*" which appears to be a reference to a Hathor fetish. According to inscriptions on the walls of the southern crypt the temple was built on a very ancient site which dated to the "*time of Horus*" a mythical time when the gods ruled on earth. When Khufu rebuilt the temple in the 4th Dynasty it was said that records of the first temple were found on rolls of leather. It was dedicated to "*Hathor, Lady of the Pillar*" and her son Ihy. This early epithet may give a clue as to why there are Hathor Head columns. The temple was reorganised by Pepy I and he gave a gold statue of Ihy to the temple. In the 11th Dynasty Mentuhotep II built a chapel. The temple was extended by several New Kingdom kings and Thutmose III rebuilt the temple and, according to inscriptions, revived some of the rituals. Even though the older buildings were demolished in the Ptolemaic Period there are still blocks containing inscriptions referring to Amenhotep III, Rameses II and III and Shabaqo (25th Dynasty).[632]

Work on the temple we have today probably began in the reign of Ptolemy XII. An inscription on the main façade of the temple says that construction began on 16th July 54 BCE and services began in 29 BCE. The foundation of the *pronaos* began in the reign of Tiberius and the decoration of various walls was completed during the reigns of Caligula, Claudius and Nero (14-68 CE). Claudius is shown presenting offerings to the deities. It was abandoned during the 1st Century CE and many of the faces on the Hathor Head columns were deliberately vandalised by the early Christians.

---

[631] *Egypt from Alexander to the Copts*, Bagnal & Rathbone, 2004:212
[632] *Revealing the Secrets of Dendera*, Taher, 2011:22-31

Structure

The temple is entered through a Roman gateway and there is a mud-brick enclosure wall. In front of the northern gate are a Roman fountain and two columns and by the fountain are two basins which were used for purification before entering the temple. Each side gate is guarded by a sphinx. The lintels and ceiling slabs are decorated with vultures and winged sun discs. This section dates to the reigns of Domitian and Trajan (81-117 CE). The outer walls show scenes of the foundation of the temple and offerings made at the time. A relief shows Cleopatra VII and Caesarean, her son by Julius Caesar, presenting offerings to Hathor and Isis.[633]

The columns in the façade and outer Hypostyle Hall have Hathor Head capitals. They are in the form of a Hathor Head surmounted by a *naos sistrum.* Each year, during the night of the eve of her birthday (New Year's Day), the priests carried the statue of Hathor to the rooftop *Chapel of the Union with the Sun's Disc.* The rising sun rejuvenated the statue as it bathed it in light. This ritual is depicted on a relief of exceptional quality on the ceiling of the Hypostyle Hall. Hathor is depicted both as the Hathor Cow and as a woman with cow's head and ears. In the ceiling representation of Hathor she wears a rectangular building as a crown. This may be an accurate representation of the chapel as well as showing the hieroglyph for the palace wall, *serekh*, which alludes to her name as *House of Horus*. A large circle represents the newly risen sun god Ra who sends his light streaming down to revive his daughter.

The Offerings Hall has depictions of the king preparing offerings. This was the entrance to the temple proper and is lit by ceiling vents. Rituals depicted include presenting *maat*, *sistra* and amulets and the burning of incense. The kings and emperors were shown participating in rituals and festivals. This was partly propaganda to show the locals that their foreign rulers had been personally selected by the Egyptian deities.

The columned Great Hall is the most impressive part of the temple. There are 24 columns, 15m high, with Hathor Head capitals. These are in the form of a *sistrum* with the cow-eared face of Hathor. The face appears on all four sides which may allude to her being the goddess of

---

[633] *Revealing the Secrets of Dendera*, Taher, 2011:22-31

the four cardinal points. The Great Hall leads on to a smaller six columned hypostyle, the *Hall of Appearances*, where statues were brought out for processions. It has inscriptions of founding ceremonies; from the king laying out the ground plan with Seshat to the purification of the temple and its presentation to Hathor and Horus. Seshat, the goddess of writing and notation, was considered present in the laying out and construction of all religious buildings. The Sanctuary held the statues of Hathor and Horus and her sacred barque. The reliefs show the presentation of offerings and the sacred barques of Hathor and Horus.[634] Eleven chapels around the central sanctuary were dedicated for the *menat* and *sistrum* and for deities associated with Hathor. Some of these were rooms "*of which no stranger knows the contents and of which the entrances are hidden*".[635]

The ceiling decoration, completed in 50 BCE, in one of the chapels has elaborate scenes of astrology with Nut's body forming the heavens. As a sky goddess they believed that Hathor would have appreciated it if her home on earth reflected her cosmic one. This depiction of the zodiac and astronomical features is a fusion of Egyptian and foreign ideas. The concept of the zodiac originated in Mesopotamia but it wasn't adopted by the Egyptians until much later, the earliest example is about 200 BCE in the temple of Khmun at Esna. It was particularly popular during the Roman Period. The original was removed by Napoleon's expedition and is now in the Louvre Museum (Paris).

The western staircase leading to the roof has depictions of the procession of Hathor (in her four forms) and Ihy ascending to the New Year Chapel on the southwest corner of the roof to reunite with the sun disc. There are six Osiris chapels on the roof which contain scenes of his resurrection and of festivals held during the month of *Khoiak*. These were decorated 50-48 BCE and inaugurated in December 47 BCE during a zenithal full moon, a conjunction that occurs only once every 1,480 years.

Crypts were used to store the treasures of the temple. Reliefs in the crypts depict the cult items that were stored there, most important of these was the *ba* statue of Hathor. This was the one used in processions and taken to the roof for uniting with the sun at the New

---

[634] *Revealing the Secrets of Dendera*, Taher, 2011:22-31

[635] *Hathor and Thoth: Two Key Figures of the Ancient Egyptian Religion*, Bleeker, 1973:78

Year festival. Some of the side chambers were used for the manufacture of perfumes and incense and for the preparation of offerings. One was used for the storage of the ornaments used to decorate cult statues.

There are two *mammisi* at Dendera. One is that of Nectanebo I (30th Dynasty) which was added to by a number of the Ptolemies. The second one is dedicated to Ihy and dates to the reign of Augustus (30 BCE – 14 CE) and was added to by Trajan and Marcus Aurelius. The decoration shows the birth of Ihy in the presence of the local gods. One relief shows Ihy being formed by Khnum, the ram-headed god who created all life on his potter's wheel. The chapel in the middle held a birthing chair. Inscriptions and scenes show that the *mammisi* was used in important rituals referencing the divine birth of kings. Hathor priestesses play drums and shake *sistra* and the emperors are shown offering to Hathor and the triad. One relief shows Hathor nursing Ihy.

Outside the main temple was a sanatorium for the accommodation and healing of pilgrims. There may have been an incubation chamber and it is believed to have been a centre for *cippus* healing. A *cippus* was a protective stele showing the Horus child which had the power to overcome hostile forces. The healing may be associated with Hathor's healing of the eyes of Horus. It was thought that pilgrims bathed in the sacred waters and spent the night in the sanatorium in the hope of receiving healing dreams from Hathor. A new theory, based on recent excavation and analysis, gives the more prosaic suggestion that rather than a sanatorium the area was a workshop for dying clothes. Basins lined with gypsum mortar were found which were connected to cisterns that provided water. There were some pottery vessels which had been used for mixing the colours used in the dying.[636] Further excavation and analysis is obviously needed.

To the south-west of the temple is the Sacred Lake which represented the primordial waters of the *Nun*. It is rectangular with low walls and an access stairway at each corner. The mud brick wall surrounding it is decorated with a wavy line pattern, the hieroglyph for water, to emphasise the symbolism.

The south exterior wall has a false door in the form of a Hathor *sistrum*. Here was a public shrine, a carved relief of Hathor protected by a gilded wooden canopy, where the general public could offer

---

[636] *Revealing the Secrets of Dendera*, Taher, 2011:22-31

prayers and petition the Goddess. This was the shrine of *"the hearing ear"* so that Hathor could hear the prayers being directed to her. The relief has been seriously eroded by pilgrims who have scraped away tiny portions of the sacred stone.[637] Excavations in 2004 uncovered the quay where Hathor's statue made its annual journey to Edfu. The river was much closer to the temple at that time. A Greek inscription on the remains of a nearby gate refers to a governor of Dendera who built a chapel for the sacred barque of Hathor in the vicinity.

To the south of the temple is a large necropolis whose tombs date from the Pre-dynastic Period through to the Greco-Roman Period. It was said that sacred cows were buried here but none have so far been excavated.[638]

OTHER HATHOR TEMPLES

Many of the Hathor temples contain a rock-cut shrine that was the original sacred focus of the temple. One spell in the *Coffin Texts* refers to the *Caverns of Hathor* and this might be an echo of the rock-cut and cave shrines. *"The mountain is broken, the stone is split, the caverns of Hathor are broken open."*[639] The term *quererts*, translated as cavern, originally applied to the burial shaft of a *mastaba* (a tomb with a low house like superstructure) but soon came to refer to the caves in the underworld. One of the later funerary texts is called the *Book of Caverns*.

Caverns are closely associated with the Great Mother Goddess. A hollow space in solid rock is seen as her womb and the seat of life and death but Hathor is not a typical Mother Goddess and as a sky and solar goddess she is definitely not a chthonic deity. The Hathor Cow is often depicted coming out of the side of a mountain, despite the fact that cows don't tend to live in caves, because her afterlife aspect connects her to the caverns of the underworld. The theme of the later funerary texts is the journey of Ra through the underworld during the twelve hours of darkness. Here he is protected by Hathor-Sekhmet in her various aspects and forms.

---

[637] *The Complete Temples of Ancient Egypt*, Wilkinson, 2000:150-151
[638] *Revealing the Secrets of Dendera*, Taher, 2011:22-31
[639] *The Ancient Egyptian Coffin Texts Volume II*, Faulkner, 2007:130. Spell 486

Abu Simbel

This is the site of Hathor's most important Nubian shrine. There is a small temple to Hathor cut into the cliff face which shows Nefertari wearing the Hathor headdress. Beside the shrine of Rameses II is a small temple dedicated to his wife, Nefertari, and to Hathor of Ibshak. Nefertari is shown making offerings to Hathor and Mut.[640] Elsewhere Hathor is depicted as a Cow emerging from the western mountain with the king standing beneath her chin.

Asyut

A temple of Hathor has recently been found here.[641]

Cusae

There is a foundation plaque in opaque glass from the temple of Aphrodite Urania. The inscription is in Greek and is dedicated by a prince to "*Hathor Who-is-in-Heaven*". Cusae was an important cult centre of Hathor and the Greeks considered it sacred to Aphrodite Urania. Another inscription found in Cusae is on the cartouche of Ptolemy I to "*Hathor of Gold*". It appears that a temple to "*Hathor of Gold*" was founded or embellished by Ptolemy I and the new shrine to Aphrodite Urania established by Ptolemy IV.[642]

Dakka

Hathor is one of the most frequently depicted deities in this Ptolemaic temple which is dedicated to Thoth of Pnubs, the site of the sycamore tree which he rested under whilst persuading the Distant Goddess to return to Egypt.[643]

---

[640] *House of Eternity: The Tomb of Nefertari*, McDonald, 1996:16
[641] *Revealing the Secrets of Dendera*, Taher, 2011:22-31
[642] *A Temple of Hathor at Kusae*, Fraser, 1956:97-98
[643] *Ancient Egypt*, Oakes & Gahlin, 2004:181

Deir el-Bahri

The area around the temple of Hatshepsut, known as Djeser-Djeseru *"Holiest of the Holy"*, appears to have been sacred to Hathor for a long time as evidenced by the large number of chapels and shrines.[644] A natural rock formation above Deir el-Bahri was said to resemble a rearing cobra, the sign of the *uraeus*, which gave it a strong link to Hathor as the Daughter and Eye of Ra. The whole area contains images of the Goddess emerging from the living rock.

The first mortuary temple on this site was that of Mentuhotep I. In the 18th Dynasty the temple was extended. The rock on the north side of the temple was cut back to make a small chapel to Hathor. The painted chapel contained a statue of a Hathor Cow which is now in the Egyptian Museum, Cairo.[645] In the southern end of Hatshepsut's mortuary temple is a complete Hathor temple. The most sacred part was the rock-cut sanctuary, here the Hathor Cow was depicted suckling and protecting Hatshepsut while Hathor and Amun consecrate her as king. There is a twelve columned hypostyle hall with Hathor Head capitals. The temple of Thutmose III also contains a chapel dedicated to Hathor which is in a similar style. Between these two mortuary temples is a small chapel built by Thutmose III. The walls show him offering to Hathor who is depicted as a woman. It also contained a statue of the Hathor Cow suckling Hatshepsut now in the Egyptian Museum, Cairo.

Inscriptions show that the Hathor cult continued in this area until the Ramesside Period when earthquakes destroyed the main temple and the entrance to the Little Chapel of the Sacred Cow was blocked. The earthquakes may have been viewed as a sign that the deities no longer wished to be worshipped in the area and that it was to be left alone. However in the Ptolemaic Period two chapels from Hatshepsut's mortuary complex were still in use. One was dedicated to *"Hathor, Mistress of the West"*. The Greeks referred to her as *"Aphrodite on the mountain"*.[646]

---

[644] *Dancing for Hathor: Women in Ancient Egypt*, Graves-Brown, 2010:152
[645] *The Complete Temples of Ancient Egypt*, Wilkinson, 2000:180
[646] *Egypt from Alexander to the Copts*, Bagnal & Rathbone, 2004:193-194

Deir el-Medina

Hathor was very popular at the workman's village for the Valley of the Kings and several chapels were dedicated to Hathor during the New Kingdom. Sety I built a Hathor chapel here for the workers and their families.[647] Rameses II endowed the chapel with offerings from his own mortuary temple. Some of the village women had the title "*Songstress of Hathor*".[648] The village was abandoned when the royal necropolis moved to Tanis. The area must have retained its sacred significance because a temple to Hathor and Maat was built there by Ptolemy IV over the remains of the New Kingdom temple.[649] The temple was decorated by several of the later Ptolemies and survives in good condition. It is a grand temple surrounded by a mud-brick wall. The columned hall opens to a narrow vestibule with three sanctuaries. The central one is dedicated to Hathor, the others to Amun-Ra-Osiris and Amun-Sokar-Osiris.[650]

Edfu: The Temple of Horus

Edfu was believed to be the location of one of the battles between Horus and Seth. The Ptolemaic temple of Horus is one of the most complete and best preserved of all Egyptian temples. Horus was worshipped alongside Hathor of Dendera and their son Harsomtus. "*The House of the Falcon rejoices after Horus-Ra has united with the Golden One.*"[651] The kings were very pleased with the temple. "*When its beautiful mistress (Hathor) sees it, she rejoices*" and the deities were willing to "*protect their beloved son...because of his monument*".[652]

One door of the main temple is inscribed "*the Portal of the Golden One, Mistress of Denderah*". This was only used during the annual *Feast of the Joyous Union* when Hathor's statue, from Dendera, was brought into the temple. It was "*her beautiful entrance for coming into*

---

[647] *The Complete Temples of Ancient Egypt*, Wilkinson, 2000:189
[648] *Ancient Egypt*, Oakes & Gahlin, 2004:176
[649] *The British Museum Dictionary of Ancient Egypt*, Shaw & Nicholson, 2008:93
[650] *The Complete Temples of Ancient Egypt*, Wilkinson, 2000:190
[651] *The Temple of Edfu*, Kurth, 2004:46
[652] *The Temple of Edfu*, Kurth, 2004:67

her house to unite with her image in the Great Seat".[653] She also left via this door when she went to the Behdet temple in the necropolis. Hathor is depicted in the main temple and in the *mammisi*. She also has a chapel in the main sanctuary along with Min, Osiris, Khonsu and Ra. Reliefs in the *mammisi* depict the Horus child being nursed by Hathor in the marshes. Unusually Hathor is shown as a woman rather than as the Hathor Cow.[654] Hathor is represented in the temple in as many forms as there are days in the year.[655]

El-Kab

This town, 32km south of Esna, was an important Pre-dynastic settlement and was the cult centre of the vulture goddess Nekhbet. A small chapel of Amenhotep III is dedicated to Hathor and Nekhbet.[656]

Faras (Nubia)

Faras is located on the modern border between Egypt and the Sudan, between the first and second cataract. Hatshepsut founded a sanctuary to Hathor here. The temple was constructed on the northern side of an isolated rock called the "*Tower of Gold*". This rock was probably a sacred site for the Nubians as it was a prominent feature in the flat landscape. The rock is a golden colour suggesting an association with Hathor. It is dedicated to "*Hathor, Lady of Ibshek*" which is the ancient name for Faras.[657] During the New Kingdom Egypt was bringing Nubia under direct control and establishing temples was one way of demonstrating power and authority. The temples also served as warehouses for goods due for export to Egypt.

---

[653] *The House of Horus at Edfu*, Watterson, 1998:56
[654] *The Complete Temples of Ancient Egypt*, Wilkinson, 2000:207
[655] *The Complete Gods and Goddesses of Ancient Egypt*, Wilkinson, 2003:32
[656] *The Complete Temples of Ancient Egypt*, Wilkinson, 2000:203
[657] *Votive Offerings to Hathor*, Pinch, 1993:26

Gebel el-Zeit

This was a mountainous area near the Red Sea coast. Mining expeditions set up shrines here to the *"lady of Galena"*. A rock-cut sanctuary dates to the late Middle Kingdom or 2nd Intermediate Period and during the 12th to 19th Dynasties large quantities of votive offerings were left at the shrines.[658]

Gebelein

Gebelein lies about 40km south of Luxor. Its religious name was Inerti which means *"twin peaks"* and its modern Arabic name means *"two mountains"*. The eastern hill is dominated by the remains of a temple of Hathor. The extant decoration dates from the 11th to 15th Dynasties but there is evidence that a temple was already in use by the late Pre-dynastic Period. A temple to Hathor was present from the 3rd Dynasty and continued in use into Roman times. It was then destroyed for its limestone. The fortified mud-brick enclosure wall dates to the 21st Dynasty.[659] Inside one of the rock-cut tombs is an inscription to Hathor. Gebelein was called Aphroditopolis and Pathyris by the Greeks emphasising the connection to the Goddess. The latter name is taken from *"Per-Hathor"*, the house or domain of Hathor.

Gerf Hussein

Now covered by Lake Nasser, there was a temple of Rameses II cut into the rock face. It was dedicated to Ptah, Ptah-Tenehn and Hathor.[660]

Heliopolis

Part of an inventory of a temple to Hathor at Heliopolis survives. It shows a diagram of the temple and lists its contents because of a decree by the king *"to carry out a review [of the temple] of the mother of*

---

[658] *Votive Offerings to Hathor*, Pinch, 1993:71

[659] *The British Museum Dictionary of Ancient Egypt*, Shaw & Nicholson, 2008:125

[660] *The Complete Temples of Ancient Egypt*, Wilkinson, 2000:219

his father Hathor Nebethetepet of Taded". *Taded* might be translated as "*the grove*". The plan shows massive rectangular gateways with vertical sided pylons (they usually have sloping sides). On the cornice of each tower are two slender poles assumed to be flag-staffs. The inscription reads "*the temple of Hathor Nebethetep [Lady of the place of Offerings] in the grove [built by] King Kheperkara*" (thought to be Senusret I). There are at least three open courts. The second court has a chapel "*for the raising of the willow tree*" and in the third court is a chapel, the "*house of Atum of the sycamore tree*". Above this inscription is the hieroglyph for the south marking the orientation of the building and recalls Hathor's Memphite epithet of "*lady of the Southern Sycamore*".[661]

Hiw

This was a Pre-dynastic cult centre of the Cow Goddess. There was a Hathor shrine which had originally been dedicated to Bat.[662]

Karnak: The Temple of Ptah

At Karnak Hathor was considered the consort of Ptah, unlike in Memphis where Sekhmet was his consort. This temple has inscriptions dating from the reign of Thutmose III through to the Emperor Tiberius. The oldest part of the temple is a triple cell structure. The central chamber is dedicated to Amun-Ra and was used as a way-station for the barque of Ra during his annual processions. The side chambers are dedicated to Hathor and Ptah. The walls of the southern courtyard were decorated by Horemheb and show Amun, Ptah, Khonsu, Mut and Hathor. The southern chapel of the Ptah temple dates to the reign of Thutmose III and he is shown seven times making offerings to Hathor. Five of these have been vandalised above the waist and the inscriptions destroyed. The two remaining depictions show Hathor as a woman with a sun disc and cow horns and the remaining inscription reads "*Hathor, Lady of Heaven, Mistress of the Gods, Beautiful of Face, Chieftainess of Thebes*".

The Hathor temple that Thutmose replaced was Middle Kingdom in date and was the principal Hathor shrine during the reign of

---

[661] *The Cult of Ra*, Quirke, 2001:103-104

[662] *Understanding Hieroglyphics: a Quick and Simple Guide*, Wilson, 1993:83-84

Hatshepsut. There is a relief on the northern wall of the entrance hall at the Deir el-Bahri shrine which depicts the arrival of the annual procession of Amun on the west side of the river. Hathor's barque is shown accompanying Amun's. The inscription reads *"shouting by the crews of the royal boats…at the time of causing this great goddess to proceed to rest in her temple in Djeser-djeseru-Amun, so that they [Hatshepsut and Thutmosis III] might achieve life forever"*. On the walls of the southern chambers of the Hathor shrine the Hathor Cow is called *"Hathor of Dendera"* whilst the female figure with the cow horn and sun disc headdress is called *"Hathor, Chieftainess of Thebes"*. This is the reverse of how they were depicted in the Hathor *speos* of Thutmose III in the 11th Dynasty temple.[663]

Kom Abu Billo

This is a town in the Delta. The Greco-Roman name, Terenuthis, is derived from Renenutet a cobra goddess linked to the harvest. There is a Ptolemaic temple dedicated to *"Hathor, Mistress of Turquoise"* and burials of scared cows have been found nearby.[664] Reliefs were found showing Ptolemy I and Hathor.

Kom el-Hisin

This town is sited at the western edge of the Delta. Senusret I established a temple dedicated to Sekhmet-Hathor.[665] Excavation work has uncovered the foundation wall of the main temple building, probably of New Kingdom date. Two statues of Rameses II were dedicated to *"Sekhmet-Hathor Mistress of Imu"*. According to the Edfu temple lists Imu was the nome capital from the New Kingdom replacing Hwt-Ihyt the House of the Cow.[666] An excavation in 1900 found many cattle bones and suggestions were made that there was an animal necropolis dedicated to Hathor in the area.

---

[663] *Senenu, High Priest of Amun at Deir el-Bahri*, Brovarski, 1976:57-73

[664] *The British Museum Dictionary of Ancient Egypt*, Shaw & Nicholson, 2008:172

[665] *The British Museum Dictionary of Ancient Egypt*, Shaw & Nicholson, 2008:172

[666] *Preliminary Report on the Survey of Kom el-Hisin, 1996*, Kirby, Oriel & Smith, 1998:23-43

Kom Ombo

There is a small chapel dedicated to Hathor in the Greco-Roman temple to Horus and Sobek.[667]

Memphis

There are a few remains of a small temple to Hathor built by Rameses II. It was constructed outside the southern enclosure wall of the temple to Ptah. The *Harris* papyrus said that the barque of Ptah went to the temple by water which has been confirmed by the archaeology.

Eight columns have been excavated in situ, all but one retains the Hathor Head capital. The head is shown on two sides, the features are similar but there are some differences most noticeably in the way that the smile is treated. The sculptors could have produced identical faces. Rather than explaining it as artistic licence it was probably done for a purpose, perhaps to show Hathor as an individual with different facial expressions or to illustrate her multiplicity of appearance. Traces of colour were found; red on the lips, green and yellow on the neck, blue on the necklace, black on the hair with some red and yellow in places.

The king is shown on various reliefs making offerings to Sekhmet and to Hathor as the "*Eye of Ra*" and the "*Mistress of the Southern Sycamore*". This is the earliest example of these two aspects of Hathor being shown together. Each is shown separately and is clearly identifiable. Most of the reliefs relate to her solar aspect from the Heliopolitan cult of Hathor which is surprising given that Memphis is the cult centre of Hathor as Mistress of the Southern Sycamore. Old records refer to a temple in the south of Memphis for the Mistress of the Southern Sycamore so it is possible that there is still an undiscovered temple in the vicinity. In the temple the Memphite Hathor is treated as another local deity in the same way that Ptah and Sekhmet are. Stelae and a statue inscription in the temple refer to both Hathors but inscriptions found in other areas of Memphis only refer to the Memphite Hathor.[668]

---

[667] *The British Museum Dictionary of Ancient Egypt*, Shaw & Nicholson, 2008:173

[668] *A New Temple for Hathor*, el-Sayed, 1978:15

Mirgissa

Located near the second cataract is an 18th Dynasty shrine dedicated to Hathor the "*Lady of Iqen*". It is a well preserved simple shrine which would have been built and run by the local community. The mud-brick shrine consists of a rectangular building split into an open forecourt and a sanctuary which was roofed by either grass or reed matting. The sanctuary was full of cult images and votive offerings. The offerings were objects in everyday use rather than specifically manufactured for use as votive offerings. At some stage the temple was abandoned but it was never vandalised. A life size cow's head made of calcite with glass inlays was found which probably came from the Hathor Cow kept in the sanctuary.[669]

Philae

Philae was a stronghold of Isis but Hathor had a small chapel at Philae, as Isis did at Hathor's cult centre of Dendera. It was built by the Ptolemies and extended by Augustus who is shown making offerings to Hathor. At Philae Hathor was commemorated as the goddess of music and dance. The hall columns are decorated with lively scenes of musicians including one of a monkey playing a lyre. Bes is shown playing the tambourine, the harp and dancing.

Qasr Ibrim (Nubia)

Hatshepsut built a temple for Hathor here.[670]

Serabit el-Khadim (Sinai)

As soon as the Egyptians started mining in Sinai they started building temples to Hathor "*Lady of Mefkat*". Serabit, 10km north of Wadi Maghara, in southern Sinai was their most important site. The impressive temple at Serabit was dedicated to the "*powerful and beautiful*" Hathor. She is depicted mostly as a woman in this temple and the offerings found either represented her or were inscribed with

---

[669] *Votive Offerings to Hathor*, Pinch, 1993:41
[670] *The Great Goddesses of Egypt*, Lesko, 1999:107

her name. Sopedu the *"Lord of the East"* and Thoth were also worshipped here.[671] Sopedu is a hawk god who guards the border lands and was closely allied with Horus. Thoth was an important god in Sinai as he looked after the control of the mining in his aspects of scribal and wisdom god.

The site is over 1000m above sea level and requires a three hour climb through the mountains to reach it. The original shrine was a sacred cave in the rock-face which was dedicated by Sneferu in the 4th Dynasty. In the 12th Dynasty Amenemhat III (12th Dynasty) enlarged the cave and set up altars and constructed a portico. The core area was extended during the Middle Kingdom and again in the New Kingdom by Hatshepsut, Thutmose III and Amenhotep III. The most important addition to the temple was of a court surrounded by four great columns with Hathor Heads. The temple contains the most Hathor Head columns of any temple.

Excavations in the Hathor cave uncovered two stone incense altars and three stone offering tables which had been dedicated by mining officials in the reign of Amenemhat III.[672] A basin for ritual washing was located in the centre of the hall. A great pylon was added later but then the temple fell out of favour and was eventually abandoned. A sandstone carved head of Hathor was found in the area. Judging by the style it is a copy of an Egyptian statue of Hathor made by the local tribesmen.[673]

Speos Artemidos

The rock-cut temple here was dedicated to the lioness goddess Pakhet whose name means *"she who scratches"*.[674] She was said to roam the wadis and sharpen her claws on the rocks, the marks left by the occasional water torrents were seen as her claw marks. This temple, like many other temples to Hathor, emerges from the living rock at the entrance to the wadi. Such a place was viewed as a liminal link between the underworld and this world. Hatshepsut explained how she had renovated the Hathor temple which had been neglected and

---

[671] *The Routledge Dictionary of Egyptian Gods and Goddesses*, Hart, 2005:151
[672] *Votive Offerings to Hathor*, Pinch, 1993:51
[673] *Gifts From the Pharaohs*, Noblecourt, 2007:108
[674] *Dancing for Hathor: Women in Ancient Egypt*, Graves-Brown, 2010:152

thus fallen into ruin. *"The serpent-goddess no longer gave terror...and its festivals no longer appeared. I sanctified it after it had been built anew...I fashioned her image from gold, with a barque for a land procession."*[675]

Timna (Sinai)

Timna, 25km from Eilat in Sinai, was an important copper mining area. A temple of Hathor was constructed beneath an overhanging rock forming the characteristic partial rock-cut sanctuary. It is thought that this particular rock was of cultic significance before the temple was built. Inscriptions cover a period of about 150 years, from Sety I to Rameses V, and show a high level of activity during this period. A basic engraving on the rock face depicts Rameses III offering to Hathor, who is depicted as a woman.[676] It was a state run temple but probably had temporary staff. The mining expeditions may have brought the cult statue of Hathor in a portable shrine from their base at Gebel Abu Hassa where the expeditions were assembled. Local mine workers used the temple leaving many votive offerings to Hathor.[677]

Wadi Abbad

The temple of Redesiyeh is a small rock-cut temple 56km east of Edfu on the road to the gold mines. It was built during the reign of Sety I and he is depicted making offerings to various deities. Ptah and Sekhmet are shown enthroned in front of an offering table. The inscription tells how Sety I had the temple set up so that travellers could rest and use water from the temple cistern. He invokes *"Hathor, Lady of Behdet"* for protection and fortune.[678]

---

[675] *The Great Goddesses of Egypt*, Lesko, 1999:107
[676] *The Complete Temples of Ancient Egypt*, Wilkinson, 2000:238
[677] *Votive Offerings to Hathor*, Pinch, 1993:62
[678] *New Renderings of Egyptian Texts*, Gunn & Gardiner, 1917:241-251

Wadi el-Hudi

This area lies in the eastern desert 35km south east of Aswan. A 13th Dynasty stele of the official Sareru tells how he performed rites in the temple of Hathor and brought *ntyw* to Hathor "*mistress of amethyst*". *Ntyw* is a form of incense. No remains of a temple have been found but an offering table was discovered. If the place was only used intermittently it might have been a very simple shrine.[679]

---

[679] *A Newly Identified Stela from Wadi el-Hudi*, Espinel, 2005:55-70

CHAPTER 24

INSIDE THE TEMPLES

"They find that there is purity and perfect order in it and excellent priests therein."[680]

Those Who Serve Hathor

The role of priests and priestesses was very different to their roles today. They had no pastoral responsibility nor did they preach, they were purely the servants of the deity. Most of the rituals they carried out were for the benefit of the deity, or the state as a whole, and they were carried out in secret without an audience.

---

[680] *The Temple of Edfu*, Kurth, 2004:67

Hierarchy

The Egyptians loved order and hierarchy and this is well illustrated in the temples with the hierarchy of staff, status and duties. However names, status and roles will have varied over time as well as over the different cults. As well as having an overall title the priests and priestesses also referred to themselves by the specific tasks they were responsible for, the length of the list appeared to show their importance. Some biographical stelae from Hathor priests of the 3rd Intermediate Period give such lists. One is an "*offering priest, lesonis priest, acolyte for the third phyle*" another is the "*overseer of the great plan of the Lady of Heaven...overseer of secrets of clothing*". Sematawy says he was a "*prophet of the living staff of Hathor...pacifier of her majesty, sistrum player...revered one before the lady of Dendera*".[681]

The *wab*-priest carried out the lesser tasks in rituals and maintenance tasks in the temple. There is no mention of *wab*-priestesses in the Old Kingdom but there is reference to women who perform *wab*-service for Hathor which is probably the same thing. They were paid the same as the *wab*-priest. The *wab*-priests of Sekhmet appear to have been doctors, as they were in her service they were considered to be more immune to her pestilence and able to appeal to her better nature. As usual some temple staff will have been more diligent than others. A 19th Dynasty letter to the *wab*-priest of Sekhmet, Sobekhotep, tells him to "*be attentive in observing the festivals of the gods and also in making their divine [offerings]*".[682]

The hm-ntr (male) and hmt-ntr (female) were the servants of the deity. They were responsible for looking after the cult statue; this consisted of making offerings, performing the liturgy and anointing the statue. During the Old Kingdom many elite women held this title, they were usually but not exclusively priestesses of goddesses. In the 25th Dynasty there is the title hmt-ntr hthr, Servant of Hathor.[683] Despite our negative associations with the word servant this was one of the higher ranks of priestess. These women will have studied the sacred documents and will have known exactly what was being done and why

---

[681] *The Libyan Anarchy: Inscriptions from Egypt's Third Intermediate Period*, Ritner, 2009:29
[682] *Letters from Ancient Egypt*, Wente, 1990:126
[683] *Temples of Ancient Egypt*, Shafer, 2005:16

when they carried out the rituals. The Greeks called such priestesses *prophetai*, prophetess.

All these people needed supervising. From the step pyramid at Saqqara, an inscription refers to an inspector of Hathor priests in the temple of Unas. The high level positions took in a number of temples. One steward of Amenhotep III had many titles including Overseer of priests of Weret-hekaw and Overseer of priests of Sekhmet.[684] There was also Senenu who was the High Priest of Amun in Djeser-djeseru as well as being the High Priest of Hathor *"in the midst of Djeser-djeseru"*.

Major temples were huge estates and centres of commerce and teaching and there were many administrative positions. In the Middle Kingdom a woman called Ib-Neith held the post of *"Trustworthy Sealer"* in a Hathor temple in Sinai.[685] The 10th Dynasty estate manager Seseni of Dendera was *"overseer of the Oarsmen of Hathor"*.[686]

The Roles of Women

Women didn't play as active a role in the temples as men did and their status seems to have declined throughout the Dynastic period. In general they held higher positions in the Old Kingdom when they were responsible for both the daily rituals and the resources needed for them. Their duties included dressing the statue and acting as incense bearer. The decline in status and number of Hathor priestesses was particularly noticeable during the Middle Kingdom and by the New Kingdom women were almost exclusively singers in her temples. This probably mirrored a decline in the status of women in general as well as the fact that the nature of the profession developed and was more suited to men. Most of the women would have been married with children and had to fit their religious duties around caring for their families. So-called 'purity rules' may have made it increasingly difficult for women to perform a full time job in a service which barred them from the temple during menstruation.

Women did not serve exclusively in the temples of goddesses although they were more prevalent there. Priestesses of all deities were

---

[684] *Egypt's Dazzling Sun: Amenhotep III and his World*, Kozloff & Bryan, 1992:54
[685] *Dancing for Hathor: Women in Ancient Egypt*, Graves-Brown, 2010:75
[686] *Ancient Egyptian Autobiographies*, Lichtcheim, 1988:133

often associated with Hathor and are sometimes depicted with a cow horn sun disc on top of a vulture cap in imitation of their Goddess. Priestesses in the sun temple at Heliopolis were called "*Hathors*". The High Priestess of Horus of Hierakonpolis was referred to as the "*wife*" of Horus which identified her with Hathor. Similarly the High Priestess of Horus of Athribus was called "*protectress*" which was the local epithet of Hathor while the High Priestess of Letopolite Haroeris was called "*Mother of the god*". An inscription of Rameses II and III mentions the "*great noble ladies of the temple of Ptah and the Hathors of the temple of Atum.*"[687] One of their functions was to greet the king as he arrived at the temple.

In the Old Kingdom priestesses of Hathor were drawn from elite families though the positions weren't necessarily hereditary. Over 400 women are recorded as holding the title priestesses of Hathor. The first known priestess of Hathor was princess Neferhetepes. In the 4th Dynasty princesses were often priestesses of Hathor. During this period many Hathor priestesses have the title *dw3t-ntr*, Worshipper of God. They were depicted in reliefs alongside priests worshipping and purifying themselves.[688]

After the title Mistress of the House, Chantress is the most common New Kingdom title for elite non-royal women. They are normally depicted as singers carrying the *sistrum* and *menat*. They were organised, like the priests, in a phyle system working one month in four. Their main role was to provide music to soothe and please the deity. They accompanied the king, or High Priest, when he made offerings and provided music for religious feasts and festivals and also sung at private funerals. The musician-priestesses acted as a stand in for Hathor so it was a prestigious position. In that capacity they were able to confer divine favour.

Hereditary Positions

Temple positions could be hereditary. Three generations of a family at Dendera held the title of Mayor and Priest of Hathor. Rameses II promised Nebwenenef that "*the temple of Hathor…will pass into the hands of your son*". Basu, a priest of Hathor in the 22nd Dynasty,

---

[687] *On the Position of Women in the Egyptian Hierarchy*, Blackman, 1921:8-30
[688] *Temples of Ancient Egypt*, Shafer, 2005:14

recorded 26 generations of his family on his statue most of whom were priests of Hathor of Dendera.[689] Whether it is genealogically accurate is another matter.

One study of people holding Hathoric titles during the Old Kingdom and 1st Intermediate Period found that only about ten percent of the positions were hereditary. When looking at married couples the study found a similar percentage where both partners held Hathoric titles. One woman from Cusae was a priestess of Hathor as were her four daughters. Another priestess had a husband, daughter and two sons who held Hathoric titles. The daughter married into one of the leading nomarch families and her husband and several of his close family had Hathoric titles. Cusae was a major cult centre for Hathor so the cult permeated all aspects of life in the area. It was politically and socially desirable to hold a Hathoric title in Cusae. Some families in other areas were deeply involved in the cult. One priestess at Dendera had a husband who was Overseer of the Priests of Hathor and Herdsman of the *Thenet*-cattle. Their son held the same titles and his wife was a Hathor priestess and the grandsons all held Hathoric titles.[690] Nek'onkh, an Old Kingdom High Priest of Hathor of Rezone, appointed all of his children to serve as priests and priestess of Hathor. There was no differentiation between his sons and daughters, they both got the same stipend and performed the same duties on a monthly rota.[691]

Important posts were the gift of the king. Somtu-tefnekht, during the Persian Period said that the Persian king *"gave me the office of the Chief Priest of Sekhmet"*.[692] For the high ranking posts being a priest or priestess was more of a career than a spiritual choice especially when the post was inherited. They may have spent all their life serving a deity who was not necessarily their personal deity, not that such a situation would have been viewed as a problem.

Individual Priests and Priestesses

We do know of individual temple staff from biographical details given in documents and on stelae. An inscription in the tomb of

---

[689] *Religion and Ritual in Ancient Egypt*, Teeter, 2011:28-29
[690] *The Hereditary Status of Titles in the Cult of Hathor*, Galvin, 1984:42-49
[691] *On the Position of Women in the Egyptian Hierarchy*, Blackman, 1921:8-30
[692] *Religion and Ritual in Ancient Egypt*, Teeter, 2011:30

Nykaiankh from Tehena explains that he was both a priest of Hathor and an overseer of the priests of Hathor and that he was appointed to the post by Userkaf. This was a hereditary post as he "*made a command for his children to serve as priests for Hathor*".[693]

An inscription on the tomb of the nomarch Pepyankhheryib at Meir says that he too was an overseer of the priests of Hathor. As a *wab*-priest he was permitted to tend to the cult statue of "*Hathor mistress of Kis, seeing her and carrying out the rituals for her with my own hands*". This was obviously appreciated because he adds "*all things I have are excellent as a result of being a wab-priest of Hathor...she has favoured me.*"[694]

In the Saqqara tomb of Hemetre the inscription tells us that she was a priestess of Hathor and called "*imakhu in the sight of Hathor*". The word *imakhu* translates as honoured or revered.[695]

Temple Rituals

"*Singers and maidens gathered together...braided, beauteous, tressed, high-bosomed, priestesses richly adorned, anointed with myrrh, perfumed with lotus, their heads garlanded with wreaths, all drunk with wine.*"[696] There were two types of ritual conducted by the temple staff; the daily rituals which ensured the continuation of cosmic order and the annual public festivals which re-enacted the principal myths. The former rituals were only performed and witnessed by a select group of priests and priestesses. Because of this there was the need for a public face to the cult something that all could participate in, these were the 'appearances' of the deity where their statue was carried in procession. The public festivals have been discussed in chapter 22.

Before he could officiate in the temple the king went through a purification ritual. A stele from the Horus temple at Edfu refers to a special place, the *pr-dw3t*, where this purification ceremony took place. The ritual alludes to the washing of Ra before he rose at dawn. In the *Hathorienne Sais* papyrus it says "*O Hathor N, thy purification is*

---

[693] *Texts From the Pyramid Age*, Strudwick, 2005:196
[694] *Texts From the Pyramid Age*, Strudwick, 2005:369-370
[695] *Texts From the Pyramid Age*, Strudwick, 2005:386
[696] *Ancient Egyptian Literature Volume III*, Lichtheim, 2006:56

performed in the pr-dw3t of the king, and thou livest". From the Old Kingdom there are references to a supervisor of the mysteries of the *pr-dw3t*. A 7th Dynasty nomarch, Emrori, was supervisor of the *pr-dw3t* he also had the title *"Chief of the Transport of Hathor Mistress of Denderah"*.[697]

The main ritual was held in the morning followed by an afternoon and short evening ritual. We know the basics of the Greco-Roman rituals as they have been inscribed on temple walls. The Dynastic rituals would have been different but the key elements were probably similar. The main daily ritual started with a purification of the temple and the preparation of the food offering. The king, or High Priest, then approached the inner sanctum of the deity accompanied by music and singing. The order of service was: bringing in water, introducing offerings, purifying offerings, consecration of offerings, daily service in the sanctuary and reversion of offerings (bringing them out from the shrine). The daily service would have covered the opening of the shrine, worshipping, presenting the meal for the deity and cleansing and purifying the statue and sanctuary. It is probable that the statue was dressed and decorated, for specific festivals if not at all times. Only the king or High Priest performed this ceremony, the ritual was considered highly sacred and they had to be initiated before they were allowed to perform it. To be allowed to unveil the statue of the deity and to contemplate and pray in their presence was a huge privilege. A text at Dendera mentions *"the gateway to go to the secret place, in order to see the Golden One"*. There is a depiction of the king opening Hathor's shrine.[698] After completing the rituals the king, or High Priest, purified the sanctuary before ritually sealing the door. High Priestesses may have performed similar tasks for Hathor or other goddesses but there is no evidence.

The secret referred to wasn't the same as the Mysteries in the Greek sense where the ceremonies are only revealed to select initiates. There is no evidence to suggest that there were closed societies who had esoteric wisdom before the Ptolemaic Period, but that is no proof that they didn't exist. It is more likely that many of the temple staff knew about the rituals but few were privileged to participate in or even

---

[697] *The House of the Morning*, Blackman, 1918:148-165

[698] *Hathor and Thoth: Two Key Figures of the Ancient Egyptian Religion*, Bleeker, 1973:81

observe them. Often in funerary texts the person will say that they know of certain mysteries but will keep them secret.

Temple Offerings

Hathor will have received the same type of offerings as the other deities. Amongst those listed for Hathor and Sekhmet were geese, gazelles, antelope, oryx, ibex, beer, wine, *sistra* and sceptres. In a fragment of painting Amenhotep III offers what looks like a perfume cone to Hathor.

The only surviving calendar of Old Kingdom festivals is from the sun temple of Niuserre at Abu Gurob. On the day of the Thoth festival offerings of 1,300 portions of bread and beer were made and "*an ox for the divine offerings of Hathor. On the barque of Hathor his majesty accomplished the escort trip.*"[699] Hathor is very much the solar goddess here, closely allied with Ra. King Sahura gave four measures of divine offerings to Hathor of Sekhetre; two *arouras* in the *ra-she* of Sahura and two in the pyramid of Sahura. A few years later he gave 204 *arouras* of land to Hathor in Upper and Lower Egypt. Neferirkare gave Ra and Hathor a daily offering of 210 portions of "*divine offerings*". He also gave a statue of Ihy to the *meret* temple of Sneferu.[700] Lists of temple donations have been found in the Atum temple at Bubastis. The 21st Dynasty king Osorkon gave a "*shrine amounting to 100,000 deben placed before Hathor Nebet-Hetepet in Hetepet*".[701]

---

[699] *Texts From the Pyramid Age*, Strudwick, 2005:87
[700] *Texts From the Pyramid Age*, Strudwick, 2005:71-73
[701] *The Libyan Anarchy: Inscriptions from Egypt's Third Intermediate Period*, Ritner, 2009:251

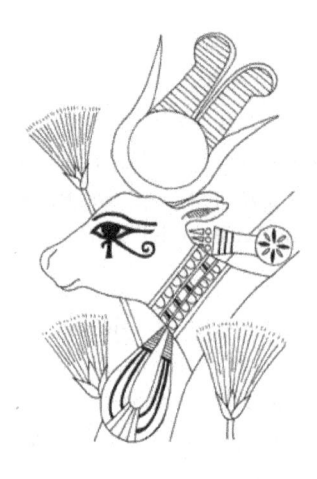

CHAPTER 25

WHAT HAPPENED TO HATHOR?

"Praise to you, Isis, the Great One, God's mother, Lady of Heaven, Mistress and Queen of the gods."[702]

The Decline of Hathor

In the Old and Middle Kingdom Hathor was the pre-eminent goddess in Egypt but by the end of the Greco-Roman Period she had been eclipsed by, and assimilated with, Isis. Despite being a goddess from the early periods Isis didn't have many cult temples of her own for most of the Dynastic period. By the Greco-Roman Period she was the ultimate life giver of all of creation; humans, animals and vegetation. How could such a great goddess as Hathor end up as an aspect of Isis?

---

[702] *Hymns to Isis in Her Temple at Philae*, Zabkar, 1988:30

Isis

The origins of Isis are uncertain but she is not attested to before the 5th Dynasty and no place is cited for her origin. Isis and her brother-husband Osiris were children of the sky goddess Nut and the earth god Geb. They ruled on earth and brought the gifts of civilization to mankind until Osiris was murdered by his jealous brother Seth. Isis was a great magician having the most magical power, *heka*, of all the goddesses. She used this to bring Osiris back to life and conceive a son, Horus, by him.

The Rise of Isis

Like all major goddesses Isis assimilated many local goddesses. As her popularity increased she was first aligned with then gradually absorbed the attributes, mythology and iconography of Hathor, Mut and Maat to become the dominant goddess. She was originally depicted as a woman wearing the hieroglyph sign for *"throne"*. During later periods she wears the cow horns and sun disc of Hathor. She has no animal form and carries only generic symbols, such as the *ankh* and papyrus staff. Later she adopted Hathor's crown, *menat* and *sistrum*. In funerary art she displaces Hathor in the solar barque and becomes the Lady of the Beautiful West. In the tomb of Thutmose III she even takes the form of a sycamore tree suckling the king.

Her assimilation of Hathor began in the New Kingdom and the two goddesses are often only distinguishable by inscriptions as their iconography became identical when Isis adopted the cow horn sun disc. Hathor and Isis are often depicted with cow horns but only Hathor, and Bat, have cow ears. Sometimes there is hieroglyph of a small throne for Isis and a square containing a falcon for Hathor.

As told in the *Contendings of Horus and Seth* Horus decapitates Isis in a fit of rage. Thoth *"transformed it through magic and restored it to her again, so that she was 'first of the cows"*.[703] He heals her by replacing her head, but with the cow head of Hathor rather than her own. Plutarch tells a more dignified version. *"Laying hands on his mother, he drew off the crown from her head. Whereupon Hermes*

---

[703] *Hathor Rising*, Roberts, 2001:106

crowned her with a head-dress of cow-horns."[704] Both may have been an attempt to explain why Isis began to wear the cow horn sun disc of Hathor. Isis and Hathor had a number of roles in common as did many goddesses. Isis was the mother of Horus and of the king. She had an afterlife role and was a guardian of women. Isis was not one of the original Solar Eye goddesses but in the New Kingdom she acquired the epithet *"Lady of Flame"* and *"Uraeus of Re, the Coiled One upon his head"*.[705]

The cult of Isis was well established at Philae during the 26th Dynasty although Hathor was the pre-eminent goddess of the island. During the reign of Nectanebo I (30th Dynasty) Isis became the principal goddess but Hathor retained her prestige and popularity. By the Ptolemaic Period epithets once associated with Hathor now become attributed to Isis. Devotion to Hathor did continue to some extent until the end of the Roman Period, this can be seen in inscriptions and reliefs in the small Hathor temple on the site. In the hymns to Isis at her temple at Philae she is often combined with Hathor as Isis-Hathor.

Hathor was not the only goddess eclipsed by Isis. By Greco-Roman times she had taken over the roles of Bastet as *"Isis-Bast"* and was also *"Isis-Sakhmet"*.[706] As the Great Goddess of Memphis she takes the roles of Mut and Hathor. As the *"Lady of Biggeh"* she assimilates Satis, Anukis, Hathor and some other southern goddesses. In the Philae texts Isis is referred to as *"Mistress of Abaton"* and *"Lady of Imu"* both epithets of Hathor.[707] As the Lady of Buto, Pe and Dep Isis takes the role and titles of Wadjet. By Roman times Isis was the cow goddess of Memphis. Ovid refers to her as the *"Cow of Memphis"*.[708] To the Greeks and Romans this further emphasised the lunar aspect of Isis due to the lunar crescent shape of her horns.

During the Ptolemaic Period Isis absorbed the Greek goddesses Demeter, Persephone, Athena, Hera, Artemis and Aphrodite. A letter from the priests of Aphrodite to Apollonius the Finance Minister of Ptolemy II asks for 100 talents of myrrh for the burial of the Hesis, the sacred cow of Hathor. He adds *"you must know that Hesis is Isis"*

---

[704] *Plutarch: Concerning the Mysteries of Isis and Osiris*, Mead, 2002:202
[705] *Hymns to Isis in Her Temple at Philae*, Zabkar, 1988:73
[706] *An Ancient Egyptian Book of Hours*, Faulkner, 1958:13
[707] *Hymns to Isis in Her Temple at Philae*, Zabkar, 1988:84&109
[708] *Isis in the Ancient World*, Witt, 1997:55

showing the Greek rulers being instructed in Egyptian religion as well as the merging of Hathor and Isis.[709]

Isis transformed into a universal goddess welcomed outside Egypt as the Queen of Heaven and the Mistress of the Sea. By late antiquity Isis was the unrivalled Great Goddess of Egypt and her cult spread across the Roman Empire and reached Britain. She also became the "*mistress of southern foreign lands*".[710]

Why Did Isis Triumph?

Isis was in her ascendance before the Greco-Roman Period so it cannot be solely explained by the new influences of the conquerors but Isis was certainly more compatible with the religious and political tone of the period. There are a number of reasons why Hathor became less popular than Isis.

Hathor is an independent goddess and functioned perfectly well without partners and children. Isis is very much more family orientated. She is the devoted wife and protective mother and is to a large extent defined by her relationships. Isis was regarded as the ideal wife and mother whereas Hathor was the epitome of female sexuality and fertility. Society was moving away from what Hathor represented, namely celebrating the sexuality of women and the enjoyment of life.

Isis embodies love, nurture, pleasure, joy and passion but also loss, suffering, healing and wholeness. Osiris was murdered and her laments over his violent death would have been empathised with by all people at all levels of society, as would her panicking distress when her child was poisoned. Isis also suffered imprisonment at the hands of her brother Seth and rape and decapitation by her son Horus. Did people feel that Isis was more able to emphasise with their own bereavement and suffering having experienced it herself? There is an unfortunate tendency for us to want, or need, the 'Goddess as Victim' and this is as true now as it was in the past. The sufferings of Isis could only be a partial explanation for her rising popularity. Hathor was very popular during the New Kingdom but people still experienced the same disasters and horrors, they suffered as much as people did in the later

---

[709] *Popular Religion in Graeco-Roman Egypt: I. The Pagan Period*, Bell, 1948: 82-97

[710] *Hymns to Isis in Her Temple at Philae*, Zabkar, 1988:95

periods. Their suffering, loss and mourning was not a barrier to worshipping Hathor and receiving comfort and support from her.

Isis through her magic, and the assistance of Thoth, is able to resurrect Osiris and conceive a son by him. She overcomes evil and death and reasserts love, rebirth and continuity. In doing so she brought hope as a saviour goddess to all who suffered. With Osiris came the promise of eternal life, although from the earliest periods Hathor was able to revive and rejuvenate the deceased. Hathor has her angry and dangerous side, particularly in her Sekhmet aspect. Was Isis seen as safer? Isis had become the more socially acceptable face of the female divine.

Isis certainly had a better fit with the Greek and Roman culture. She was probably more similar to the Greco-Roman goddesses than Hathor was. Demeter was very popular and it is possible to find a lot more of Demeter in Isis than in Hathor, who was equated to Aphrodite and thus appeared to have little to offer apart from sex. Hathor liked a good party and wouldn't be offended by pre-marital sex and she certainly wouldn't have supported the obsession with virgin brides. The position of women in Greece and Rome was very different to that of the Egyptian women despite their status having declined since the Old Kingdom. These societies did not want independent women and certainly didn't want their wives and daughters to enjoy themselves too much. Isis was a much better role model than the independent and sexually active Hathor. She just wasn't respectable enough or dependent enough for the cultures that welcomed Isis. The Greco-Roman world, and I suspect most of the rest of it, wasn't ready for the freedom-loving, fun-loving, women-loving Hathor. They wanted more piety and chastity amongst women and a good role model of devoted wife and mother and sometime victim. Hathor's independence and dazzling power frightened them and ran the risk of empowering women.

The cult of Isis and Osiris became a mystery religion which in itself was more appealing because of its secrecy and exclusivity. The Greek and Roman cultures in particular had a hunger for the new mystery religions which gave individuals more comfort and meaning than the existing state religions. Was there an undercurrent in religion and society that was drifting towards monotheism? Until the end of the Pagan period many deities were worshipped but in some instances they were seen as manifestations of the same deity. In Apuleius' *The Golden*

Ass Isis says *"I am the loftiest of deities...the single embodiment of all gods and goddesses"*.[711]

Conclusion

The question of what happened to Hathor can be answered in one word. Isis. Even today Isis is the pre-eminent Egyptian Goddess of the Goddess Revival. Bastet and Sekhmet are popular as a result of their cat and lion imagery. The response to Hathor is, all too often, just 'isn't she the one with the cow's head?' and as a culture we have little regard for cows.

---

[711] *The Golden Ass*, Apuleius & Walsh, 1994:220

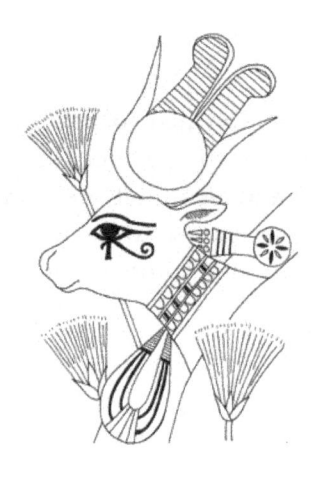

CHAPTER 26

CONCLUSION

"I am the Woman who lightens darkness."

This book has looked at the aspects of Hathor as the Divine Cow, the tree goddess, the sky and solar goddess and at her varying roles from birth through to the afterlife. One thing is outstandingly apparent. Hathor aroused feelings of great reverence and gratitude amongst her worshippers. She was benevolent and merciful and wanted people to be happy and to enjoy themselves. Hathor listened to their prayers and answered them, desiring always to bring her uplifting solar energies back into their lives. *"I have lightened the darkness, I have overthrown the destroyers, I have adorned those who are in the darkness. I have made to stand those who weep, who hid their faces, who had sunk down."*[712]

---

[712] *The Egyptian Book of the Dead,* Budge, 1967:183

Hathor

Hathor touched the hearts and souls of the Egyptians from the earliest times. Whether as a local goddess or a cosmic power, she was ever present in all aspects of their lives. Despite being such a pre-eminent and imposing Goddess she was very popular at all levels of society from kings to poor labourers and she was especially adored by women. Her cult was widespread and impressive and her festivals joyful and exuberant. Hathor was loved by the living and the dead. The deceased hoped to be in her service and the living desired to be swept along by her enthusiasm for life. How sad it is that she was eclipsed by Isis (while meaning no disrespect to the *"Great Isis, Mother of the God"*[713]) and has slowly faded out of our lives. Or has she?

If I could use only one word to describe Hathor it would be energy. This is particularly apparent as a solar goddess but her never ceasing power flows through all her aspects. She is the Eye of the Sun, the active principle of divinity. Without the energising force of Hathor the sun god is devoid of life and power. The cycles of the natural world depend upon her infinite pulsating energy. Hathor can never be static for this reason, neither can she be unvarying. Cycles by their very nature grow and decline; the weather veers from too hot through to too cold and food supplies swing between glut and famine. A protector is one step away from a predator.

Maat and Thoth, with their unyielding devotion to *maat*, form the staff of the universe, the *djed* pillar that ensures the continuation of creation. They keep societies in order and maintain the laws of physics and nature. Hathor is the endlessly winding serpent who entwines that staff causing the animating cycles which breathe life into creation. Without Hathor's enlivening energy creation would be a mechanical not a living entity and without her ferocity chaos would drive creation back into the featureless *Nun*.

Hathor's energy continues unabated and unimpeded. It is up to us to recognise it and acknowledge it and having done that to enjoy the pleasures which she brings.

"Gold will rise beside her father."[714]

---

[713] *Isis in the Ancient World*, Witt, 1997:18
[714] *Hymns to Isis in Her Temple at Philae*, Zabkar, 1988:111

Lesley Jackson

APPENDICES

APPENDIX 1
HATHOR FESTIVALS

Hathor Festivals from the Temple Calendar of Edfu

These tables have been derived from El-Sabban (2000) *Temple Festival Calendars of Ancient Egypt*. Liverpool, Liverpool University Press. (Pages 174-184)

Hathor

Month[715]	Day	Details
Djehuti - 1st Month of *Akhet* (inundation)	9th	Procession of the statue of Hathor, via the *mammisi* and a public festival. The text refers to a choir with musicians. During all processions various rituals will have been held.
	12th	Milk offering in the temple.
	18th	This was a feast of Shu and Tefnut but if it coincided with a full moon it became a full festival day. Two *men*-vases were offered to Hathor.
	20th	Procession of the statue of Hathor.
	22nd	As above.
Paope – 2nd Month of *Akhet* (inundation)	5th	Procession of the statue of Hathor. Various rituals and offerings were made. The text reads *"it is the phallus that fertilises all that exists"*. Hathor is referred to as *"she who opens the (new) Year"*.
	8th	Procession of the statue of Hathor, via the barque sanctuary. Offerings included bread, beer, oxen and fowl.
	19th	Procession of the statue of Hathor. Rituals were performed at the quayside each day for 15 days after which the level of the inundation was recorded.

---

[715] *The Practices of Ancient Egyptian Ritual & Magic*, Rankine, 2006:137-148

Month	Day	Details
Hathor – 3rd Month of *Akhet* (inundation)	1st	The festival of Hathor ran from 1st to 30th of this month.
Hathor – 3rd Month of *Akhet* (inundation)	29th	Procession of the statue of Hathor via the royal way-station to celebrate the inundation, returning via the barque sanctuary.
	30th	Second day of the procession of Hathor. The ritual of *"opening the breast of the women"* was performed.
Koiahk – 4th Month of *Akhet* (inundation)	1st	As above.
	9th	Procession of the statue of Hathor.
	28th	*"Feast of offerings on the altar"*. Various rituals were performed.
	29th	Procession of the statue of Hathor to the royal way-station as part of the feast of Nehebkau.
	30th	Second day of the festival. Procession of the statue of Hathor via the barque sanctuary. There was a feast to celebrate the raising of the *djed*-pillar.

Month	Day	Details
Tobe – 1st month of *Peret* (emergence)	3rd	Festival of drunkenness for the Eye of Ra.
	5th	Festival of Hathor.
	9th	Festival of Hathor.
	15th	Festival of Hathor.
	19th – 21st	Festival of the navigation of Hathor. Procession to the quay where rituals were performed. The text says the festival was decreed by Ra to celebrate her return from Nubia *"that the Nile-flood may be (given) to Egypt…and that she might turn her back on Nubia"*.
	25th	Festival of Hathor.
Mshir – 2nd month of *Peret* (emergence)	4th	The festival is described as *"very, very great"*. There were offerings of oxen, fowl, oryx, gazelles and ibex and *"singing, dancing, prancing and rejoicing by the braided dancers of the town"*.
	21st – 30th	This festival was a voyage by the statue of Hathor to visit Pakhet and the temple of the Seven Hathors.

Month	Day	Details
Pashons – 1st month of *Shemu* (harvest)	Full moon	*"A great feast in all the land."* Offerings were made of bread, oxen, fowl, oryx, beer and wine. The festival was to celebrate the birth of Harsomtus. *"Fruit-seeds are let fall...the goddess's garments are removed."* The statue of Harsomtus was taken in procession to the royal way-station, via the *mammisi*.
	11th	This festival celebrated the *"birth-giving"* of Iusaas.
Paone – 2nd month of *Shemu* (harvest)	1st	Festival of Hathor as the Eye of Ra. The text says that candles in the sanctuary were lit by special torch-bearers.
Epep – 3rd month of *Shemu* (harvest)	4th	A celebration of the conception of Horus. The text shows the confusion between Horus as son of Isis and of Hathor. Horus is called the son of Isis but the text also says *"in the womb of the goddess, he forms an 'abode of Horus within her: the name 'Hathor' is because of this"*. The text mentions a levy of food offerings for the temple.
	New moon	The start of the festival of the New Moon or Feast of Reunion. As well as Hathor's visit to Horus of Edfu it was a celebration of the first harvest. Hathor's statue was processed through the town then she was placed in her barque and set sail for Edfu. The festival lasted fourteen days.

Month	Day	Details
Epep – 3rd month of *Shemu* (harvest)	27th	Statues of Hathor and Harsomtus were processed through the town. *"The face of the goddess is turned to the South."*
	28th	As above.
	29th	As above.
	30th	Fourth day of the procession of Hathor. A procession to the royal way-station was led by torch-bearers.
Mesore – 4th month of *Shemu* (harvest)	1st	Fifth day of the procession of Hathor. This harvest celebration included reaping barley and releasing *aper*-geese.
	2nd	Sixth day of the procession of Hathor.
	3rd – 7th	Repeat of last five days.
Epagomenal or Demon days	2nd	Procession of the statue of Hathor to celebrate the birth of Horus the Elder.
	3rd	Procession of the statue of Hathor. Part of the festival centred upon an evening meal and there is mention of large quantifies of burnt offerings.

Hathor Festivals from the Temple Calendar of Dendera

Month	Day	Details
Djehuti - 1st Month of *Akhet* (Inundation)	1st	Festival for all the deities to celebrate the start of the New Year. Procession of the statue of Hathor in her barque to the temple roof for union with the sun disc.
	2nd	Procession of the statue of Hathor via the *mammisi*. A public procession of the statue of Ihy.
	9th	Procession of the statue of Hathor via the Mansion of the Bier.
	20th	Festival of the Purification of Ra and Drunkenness of Hathor. Her statue was processed to the temple roof for union with the sun disc. The festival lasted five days.
Paope – 2nd Month of *Akhet* (Inundation)	5th	Procession of the statue of Hathor to the hypostyle where offerings were made to *"her father Nun"*.
Koiahk – 4th Month of *Akhet* (Inundation)	26th	Hathor's statue was processed to the temple roof for union with the sun disc. The festival lasted two days.
Tobe – 1st month of *Peret* (emergence)	19th	Procession of the statue of Hathor to the quayside. *"Her beautiful face being turned north."* Then the *"ritual of the navigation"* was performed.
	20th – 22nd	As above.
	28th – 30th	As above.

Month	Day	Details
Mshir – 2nd month of *Peret* (emergence)	1st – 3rd	As above.
	4th	Procession of the statue of Hathor to the quayside.
	21st	Procession of the statue of Hathor to the temple roof. Various rituals for the Feast of Victory were held. This was followed by a further procession via the *mammisi*. The festival lasted five days.
Parmouter – 4th month of *Peret* (emergence)	New moon	Procession of the statue of Hathor via the *mammisi*. The festival lasted two days.
	28th	As above.
Pashons – 1st month of *Shemu* (harvest)	11th	Procession of the statue of Hathor to the temple roof for union with the sun disc then a procession to the Mansion of the Bier.
	Full moon	"A great festival in the whole land." Procession of the statue of Hathor, union with the sun disc and then to the *mammisi*. The festival lasted three days.
Paone – 2nd month of *Shemu* (harvest)	27th	The statues of Hathor and Horus were carried in their sacred barques in a procession around the town. The festival lasted four days.
	28th – 30th	As above.

Month	Day	Details
Epep – 3rd month of *Shemu* (harvest)	New moon	The Feast of the Happy Reunion. Procession of the statue of Hathor to the temple roof for union with the sun disc.
Mesore – 4th month of *Shemu* (harvest)	1st	Procession of the statue of Hathor. *"Performing all the rites of the ritual for the Feast of Her Majesty."*
	27th	Procession of the statue of Hathor into the Hall of Appearance.
Epagomenal or Demon days	4th	*"This beautiful day of the night of the child in his nest. A great feast in the whole land."* Procession of the statue of Hathor at night.

APPENDIX 2
CHRONOLOGY

Predynastic 5500-3100 BCE

Early Dynastic Period 1st - 2nd Dynasty 3100-2686 BCE

Old Kingdom 3rd - 6th Dynasty 2686-2181 BCE

First Intermediate Period 7th - 11th Dynasty 2181-2055 BCE

Middle Kingdom 11th - 14th Dynasty 2055-1650 BCE

Second Intermediate Period 15th - 17th Dynasty 1650-1550 BCE

New Kingdom 18th - 20th Dynasty 1550-1069 BCE

Third Intermediate Period 21st - 24th Dynasty 1069-747 BCE

Late Period 25th - 31st Dynasty 747-332 BCE

Ptolemaic Period 332-30 BCE

Roman Period 30 BCE-395 CE

APPENDIX 3

PLACE NAMES IN THE TEXT

Modern Egyptian	*Ancient Egyptian*	*Classical*
Abu Gurob		
Abu Simbel		
Abusir (necropolis of Memphis)		
Abydos	*Abdjw*	
Akhmim	*Ipu*	*Panopolis*
Amarna	*Akhetaten*	
Aswan	*Swenet*	*Syene*
Asyut	*Djawty*	*Lykopolis*
Atfih		
Beni Hasan		
Biga (Biggeh) an island near Philae		
Bir Kisseibaq		
Cusae	*Qis*	
Dakhla (Oasis)		

Hathor

Dakka (Nubia)		
Deir el-Bahri (opposite Luxor)		
Deir el-Medina (opposite Luxor)		
Deir el-Gebrawi		
Dendera	*Iunet (or Tanter)*	*Tentyris*
Edfu	*Djeb*	*Apollonopolis*
el-Ashmunein	*Khmun*	*Hermopolis Magna*
Elephantine	*Abu*	
el-Kab (or Elkab)	*Nekheb*	
el-Maragha		*Kynopolis*
Esna	*Iunyt*	*Latopolis*
Faras	*Pachoras*	
Fayum	*Ta-she*	*Moeris*
Gebel Abu Hassa		
Gebel Ahmar		
Gebel el-Zeit		
Gebelein	*Inerti*	*Aphroditopolis, Pathyris or Per-Hathor*
Gerf Hussein		
Giza		
Hiw		

Ihnasya el-Medina	*Henen-nesw*	*Herakleopolis*
Karnak	*Ipet-isut*	
Khargo Oasis		
Kom Abu Billo		*Terenuthis*
Kom Ausim		*Letopolis*
Kom el-Ahmar	*Nekhen*	*Hierakonpolis*
Kom el-Hisin	*Imu*	
Kom Ombo	*Pa-Sebek*	*Ombus*
Kosseir		
Lahun		
Luxor	*Waset*	*Thebes*
Medinet Habu	*Djamet (or Djeme)*	
Meir (necropolis of Cusea)		
Memphis	*Men-nefer*	
Merimda Beni Salama		
Mirgissa	*Iken?*	
Nabta Playa		
Nag Hammadi		
Nagada	*Nubt*	*Ombos*
Nefrusy		
New Kalabsha		

Philae		
Qasr Ibrim	*Pedeme*	*Primis*
Qertassi		
Saqqara (necropolis of Memphis)		
Serabit el-Khadim (Sinai)		
Sharuna		
Speos Artemidos (near Beni Hasan)		
Tell Basta		*Bubastis*
Tell el-Far'in	*Pe and Dep*	*Buto*
Tell el-Muqdan		*Leonopolis*
Tell Hisn	*Iunu (or On)*	*Heliopolis*
Tell Nabasha	*Imet*	
Timna		
Wadi Abbad		
Wadi el-Hudi		
Wadi el-Subua		
Wadi Hammamat		
Wadi Maghara (Sinai)		

APPENDIX 4

SACRED GEOGRAPHY

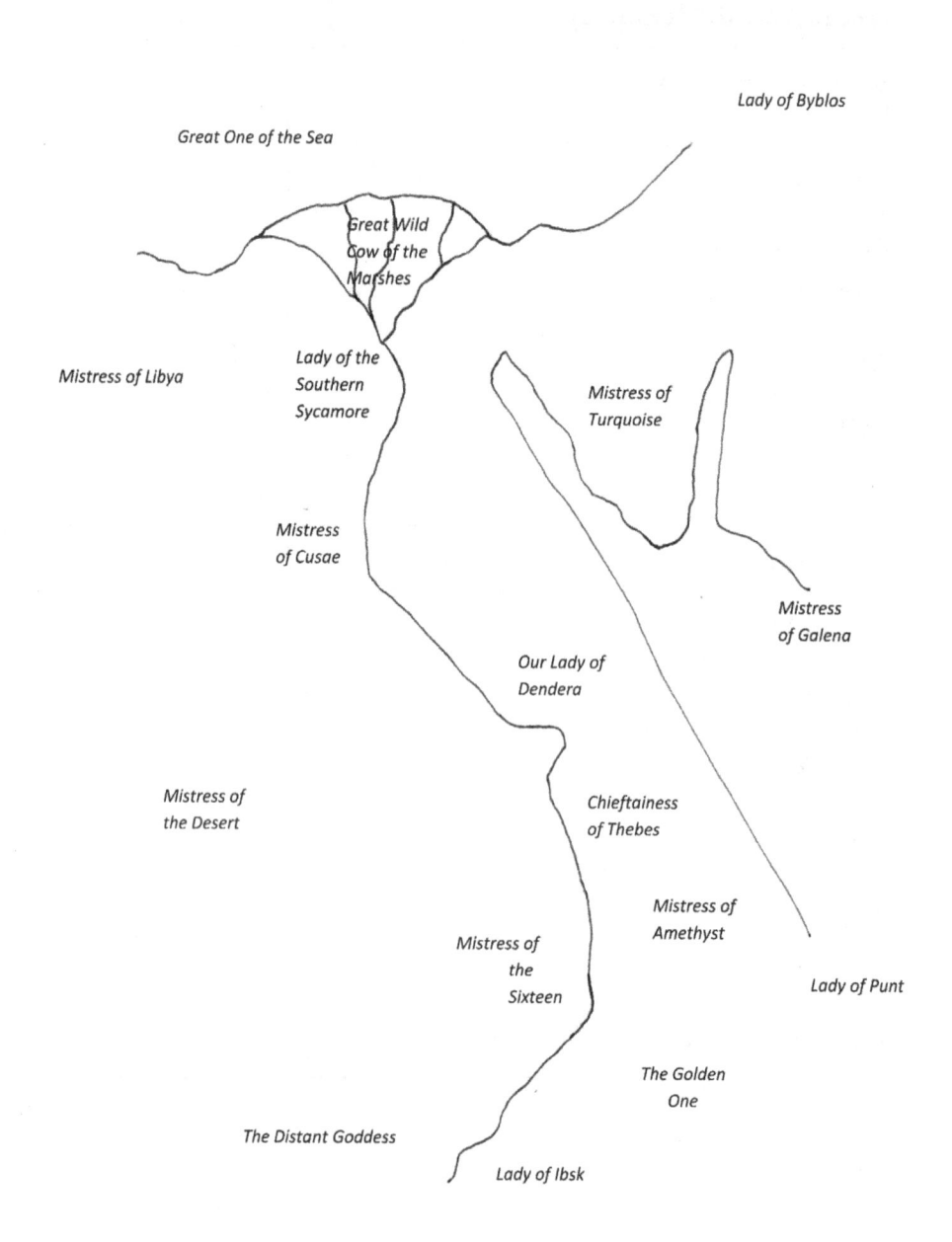

Lady of Byblos

Great One of the Sea

Great Wild Cow of the Marshes

Mistress of Libya

Lady of the Southern Sycamore

Mistress of Turquoise

Mistress of Cusae

Mistress of Galena

Our Lady of Dendera

Mistress of the Desert

Chieftainess of Thebes

Mistress of Amethyst

Mistress of the Sixteen

Lady of Punt

The Golden One

The Distant Goddess

Lady of Ibsk

BIBLIOGRAPHY

Abt, T. & Hornung, E. (2003) *Knowledge for the Afterlife*. Zurich, Living Human Heritage Publications

Abt, T. & Hornung, E. (2007) *The Egyptian Amduat*. Zurich, Living Human Heritage Publications

Aelian & Scholfield A. F. (Trans.) *On the Characteristics of Animals Volume I*. London, William Heinemann Ltd 1957.

Aelian & Scholfield A. F. (Trans.) *On the Characteristics of Animals Volume III*. London, William Heinemann Ltd 1957.

Allam, S. (1991) *Egyptian Law Courts in Pharaonic and Hellenistic Times*. In *Journal of Egyptian Archaeology*, Vol 77:109-127

Allen, T. A. (1974) *The Book of the Dead or Going Forth by Day*. Chicago, University of Chicago Press

Apuleius & Walsh, P. G. (trans.) (1994) *The Golden Ass*. Oxford, Oxford University Press

Arkell, A. J. (1955) *An Archaic Representation of Hathor*. In *Journal of Egyptian Archaeology*, Vol 41:125-126

Assmann, J. (1995) *Egyptian Solar Religion in the New Kingdom*. London, Kegan Paul International Ltd

Bagnal, R.S. & Rathbone, D.W. (2004) *Egypt from Alexander to the Copts*. London, British Museum Press

Bell, H. (1948) *Popular Religion in Graeco-Roman Egypt: I. The Pagan Period*. In *Journal of Egyptian Archaeology*, Vol 34:82-97

Betro, M. C. (1996) *Hieroglyphics: The writings of Ancient Egypt*. New York, Abbeville Press

Blackman, A. M. & Fairman, H. W. (1944) *The Myth of Horus at Edfu: II. C. The Triumph of Horus Over His Enemies. A Sacred Drama (Concluded)*. In *Journal of Egyptian Archaeology*, Vol 30:5-22

Blackman, A. M. & Fairman, H. W. (1949) *The Significance of the Ceremony Hwt Bhsw in the Temple of Horus at Edfu*. In *Journal of Egyptian Archaeology*, Vol 35:98-112

Blackman, A. M. (1918) *The House of the Morning*. In *Journal of Egyptian Archaeology*, Vol 5:148-165

Blackman, A. M. (1921) *On the Position of Women in the Egyptian Hierarchy*. In *Journal of Egyptian Archaeology*, Vol 7:8-30

Blackman, A. M. (1945) *The King of Egypt's Grace Before Meat*. In *Journal of Egyptian Archaeology*, Vol 31:57-73

Bleeker, C. J. (1967) *Egyptian Festivals*. Leiden, E J Brill

Bleeker, C. J. (1973) *Hathor and Thoth: Two Key Figures of the Ancient Egyptian Religion*. Leiden, E J Brill

Bomhard, A. S. (1999) *The Egyptian Calendar A Work For Eternity*. London, Periplus Publishing

Borghouts, J. F. (1973) *The Evil Eye of Apophis*. In *Journal of Egyptian Archaeology*, Vol 59:114-150

Borghouts, J. F. (1978) *Ancient Egyptian Magical Texts*. Leiden, E J Brill

Brovarski, E (1976) *Senenu, High Priest of Amun at Deir el-Bahri*. In *Journal of Egyptian Archaeology*, Vol 62:57-73

Budge, E.A.W. (1969) *The Egyptian Book of the Dead*. London, Dover Publications

Budge, E.A.W. (1969) *The Gods of the Egyptians Vol I*. London, Dover Publications

Buhl, N. (1947) *The Goddesses of the Egyptian Tree Cult*, In *Journal of Near Eastern Studies*, Vol 6:80-97

Capel, A. K. & Markoe, G. E. (1997) *Mistress of the House, Mistress of Heaven: Women in Ancient Art*. Easthampton, Hudson Hills Press Inc.

Cerny, J. (1952) *Ancient Egyptian Religion*. London, Hutchinson's University Library

Clark, R. T. (1978) *Myth and Symbol in Ancient Egypt*. London, Thames & Hudson

Davis N. G. (1915) *The Tomb of Amenemhet*. London, Egypt Exploration Fund

Davis N. G. (1920) *An Alabaster Sistrum Dedicated by King Teta*. In *Journal of Egyptian Archaeology*, Vol 6:69-72

Davis N. G. (1920) *The Tomb of Antefoker, Vizier of Setostris I, and of His Wife, Senet*. London, Allen & Unwin

Davis, N. G. (1925) *The Tomb of Tetaky at Thebes (no. 15)*. In *Journal of Egyptian Archaeology*, Vol 11:10-18

Dennis, J. T. (1910) *The Burden of Isis*. London, John Murray

Dorman, P. F. (1999) *Creation on the Potter's Wheel at the Eastern Horizon of Heaven*. In Teeter, E. & Larson, J. A. (eds.) (1999) *Studies on Ancient Egypt in Honour of Edward F. Wente*. Chicago, University of Chicago Press

Dunand, F. & Zivie-Coche, C. (2004) *Gods and Men in Egypt 3000 BCE to 395 CE*. Ithaca, Cornell University Press

Dunham, D. (1935) *Four New Kingdom Monuments in the Museum of Fine Arts, Boston*. In *Journal of Egyptian Archaeology*, Vol 21:147-151

el-Khouly, A. (1973) *Excavations East of the Serapeum at Saqqara*. In *Journal of Egyptian Archaeology*, Vol 59:151-155

el-Saady, H. M. (1990) *Two Minor Monuments of Sety I*. In *Journal of Egyptian Archaeology*, Vol 76:186-188

el-Sabban (2000) *Temple Festival Calendars of Ancient Egypt*. Liverpool, Liverpool University Press

el-Sayed, M.A. (1978) *A New Temple for Hathor at Memphis*. Warminster, Aris & Phillips Ltd.

Ellis, C. (1984) *A Bronze Mirror with the Titles rht-nsw hm(t)-ntr Hwt-hr*. In *Journal of Egyptian Archaeology*, Vol 70:139-140

Erman, A. (1995) *Ancient Egyptian Poetry and Prose*. New York, Dover Publications.

Espinel, A. D. (2005) *A Newly Identified Stela from Wadi el-Hudi*. In *Journal of Egyptian Archaeology*, Vol 91:55-70

Fairman, H. W, (1974) *The Triumph of Horus*. London, Batsford

Fairman, H. W. & Grdseloff, B (1947) *Texts of Hatshepsut and Sethos I Inside Speos Artemidos*. In *Journal of Egyptian Archaeology*, Vol 33:12-33

Faulkner, R. O. (1937) *The Bremner-Rhind Papyrus: II*. In *Journal of Egyptian Archaeology*, Vol 23:10-16

Faulkner, R. O. (1937) *The Bremner-Rhind Papyrus: III: D. The Book of Overthrowing Apep*. In *Journal of Egyptian Archaeology*, Vol 23:166-185

Faulkner, R. O. (1938) *The Bremner-Rhind Papyrus: IV*. In *Journal of Egyptian Archaeology*, Vol 24:41-53

Faulkner, R. O. (1944) *The Rebellion in the Hare Nome*. In *Journal of Egyptian Archaeology*, Vol 30:61-63

Faulkner, R. O. (1958) *An Ancient Egyptian Book of Hours*. Oxford, Griffith Institute

Faulkner, R. O. (1989) *The Ancient Egyptian Book of the Dead*. London, British Museum Publications

Faulkner, R. O. (2007) *The Ancient Egyptian Coffin Texts*. Oxford, Aris & Phillips

Faulkner, R. O. (2007) *The Ancient Egyptian Pyramid Texts*. Kansas, Digireads.com Publishing

Finnestad, R. B. *Enjoying the Pleasures of Sensation: Reflections on a Significant Feature of Egyptian Religion*. In Teeter, E. & Larson, J. A. (eds.) (1999) *Studies on Ancient Egypt in Honour of Edward F. Wente*. Chicago, University of Chicago Press

Fletcher, J. (1999) *Oils and Perfumes of Ancient Egypt*. New York, Harry N Abrams Inc.

Foreman, W. & Quirke, S. (1996) *Hieroglyphs & the Afterlife in Ancient Egypt*. London, Opus Publishing Ltd

Foster, J. L. (1992) *Echoes of Egyptian Voices*. Oklahoma City, University of Oklahoma Press

Foster, J. L. (1995) *Hymns, Prayers and Songs*. Atlanta, Scholars Press

Foster, J. L. (2001) *Ancient Egyptian Literature*. Austin, University of Texas Press

Fox, M. V. (1985) *The Song of Songs and the Egyptian Love Songs*. Madison, University of Wisconsin Press

Frandsen, P. J. (1999) *On Fear of Death and the Three Bwts connected with Hathor*. In Teeter, E. & Larson, J. A. (eds.) (1999) *Studies on Ancient Egypt in Honour of Edward F. Wente*. Chicago, University of Chicago Press

Frankfort, H. (1928) *The Cemeteries of Abydos: Work of the Season 1925-26*. In *Journal of Egyptian Archaeology*, Vol 14:235-245

Frankfort, H. (1948) *Kingship and the Gods*. Chicago, University of Chicago Press

Frankfurter, D. (1998) *Religion in Roman Egypt*. Princeton, Princeton University Press

Fraser, P. M. (1956) *A Temple of Hathor at Kusae*. In *Journal of Egyptian Archaeology*, Vol 42:97-98

Friedman, F. D. (Ed.) (1998) *Gifts of the Nile: Ancient Egyptian Faience*. London, Thames & Hudson

Frood, E. & Baines, J. (2007) *Biographical Texts from Ramessid Egypt*. Atlanta, Society of Biblical Literature

Gaballa, G. A. (1969) *Minor War Scenes of Ramesses II at Karnak*. In *Journal of Egyptian Archaeology*, Vol 55:82-88.

Galvin, M. (1984) *The Hereditary Status of Titles in the Cult of Hathor.* In *Journal of Egyptian Archaeology*, Vol 70:42-49

Gardiner, A. H. (1918) *The Delta Residence of the Ramessides.* In *Journal of Egyptian Archaeology*, Vol 5:179-200

Gardiner, A. H. (1938) *The Mansion of Life and the Master of the King's Largess, Gardiner.* In *Journal of Egyptian Archaeology*, Vol 24.1:83-91

Gardiner, A. H. (1941) *Ramesside Texts Relating to the Taxation and Transport of Corn.* In *Journal of Egyptian Archaeology*, Vol 27:19-73

Gardiner, A. K. (1917) *The Tomb of a Much-Travelled Theban Official.* In *Journal of Egyptian Archaeology*, Vol 4:28-38

Giveon, R. (1982) *A God Who Hears.* In van Voss, M. H., & Hoens, D. J., & Mussies, G., & van der Plas, D. & te Velde, H. (eds.) *Studies in Egyptian Religion: Dedicated to Professor Jan Zandee.* Leiden, E. J. Brill

Goedicke, H (1991) *The Prayers of Wakh-ankh-antef-Aa,* In *Journal of Near Eastern Studies*, Vol 50:235-253

Goodison, L. & Morris, C. (eds.) (1998) *Ancient Goddesses.* London, British Museum Press

Graves-Brown, C. (2010) *Dancing for Hathor: Women in Ancient Egypt.* London, Continuum

Griffith, F. L. & Thompson, H. (1974) *The Leyden Papyrus.* London, Dover Publications

Griffiths, J. G. (1982) *Eight Funerary Paintings with Judgement Scenes in the Swansea Wellcome Museum.* In *Journal of Egyptian Archaeology*, Vol 68:228-252

Gunn, B. & Gardiner, A. H. (1917) *New Renderings of Egyptian Texts.* In *Journal of Egyptian Archaeology*, Vol 4:241-251

Hart, G. (2005) *The Routledge Dictionary of Egyptian Gods and Goddesses.* Abingdon, Routledge

Hawass, Z. (1994) *A Fragmentary Monument of Djoser from Saqqara.* In *Journal of Egyptian Archaeology*, Vol 80:45-56

Hayes, W. C. (1948) *A Foundation Plaque of Ptolemy IV.* In *Journal of Egyptian Archaeology*, Vol 34:114-115

Herodotus & Selincourt, A. (trans.) (2003) *The Histories.* London, Penguin Books

Hornung, E. & Bryan, B. M. (eds.) (2002) *The Quest for Immortality: Treasures of Ancient Egypt.* London, Prestel Publishers

Hornung, E. (1996) *Conceptions of God in Ancient Egypt*. Ithica, Cornell University Press

Houlihan, P. F. (1996) *The Animal World of the Pharaohs*. London, Thames & Hudson

Jacq, C. (1999) *The Living Wisdom of Ancient Egypt*. London, Simon & Schuster

James, E. O. (1959) *The Cult of the Mother-Goddess*. London, Thames & Hudson

James, T. G. H. (1982) *A Wooden Figure of Wadjet with Two Painted Representations of Amasis*. In *Journal of Egyptian Archaeology*, Vol 68:156-165

Janssen, J. J. (1968) *The Smaller Dakhla Stela (Ashmolean Museum No. 1894. 107b)*. In *Journal of Egyptian Archaeology*, Vol 54:165-172

Johnson, S. B. (1990) *The Cobra Goddesses of Ancient Egypt*. London, Kegan Paul International

Kakosy, L. (1980) *A Memphite Triad*. In *Journal of Egyptian Archaeology*, Vol 66:48-53

Kakosy, L. (1982) *The Nile, Euthenia and the Nymphs*. In *Journal of Egyptian Archaeology*, Vol 68:290-298

Kaster, J. (1993) *The Wisdom of Ancient Egypt*. New York, Barnes & Noble Books

Kemp, B. (2006) *100 Hieroglyphs: Think Like an Egyptian*. London, Granta Books

Kirby, C. J., Oriel, S. E. & Smith, S. T. (1998) *Preliminary Report on the Survey of Kom el-Hisin, 1996*. In *Journal of Egyptian Archaeology*, Vol 84:23-43

Kozloff, A. P. & Bryan, B. M. (1992) *Egypt's Dazzling Sun: Amenhotep III and his World*. Cleveland, Cleveland Museum of Art

Kurth, D. (2004) *The Temple of Edfu*. Cairo, The American University in Cairo Press

Leahy, A. (2006) *A Battered Statue of Shedsunefertem, High Priest of Memphis*. In *Journal of Egyptian Archaeology*, Vol 92:169-184

Lesko, B. S. (1999) *The Great Goddesses of Egypt*. Norman, University of Oklahoma Press

Lesko, L. H. (1991) *Ancient Egyptian Cosmogonies and Cosmology*. In Shafer, B. E. (ed.) (1991) *Religion in Ancient Egypt*. Ithica, Cornell University Press

Lichtheim, M. (1988) *Ancient Egyptian Autobiographies.* Switzerland, Biblical Institute of the University of Fribourg

Lichtheim, M. (2006) *Ancient Egyptian Literature Volume I.* California, University of California Press

Lichtheim, M. (2006) *Ancient Egyptian Literature Volume II.* California, University of California Press

Lichtheim, M. (2006) *Ancient Egyptian Literature Volume III.* California, University of California Press

Lilyquist, C. (1979) *Ancient Egyptian Mirrors from the Earliest Times through the Middle Kingdom.* Berlin, Deutscher Kunstverlag

Lindsay, J. (1968) *Men and Gods on the Roman Nile.* London, Frederick Muller

Lord, C. (2010) *How Now Sick Cow?* In *Ancient Egypt,* Vol 11.1 Issue 61:20-24

Lurker, M. (1986) *The Gods and Symbols of Ancient Egypt.* London, Thames & Hudson

Mace, A. C. (1920) *Hathor Dances.* In *Journal of Egyptian Archaeology,* Vol 6:297

Malek, J. (1974) *Two Monuments of the Tias.* In *Journal of Egyptian Archaeology,* Vol 60:161-167

Malek, J. (1993) *The Cat in Ancient Egypt.* London, British Museum Press

Manniche, L. (1986) *The Tomb of Nakht, the Gardener, at Thebes (no. 161) as Copied by Robert Hay.* In *Journal of Egyptian Archaeology,* Vol 72:55-78

Manniche, L. (1999) *Sacred Luxuries.* Ithica, Cornell University Press

Martin, G. T. (2012) *The Tomb of Maya and Meryt I: The Reliefs Inscriptions, and Commentary.* London, Egypt Exploration Society

McDonald, J. K. (1996) *House of Eternity: The Tomb of Nefertari.* London, Thames & Hudson

McDowell, A. (1992) *Agricultural Activity by the Workman of Deir el-Medina.* In *Journal of Egyptian Archaeology,* Vol 78:195-206

Mead, G. R. S. (2002) *Plutarch: Concerning the Mysteries of Isis and Osiris.* Montana, Kessinger Publishing (Reprints)

Morenz, S. (1992) *Egyptian Religion.* Ithica, Cornell University Press

Muhs, B (1998) *Partisan Royal Epithets in the Late Third Intermediate Period and the Dynastic Affiliations of Pedubast I and Iuput II.* In *Journal of Egyptian Archaeology,* Vol 84:220-223

Muller, H. W. & Theim, E. (1999) *The Royal Gold of Ancient Egypt*. London, I. B. Tauris

Mumford, G. D. & Parcak, S. (2003) *Pharaonic Ventures into Southern Sinai, el-Markha Plain Site 346*. In *Journal of Egyptian Archaeology*, Vol 89:83-116

Murray, M. A. (1956) *Burial Customs and Beliefs in the Hereafter in Predynastic Egypt*. In *Journal of Egyptian Archaeology*, Vol 42:86-96

Myers, O. H. & Fairman, H. W. (1931) *Excavations at Armant, 1929-31*. In *Journal of Egyptian Archaeology*, Vol 17:223-232

Noblecourt, C. D. (2007) *Gifts From the Pharaohs*. Paris, Flammarion

Oakes, L. & Gahlin, L. (2004) *Ancient Egypt*. London, Hermes House 2004.

Parkinson, R. (1999) *Cracking Codes: The Rosetta Stone and Decipherment*. London, British Museum Press

Parkinson, R. (1991) *Voices from Ancient Egypt*. London, British Museum Press

Peet, T. E. (1920) *A Stela of the Reign of Sheshonk IV*. In *Journal of Egyptian Archaeology*, Vol 6:56-57

Pestman, P. W. (1969) *A Greek Testament from Pathyris*. In *Journal of Egyptian Archaeology*, Vol 55:129-160

Piankoff, A. & Clere, J. J. (1934) *A Letter to the Dead on a Bowl in the Louvre*. In *Journal of Egyptian Archaeology*, Vol 20:157-169

Piankoff, A. (1972) *The Wandering of the Soul*. New Jersey, Princeton University Press

Pinch, G. (1993) *Votive Offerings to Hathor*. Oxford, Griffith Institute

Pinch, G. (2002) *Egyptian Mythology*. Oxford, Oxford University Press

Pinch, G. (2004) *Egyptian Myth: A Very Short Introduction*. Oxford, Oxford University Press

Pinch, G. (2006) *Magic in Ancient Egypt*. London, The British Museum Press

Poo, M. (1995) *Wine and Wine Offering in the Religion of Ancient Egypt*. London, Kegan Paul International

Quirke, S. (1992) *Ancient Egyptian Religion*. London, The British Museum Press

Quirke, S. (2001) *The Cult of Ra*. London, Thames & Hudson

Rankine, D. (2006) *Heka: The Practices of Ancient Egyptian Ritual & Magic*, London, Avalonia

Ray, D. J. (1987) *A Pious Soldier: Stele Aswan 1057*. In *Journal of Egyptian Archaeology*, Vol 73:169-180

Reader, C. (2008) *Pharaoh's Gold*. In *Ancient Egypt*, Vol 9.2 Issue 50:15-21

Ritner, R. K. (2009) *The Libyan Anarchy: Inscriptions from Egypt's Third Intermediate Period*. Atlanta, Society of Biblical Literature

Roberts, A. (2001) *Hathor Rising*. Rottingdean, Northgate Publishers

Sauneron, S. (2000) *The Priests of Ancient Egypt*. Ithica, Cornell University Press

Schweizer, A. (2010) *The Sungod's Journey Through the Netherworld*. Ithaca, Cornell University Press

Shafer, B. E. (Ed.) (2005) *Temples of Ancient Egypt*. London, Tauris & Co Ltd

Shaw, I. & Nicholson, P. (2008) *The British Museum Dictionary of Ancient Egypt*. London, British Museum Press

Shorter, A. W. (1935) *The God Nehebkau*. In *Journal of Egyptian Archaeology*, Vol 21:41-48

Simpson, W. K., Ritner, R. K., Tobin, V.A. & Wente, E. F. (2003) *The Literature of Ancient Egypt*. London, Yale University Press

Smith, M. (1993) *The Liturgy of Opening the Mouth for Breathing*. Oxford, Griffith Institute

Smith, M. (2009) *Traversing Eternity*. Oxford, Oxford University Press

Snape, S. (2011) *Ancient Egyptian Tombs*. Chichester, John Wiley & Sons Ltd

Stevens, A. (2007) *Private Religion at Amarna: the Material Evidence*. Oxford, Archeapress

Strudwick, N. (2005) *Texts From the Pyramid Age*. Atlanta, Society of Biblical Literature

Szpakowska, K (2003) *Behind Closed Eyes*. Swansea, The Classical Press of Wales

Szpakowska, K. (2008) *Daily Life in Ancient Egypt*. Oxford, Blackwell Publishing

Szpakowska, K. (Ed.) (2006) *Through a Glass Darkly*. Swansea, The Classical Press of Wales

Taher, A. W. (2010) *News From Egypt*. In *Ancient Egypt*, Vol 11.3 Issue 63:9-16

Taher, A. W. (2011) *Revealing the Secrets of Dendera*. In *Ancient Egypt*, Vol 12.1 Issue 67:22-31

Taylor, J. H. (2001) *Death and the Afterlife in Ancient Egypt*. London, British Museum Press.

Taylor, J. H. (ed) (2010) *Journey Through the Afterlife: Ancient Egyptian Book of the Dead*. London, British Museum Press.

Teeter, E. & Johnson, J. H. (Eds.) (2009) *The Life of Meresamun*. Chicago, University of Chicago

Teeter, E. (2011) *Religion and Ritual in Ancient Egypt*. Cambridge, Cambridge University Press

Thiers, C. & Zignani, P. (2011) *The Temple of Ptah at Karnak*. In *Egyptian Archaeology*, No. 38:20-24

Torpey, A. (2011) *Gardens in Ancient Egypt*. In *Ancient Egypt*, Vol 12.1 Issue 67:32-37

Tyldesley, J (2010) *Myths & Legends of Ancient Egypt*. London, Allen Lane

Tyldesley, J. (1995) *Daughters of Isis*. London, Penguin Books 1995.

Velde te, H. (1971) *Some Remarks on the Structure of Egyptian Divine Triads*. In *Journal of Egyptian Archaeology*, Vol 57:80-86

Vernus, P. (1998) *The Gods of Ancient Egypt*. London, Tauris Parke Books

Ward, W. A. (1970) *The Origins of Egyptian Design Amulets*. In *Journal of Egyptian Archaeology*, Vol 56:65-80

Watterson, B. (1998) *The House of Horus at Edfu*. Stroud, Tempus Publishing Limited

Watterson, B. (2003) *Gods of Ancient Egypt*. Stroud, Sutton Publishing Ltd

Weeks, K. R. (Ed.) (2010) *Valley of the Kings*. Italy, White Star Publishers

Wente, E. (1990) *Letters from Ancient Egypt*. Atlanta, Scholars Press

Whitehouse, H. (2009) *Ancient Egypt and Nubia*. Oxford, Ashmolean Museum

Wilkinson, R. H. (2000) *The Complete Temples of Ancient Egypt*. London, Thames & Hudson

Wilkinson, R. H. (2003) *The Complete Gods and Goddesses of Ancient Egypt*. London, Thames & Hudson

Wilkinson, R. H. (2011) *Reading Egyptian Art*. London, Thames & Hudson

Williams, C. R. (1918) *The Egyptian Collection in the Museum of Art at Cleveland, Ohio*. In *Journal of Egyptian Archaeology*, Vol 5:166-178

Wilson, A. (1952) *A Note on the Edwin Smith Surgical Papyrus*, In *Journal of Near Eastern Studies*, Vol 11:76-80

Wilson, H. (1993) *Understanding Hieroglyphics: a Quick and Simple Guide*. London, Michael O'Mara Books Ltd.

Wilson, H. (2009) *The Sycamore and the Fig*. In *Ancient Egypt*, Vol 10.2 Issue 56:41-43

Wilson, H. (2010) *A Sense of Smell*. In *Ancient Egypt*, Vol 10.5 Issue 59:32-33

Witt, R. E. (1997) *Isis in the Ancient World*. Baltimore, The John Hopkins University Press

Wood W. (1974) *A Reconstruction of the Triads of King Mycerinus*. In *Journal of Egyptian Archaeology*, Vol 60:82-93

Zabkar, L. V. (1980) *Adaption of Ancient Egyptian Texts to the Temple Ritual at Philae*. In *Journal of Egyptian Archaeology*, Vol 66:127-136

Zabkar, L. V. (1988) *Hymns to Isis in Her Temple at Philae*. Hanover, University Press of New England

INDEX

A

Abu Gurob 263, 284
Abu Simbel 140, 236, 244, 284
Abusir 106, 178, 225, 284
Abydos 16, 119, 175, 181, 207, 284
acacia 61, 62, 68, 161
Aelian 166
afterlife.12, 24, 31, 36, 37, 38, 45, 63, 66, 67, 77, 80, 81, 84, 87, 97, 108, 122, 130, 136, 142, 143, 144, 145, 146, 147, 148, 149, 151, 152, 153, 154, 157, 161, 162, 190, 197, 208, 214, 235, 243, 266, 270
akh 145, 148
Akhenaten 205
Akhmim 97, 284
alabaster 75, 112, 115
Amarna 205, 206, 284
Amduat 21, 127
Ameneminet 216
Amenhotep II 37, 131, 153
Amenhotep III 93, 133, 169, 179, 180, 193, 202, 203, 204, 206, 233, 239, 247, 253, 258, 263
Amratian 31, 33
amulets 34, 67, 76, 85, 133, 146, 168, 177, 181, 194, 207, 208, 209, 212, 213, 216, 218, 240
Amun 17, 23, 48, 72, 73, 75, 98, 113, 114, 122, 147, 177, 178, 184, 185, 200, 205, 208, 209, 211, 221, 222, 224, 245, 246, 249, 250, 258
Amunemhet 211
Anastasi III Papyrus 233
Anastasi Papyrus 157
Anat 140, 192, 193, 196
Angry Eye 53, 65, 189, 226
ankh 76, 77, 80, 82, 113, 153, 175, 179, 195, 202, 265
Ankh Tawy 180
Ankhesenamun 77
Antef-iker 94
Antefoker 95
Anubis 38, 108, 146, 147, 148, 153
Anukis ... 83, 123, 192, 193, 196, 222, 266
Aphrodite 14, 42, 100, 193, 230, 244, 245, 266, 268
Aphroditopolis 32, 248, 285
Apophis 87, 123, 126, 128, 174, 189, 217
Aspalathos 114
Aspersion of the Dead 150
Astarte 192, 196
Aswan 135, 192, 193, 196, 255, 284
Asyut 244, 284
Aten 48, 205
Atfih 284
Atum 43, 49, 52, 89, 97, 101, 147, 249, 259, 263
August Lady 17
Augustus 128, 242, 252

B

ba 12, 32, 67, 145, 148, 236, 237, 241
Baal 193
Baalat 140, 193
Baalat Gebal 140
Baba 100
Babi 50, 51
baboon 51, 56, 57, 65, 127
barque .. 36, 41, 48, 57, 58, 126, 127, 139, 156, 157, 181, 188, 189, 203, 207, 221, 237, 241, 243, 249, 250, 251, 254, 263, 265, 275, 276, 278, 280
Bastet .12, 19, 21, 33, 53, 72, 84, 99, 112, 115, 168, 169, 172, 175, 176, 181, 194, 195, 266, 269
Bat 34, 35, 37, 72, 249, 265
Baubo 50
Beautiful Feast of the Valley 150, 221
Beautiful of Face 17, 249
Beef 31
beer 54, 55, 67, 79, 103, 104, 105, 106, 107, 109, 149, 152, 157, 169, 186, 224, 263, 275, 278
beetles 114
Behdet 18, 223, 247
Beni Hasan 181, 226, 284, 287
Bes 20, 25, 61, 73, 83, 92, 96, 97, 98, 108, 119, 120, 187, 188, 196, 209, 216, 218, 219, 252
besbes 61
Biga 284
Bir Kisseibaq 28, 284
birth 12, 24, 31, 34, 36, 38, 44, 48, 56, 76, 77, 96, 114, 116, 118, 119, 120, 136, 160, 170, 186, 200, 202, 208, 233, 235, 242, 270, 278, 279
black 43, 68, 178, 179, 180, 214, 251
blood 21, 54, 55, 106, 175
blue 32, 40, 68, 85, 113, 114, 134, 137, 176, 236, 251
blue lotus 113, 176, 236

Book of Gates 173
Book of Overthrowing Apep 126, 174
Book of the Amduat. 53, 126, 139, 144, 174
Book of the Dead 39, 42, 44, 46, 68, 73, 89, 144, 146, 148, 151, 154, 155, 156, 161, 173, 186, 194, 197
Book of the Last Day of the Year 169
Book of Two Ways 144
breasts 35, 56
Bremner-Rhind Papyrus 19, 43, 126, 174
Bubastis 194, 263, 287
Busiris 152
Buto 58, 84, 176, 192, 266, 287
Bwgm 56, 104, 227
Byblos 140, 193

C

calf 24, 32, 216
Caligula 239
Canaan 192
canine 21
cat 12, 73, 115, 194, 217, 269
cedar 113, 193
Celestial Cow ... 17, 23, 28, 34, 35, 36, 37, 38, 40, 41, 42, 44, 46, 48, 235
Chester Beatty Papyrus 18, 210
Chieftainess of Thebes 202
childbirth 8, 116, 119
Christians 112, 188, 239
Claudius 239
Cleopatra VII 240
cobra .. 12, 20, 46, 52, 53, 57, 58, 72, 124, 160, 175, 182, 207, 217, 245, 250
Cobra 57
Coffin Texts 32, 42, 66, 132, 134, 144, 150, 151, 154, 156, 157, 162, 186, 217, 243
Coming Forth by Day 153
constellation 35, 43, 165
cow. 12, 14, 19, 20, 22, 23, 24, 25, 26, 27, 28, 31, 32, 33, 34, 35, 36, 37, 38, 41, 44, 45, 46, 58, 60, 65, 66, 68, 74, 76,

79, 118, 122, 123, 124, 126, 140, 146, 148, 150, 151, 167, 170, 185, 199, 201, 205, 212, 215, 221, 234, 240, 249, 250, 252, 259, 265, 266, 269
Crete 141
crocodile 160, 171, 185
crown .20, 23, 58, 62, 65, 66, 67, 77, 122, 143, 148, 165, 185, 189, 240, 265
Cusae 32, 42, 238, 244, 260, 284
Cyprus 141

D

Dakhla 65, 105, 284
dance 81, 87, 89, 90, 91, 92, 93, 94, 95, 96, 97, 98, 104, 150, 162, 220, 252
dancers 34, 78, 79, 92, 94, 95, 96, 149, 277
date palm 61, 62, 68
death 21, 31, 43, 63, 65, 66, 77, 80, 87, 106, 143, 145, 147, 148, 153, 160, 199, 203, 205, 219, 220, 226, 235, 243, 267, 268
Deir el-Bahri ... 16, 17, 32, 37, 48, 78, 93, 113, 122, 202, 208, 209, 212, 214, 215, 216, 221, 233, 235, 236, 245, 250, 285
Deir el-Gebrawi 195, 285
Deir el-Medina 19, 24, 42, 136, 147, 196, 207, 212, 218, 238, 246, 285
Delta...28, 30, 41, 55, 59, 73, 84, 85, 105, 132, 138, 182, 185, 192, 193, 194, 225, 233, 250
Demeter 50, 266, 268
demons .73, 154, 155, 167, 173, 174, 187
Dendera25, 32, 37, 42, 44, 55, 56, 62, 74, 77, 79, 81, 93, 107, 108, 114, 117, 119, 120, 126, 128, 139, 140, 149, 184, 185, 186, 187, 189, 195, 197, 201, 203, 204, 210, 212, 222, 223, 224, 227, 236, 237, 238, 239, 242, 243, 246, 250, 252, 257, 258, 259, 260, 262, 280, 285

Distant Goddess44, 55, 56, 57, 104, 187, 189, 196, 226, 227, 244
djed 85, 175, 203, 236, 271, 276
Djehutiemhab 19, 209
Djeser-Djeseru 32, 245
dog 160
Domitian 240
doum palms 63
drunkenness 55, 86, 88, 103, 106, 107, 108, 109, 220, 223, 277
dryads 63
duck 73
dwarf 20, 119, 120, 187
Dynastic Period. 33, 35, 46, 64, 140, 220, 283

E

ebony 37, 98, 141, 218
Edfu 18, 21, 27, 56, 98, 112, 114, 117, 128, 169, 172, 184, 185, 186, 197, 205, 222, 223, 225, 230, 235, 238, 239, 243, 246, 250, 254, 261, 274, 278, 285
Edjo .... *See* Wadjet
egg 16
el-Ashmunein 285
Elephantine 54, 192, 196, 285
el-Kab 247, 285
el-Maragha 285
el-Markha 131
Esna 56, 241, 247, 285
evil eye 51, 168, 170
Eye of Horus 154
Eye of Ra. 17, 18, 46, 49, 51, 52, 53, 104, 124, 126, 128, 136, 154, 164, 165, 174, 180, 181, 182, 204, 235

F

faience 71, 72, 78, 85, 132, 137, 206, 212, 215, 217
falcon ... 14, 23, 38, 42, 52, 131, 143, 184, 218, 265

Faras 212, 217, 233, 247, 285
Fayum 134, 285
feathers 21, 23, 24, 65, 146
fertility .. 21, 26, 31, 35, 37, 44, 75, 77, 78, 87, 92, 104, 116, 117, 118, 123, 135, 185, 206, 212, 213, 216, 217, 218, 222, 223, 236, 267
Festival of Eternity 95
fig61
fish 83, 113, 156, 207, 216
foreigners 12, 173
Foremost in Thebes 15
four pillars 41

G

gazelle 83, 123, 193
Geb 37, 116, 222, 265
Gebel Abu Hassa 131, 254, 285
Gebel Ahmar 136, 285
Gebel el-Zeit 135, 212, 248, 285
Gebelein 16, 35, 238, 248, 285
Gerf Hussein 248, 285
Gerzean 34, 35, 134
Giza 81, 204, 225, 285
Gleaming One 17
Goddess of drunkenness 17
gold 16, 18, 19, 49, 79, 101, 132, 133, 211, 215, 234, 237, 247, 271
Gold of the gods in Wetjset-Hor 17
Golden Goddess 12, 95
Golden Lady 17
Golden One 12, 17, 77, 93, 96, 101, 210, 223, 246, 262
Great Flood 36
Greco-Roman Period 35, 45, 97, 107, 109, 128, 151, 186, 219, 220, 233, 235, 243, 264, 267
green ... 20, 64, 68, 84, 107, 135, 148, 175, 182, 221, 251
Guardian of the West 142

H

hair 21, 34, 73, 83, 98, 102, 112, 113, 119, 129, 160, 165, 179, 186, 196, 207, 213, 217, 234, 235, 251
hairstyle 102
Hapy 44, 104
harp 93, 97, 98, 149, 252
Harris Papyrus 49
Harsomtus 48, 74, 76, 184, 186, 188, 202, 246, 278, 279
Hathor Cow 18, 23, 24, 26, 29, 32, 35, 36, 37, 43, 44, 47, 57, 61, 73, 76, 83, 84, 107, 115, 122, 136, 140, 143, 146, 148, 155, 161, 164, 202, 206, 208, 215, 216, 240, 243, 245, 247, 250, 252
Hathor Head 20, 32, 77, 80, 97, 146, 206, 232, 234, 235, 236, 239, 240, 245, 251, 253
Hathor Heads 20, 25, 105, 119, 196, 203, 206, 212, 235, 253
Hathor of Bhdt 15
Hathor of Gold 244
Hathoremheb 20
Hathor-Sekhmet 243
Hatshepsut 62, 67, 102, 108, 122, 131, 149, 181, 201, 202, 208, 221, 232, 235, 245, 247, 250, 252, 253
healing ... 65, 77, 120, 123, 124, 154, 156, 167, 170, 176, 212, 242, 267
heb-sed 93, 203, 205
heiros gamos 117
heka 124, 162, 265
Heka 171
Heket 116
Heliopolis 56, 62, 152, 166, 197, 248, 259, 287
Hely 19
Herakleopolis 54, 226, 286
Hermes 144, 265
Hesat 38
heset 99

High Priest 17, 73, 98, 164, 204, 229, 258, 259, 260, 262
Hiw 72, 81, 249, 285
Horurre 130
Horus ... 14, 18, 24, 27, 32, 38, 42, 48, 49, 50, 51, 52, 76, 84, 96, 98, 99, 100, 106, 107, 114, 117, 122, 123, 124, 128, 137, 172, 174, 182, 183, 184, 185, 186, 187, 201, 202, 204, 208, 215, 218, 222, 223, 225, 238, 239, 240, 241, 242, 246, 247, 251, 253, 259, 261, 265, 267, 278, 279, 281
House of Horus 14
Hwt Sekhem 72
Hwt-Hr 14
Hwt-hrw 14
Hyksos 192

I

ibis 16
Ihet 38, 122
Ihnasya el-Medina 286
Ihy . 48, 72, 76, 77, 92, 98, 114, 119, 157, 184, 186, 188, 239, 241, 242, 263, 280
Inanna 117
incense 62, 82, 89, 97, 107, 111, 112, 113, 114, 139, 141, 151, 155, 169, 233, 240, 242, 253, 255, 258
intoxication 89, 90, 97, 106, 109
inundation . 21, 43, 44, 55, 56, 57, 62, 87, 104, 105, 117, 122, 168, 185, 196, 199, 221, 233, 275, 276
Irynefer 24, 153
Isis . 14, 20, 23, 38, 43, 48, 64, 68, 72, 84, 113, 116, 119, 122, 123, 124, 125, 127, 139, 148, 174, 176, 183, 184, 186, 187, 192, 202, 204, 213, 218, 226, 240, 252, 264, 265, 266, 267, 268, 269, 271, 278, 298
Iusaas 49, 101, 278
ivory 23, 33, 34, 37, 44, 79, 97, 213

Iy-mery 95

J

Julius Caesar 240
Jusas 68

K

ka 33, 69, 74, 80, 82, 107, 108, 145, 147, 148, 150, 173, 195, 211, 215, 227, 237
Karnak . 98, 168, 178, 194, 202, 209, 224, 249, 286
Khafra 195
Khemmis .. 24, 38, 84, 122, 182, 186, 202
khener 79, 83, 99
Khepri 114
Khnum 48, 101, 160, 202, 230, 242
Khonsu 44, 113, 170, 184, 185, 200, 205, 211, 247, 249
kingship 57, 166, 184, 223
kitten 73
knot 156, 161
Kom Abu Billo 250, 286
Kom Ausim 286
Kom el-Ahmar 286
Kom el-Hettan 180
Kom el-Hisin 179, 250, 286
Kom Ombo 184, 185, 251, 286
Kosseir 286
Kyphi 115

L

Lady of Agny 15
Lady of All 17
Lady of Aphroditopolis 15
Lady of Behdet 254
Lady of Byblos 140
Lady of Djeser 15
Lady of Faience 137
Lady of Galena 248
Lady of Gebelein 15

Lady of Heaven ...17, 101, 136, 148, 172, 204, 212, 215, 249, 257, 264
Lady of Hetepet............................15
Lady of Horns 17, 27
Lady of Ibshek............................217, 247
Lady of Ibsk............................ 140
Lady of Imet 15
Lady of Iunt 140
Lady of Mefkat 252
Lady of Memphis 15
Lady of Mining.. 132
Lady of Nefrusi 15
Lady of Sinai 15
Lady of Sycamore-town 15, 64
Lady of the Pillar............................ 17, 239
Lady of the Red Mountain............ 15, 136
Lady of the Sky............................ 18, 40
Lady of the Southern Sycamore 147
Lady of the temple of Herakleopolis...15
Lady of the town of Atfih....................15
Lady of the two Egg-shells 16
Lady of the West............................ 148
Lady of Wawat..15
Lahun............................226, 286
lapis lazuli 137
Late Period...... 17, 23, 56, 71, 82, 85, 93, 115, 137, 146, 166, 193, 221, 238, 283
laughter..11
Lebanon.. 140
Letopolis..179, 286
Leyden Hymns 58
Leyden Papyrus............................ 119, 170
lion 41, 96, 114, 115, 127, 166, 167, 172, 175, 176, 187, 194, 195, 196, 239, 269
lioness 12, 25, 26, 56, 57, 73, 104, 115, 125, 165, 166, 167, 175, 180, 181, 182, 194, 195, 206, 234, 253
lion-headed............96, 114, 127, 175, 239
lions............................72, 146, 165, 166, 167
Little People..14

lotus ... 24, 48, 67, 83, 107, 113, 114, 115, 124, 175, 176, 186, 196, 216, 234, 236, 261
love. 11, 14, 26, 49, 50, 77, 78, 86, 87, 90, 91, 98, 100, 101, 112, 113, 117, 135, 160, 161, 175, 176, 184, 193, 206, 208, 211, 215, 221, 222, 238, 267, 268
Luxor 180, 202, 238, 248, 285, 286

M

maat 55, 123, 124, 189, 199, 204, 240, 271
Maat 23, 148, 151, 156, 188, 189, 204, 206, 246, 265, 271
Maat-Hathor..189
malachite 129, 135
mammisi 25, 186, 187, 188, 202, 233, 242, 247, 275, 278, 280, 281
Mansion of kas
  One of the Seven Hathors 161
Marcus Aurelius 242
masks 96, 119
Maya..67
Medamud 93
medicine 109, 169
Medinet Habu............. 118, 185, 218, 286
Mehet-Weret.......... 24, 36, 38, 39, 42, 153
mehyt 84
Meir....................73, 78, 95, 149, 261, 286
Meketra..63
Memphis . 32, 64, 65, 147, 164, 175, 176, 177, 178, 180, 185, 223, 238, 249, 251, 266, 284, 286, 287
menat 24, 32, 70, 73, 75, 76, 77, 78, 97, 98, 148, 149, 153, 186, 206, 216, 241, 259, 265
Mentuhotep I..245
Mentuhotep II.............. 67, 201, 202, 239
merchants................. 12, 87, 125, 139, 140
Mereru-ka..95
Meretseger..207
Merimda Beni Salama................... 30, 286

Meskhenet 160
Mestjet 181
meteorite 41, 135, 170
Middle Kingdom ... 32, 36, 38, 49, 58, 63, 79, 98, 99, 102, 105, 106, 109, 122, 130, 131, 132, 134, 143, 144, 149, 170, 188, 192, 199, 214, 217, 226, 235, 248, 249, 253, 258, 264, 283
midwife ... 12, 87, 119, 122, 145, 152, 235
milk 30, 31, 38, 61, 122, 123, 150, 202, 203, 216
Milky Way 35, 151
Min 117, 187, 196, 247
mines 86, 87, 129, 130, 133, 134, 254
Mirgissa 78, 136, 252, 286
mirror 25, 78, 79, 80, 81, 82, 83, 203
Mistress of all the Gods 18
Mistress of Biggeh 15
Mistress of Cusae 15
Mistress of Dendera 15, 187, 223, 225
Mistress of Desert Borders 15
Mistress of Fear 18, 58
Mistress of Galena 135
Mistress of Hu-Sekhem 16
Mistress of Libya 16, 141
Mistress of Manu 16
Mistress of Music 92
Mistress of Punt 139
Mistress of the Barque 139
Mistress of the Date Palms 18, 62
Mistress of the High House 16
Mistress of the Incense 139
Mistress of the Lapis Lazuli 137
Mistress of the Malachite Country 135
Mistress of the North Wind 19
Mistress of the Northern Sky 18
Mistress of the Songs 92
Mistress of the Southern Sycamore 18, 64, 251
Mistress of the Sycamore 185
Mistress of the Sycamore Shrine 16
Mistress of the Two Lands 18, 23, 163

Mistress of the Two Lands 136
Mistress of the West 18, 23, 148, 150, 245
Mistress of the Western Dead 142
Mistress of Turquoise 130, 131, 132, 134, 250
monkey 252
Montu 205
moon . 25, 35, 38, 44, 52, 57, 78, 89, 124, 137, 184, 185, 194, 201, 213, 221, 222, 241, 275, 278, 281, 282
mother . 16, 18, 19, 24, 36, 37, 38, 42, 47, 48, 62, 67, 74, 76, 88, 96, 117, 119, 122, 123, 124, 147, 149, 152, 160, 171, 172, 176, 180, 183, 186, 192, 193, 195, 201, 202, 204, 207, 216, 225, 236, 248, 264, 265, 267, 268
Mother 14, 48, 59, 88, 192, 243, 259, 271 Much Beloved
  One of the Seven Hathors 161
mulberry 61
music 11, 56, 73, 77, 87, 89, 91, 92, 93, 94, 96, 97, 98, 99, 104, 119, 135, 150, 187, 188, 252, 259, 262
musician-priestesses 73, 98, 224, 259
musicians .. 92, 93, 98, 149, 221, 252, 275
Mut 19, 23, 53, 80, 113, 165, 168, 178, 180, 185, 192, 194, 195, 200, 205, 211, 222, 244, 249, 265, 266
myrrh 62, 112, 113, 169, 221, 261, 266

N

Nabta Playa 28, 286
Nag Hammadi 37, 286
Nagada 134, 286
naked 23, 25, 100, 186, 196, 213
Nakht 67, 68, 108, 132
name 13, 14, 20, 21, 32, 35, 36, 38, 42, 48, 53, 58, 61, 68, 72, 73, 79, 81, 87, 96, 98, 107, 112, 125, 126, 134, 140, 145, 155, 161, 164, 170, 172, 173, 174,

176, 180, 182, 185, 186, 192, 196, 208, 210, 223, 225, 231, 238, 240, 247, 248, 250, 253, 278
naos 71, 72, 74, 75, 220, 231, 238, 240
Naqada 31, 33, 34, 35
Narmer 34, 43, 203
Narmer palette 34, 43
Near East 30, 59, 133, 137, 146, 192
Nebethetepet 49, 101, 249
Nectanebo I 242, 266
Nefertari 148, 161, 235, 244
Nefertem 48, 114, 175, 176, 195
Nefrusy 286
nehet 61, 68, 209
Neith 21, 84, 147, 194, 214, 258
Neolithic 23, 28, 30, 35
Nephthys 23, 127, 186
Nero 239
New Kalabsha 135, 286
New Kingdom 16, 18, 21, 24, 26, 28, 36, 67, 76, 79, 85, 99, 102, 115, 124, 126, 129, 131, 134, 140, 144, 147, 175, 177, 178, 180, 184, 193, 194, 196, 200, 201, 204, 206, 208, 209, 212, 213, 214, 217, 231, 233, 235, 239, 246, 247, 250, 253, 258, 259, 265, 266, 267, 283
New Year's Day 93, 150, 224, 240
nht 61, 67
Nile 21, 28, 30, 31, 35, 41, 44, 54, 55, 56, 57, 64, 84, 104, 117, 121, 122, 130, 135, 139, 142, 143, 151, 166, 185, 199, 207, 220, 221, 237, 238, 277
Nofretari 32
north wind 19, 185, 189
Nubia ... 14, 44, 56, 65, 94, 104, 133, 134, 140, 196, 211, 217, 247, 252, 277, 285
Nubt 134, 286
nude 23, 33
Nun ...24, 36, 38, 42, 48, 52, 54, 129, 137, 199, 220, 233, 236, 242, 271, 280
Nut 14, 23, 35, 36, 39, 41, 45, 64, 68, 82, 146, 241, 265

Nwbt 16

O

Old Kingdom ..26, 30, 38, 47, 51, 64, 72, 76, 79, 81, 82, 99, 102, 112, 142, 144, 146, 150, 152, 170, 196, 201, 214, 235, 257, 258, 259, 260, 262, 263, 268, 283
Old Nick 14
Old Testament 66
Opening of the Mouth for Breathing 144
Orion 35
Osiris 14, 43, 50, 65, 85, 89, 108, 116, 117, 145, 146, 147, 148, 149, 153, 169, 174, 175, 183, 184, 187, 189, 200, 202, 203, 206, 226, 236, 241, 246, 247, 265, 267, 268
ostracon 56
Our Lady of Denderah 18

P

Pakhet 172, 180, 181, 194, 253, 277
papyrus 18, 19, 21, 23, 24, 29, 38, 43, 49, 56, 57, 62, 64, 66, 72, 73, 75, 77, 79, 83, 84, 85, 107, 119, 126, 133, 135, 139, 143, 146, 153, 165, 168, 170, 172, 175, 178, 182, 196, 198, 203, 215, 216, 218, 225, 230, 234, 251, 261, 265
Papyrus of Kahun 170
Paris 26, 153, 241
Pathyris 16, 230, 248, 285
Pepy I 47, 195, 201, 239
perfume making 114
persea 62
Persephone 50, 266
phallus 118, 275
Philae 56, 97, 108, 115, 167, 174, 195, 218, 219, 227, 252, 266, 284, 287
Pi-Hathor 16
plagues 55, 167, 168, 169
Plutarch 74, 75, 265
Port Kosseir 134

Pre-dynastic Period 25, 28, 35, 47, 57, 59, 64, 105, 112, 133, 134, 135, 137, 166, 220, 243, 248
pregnancy 100, 117, 214
pregnant 119
priestess . 64, 99, 114, 178, 237, 257, 259, 260, 261
priests ... 47, 73, 97, 98, 99, 128, 168, 170, 177, 199, 212, 220, 224, 234, 237, 240, 256, 257, 258, 259, 260, 261, 266
procreation 87, 116, 117, 190
Ptah 64, 65, 113, 164, 175, 176, 177, 178, 185, 203, 223, 238, 248, 249, 251, 254, 259
Ptolemaic 24, 38, 56, 72, 98, 107, 125, 137, 145, 170, 236, 239, 244, 245, 246, 250, 262, 266, 283
Ptolemy I 244, 250
Ptolemy IV 42, 128, 244, 246
Ptolemy XII 239
Punt 62, 113, 182
Pyramid Texts 23, 37, 38, 42, 52, 65, 68, 144, 176, 201, 203, 225

Q

Qadesh 196
Qasr Ibrim 252, 287
Qertassi 135, 287
quartz 133, 137
quartzite 136

R

Ra .. 17, 23, 24, 35, 36, 42, 47, 48, 49, 50, 51, 52, 53, 54, 56, 57, 58, 59, 62, 87, 88, 100, 104, 113, 114, 119, 123, 125, 126, 127, 128, 146, 156, 161, 164, 166, 167, 169, 174, 176, 179, 180, 184, 185, 188, 189, 192, 194, 196, 204, 207, 208, 217, 223, 224, 225, 229, 235, 236, 237, 240, 243, 245, 246, 247, 249, 251, 261, 263, 277, 278, 280

Raet 58
Raettawy 58
Ra-Harakhti 49, 136, 147
Raiyt 58
Rameses II ... 24, 136, 148, 179, 194, 201, 239, 244, 246, 248, 250, 251, 259
Rameses III 114, 175, 239, 254
Ramesside Period 143, 245
rape 50, 90, 267
rebirth .. 24, 31, 35, 65, 68, 77, 78, 87, 88, 106, 114, 136, 137, 150, 152, 153, 203, 207, 213, 225, 235, 268
red 21, 23, 24, 32, 54, 55, 57, 97, 104, 105, 132, 136, 148, 160, 161, 164, 165, 179, 251
Renenutet 116, 160, 250
Reshep 196
ribbons 65, 160
Roman Catholic 89, 178
royal child 122

S

sacrificial food 113
Sahara 28, 30
Sahura 178, 263
Saite Period 57
Sallier Papyrus 175
Saosis 68
Saqqara 81, 95, 96, 139, 166, 258, 261, 287, 291
Sareru 131, 255
Satis 196, 266
scarab 114, 127, 146, 206, 209
scented oil 113
sceptre 21, 136, 165, 175, 178
Scintillating One 137
scorpion 124, 148, 161
scorpion sting 124, 161
Sehet Island 193
Sekhathor 44
Sekhat-Hor 18, 202, 208

sekhem 21, 72
Sekhmet . 8, 12, 19, 21, 24, 47, 49, 51, 53, 54, 55, 73, 78, 94, 96, 104, 106, 107, 123, 124, 125, 126, 127, 128, 144, 154, 159, 163, 164, 165, 167, 168, 169, 170, 171, 172, 173, 174, 175, 176, 177, 178, 179, 180, 181, 182, 185, 186, 189, 194, 195, 196, 199, 200, 206, 224, 249, 250, 251, 254, 257, 258, 260, 263, 268, 269
Sekhmet-Hathor 164, 250
sensual 87, 89, 91, 193
Senusret I 78, 95, 134, 249, 250
Serabit el-Khadim 131, 134, 193, 208, 233, 252, 287
Serket 148
Serpent-Goddess 58, 254
Seshat 196, 241
seshen 113
Seth 21, 50, 51, 74, 90, 100, 110, 123, 124, 127, 128, 146, 173, 174, 175, 187, 193, 246, 265, 267
Sethnakhte 190
Sety I 15, 153, 172, 175, 246, 254
Seven Hathors 8, 120, 125, 159, 160, 161, 162, 168, 226, 277
seven sacred oils 113
sex 87, 89, 90, 91, 117, 118, 145, 184, 268
sexual love 86
sexual pleasure 100, 196
Shabaqo 239
shabti 143
Shalim 208
Sharuna 234, 287
She of Chemnis
 One of the Seven Hathors 161
She who protects
 One of the Seven Hathors 161
She whose name has power
 One of the Seven Hathors 161
shemayet, ... 99
Shesmetet 175, 182
Shu 44, 52, 56, 207, 226, 275

Silent One
 One of the Seven Hathors 161
Sinai 14, 108, 130, 131, 134, 141, 185, 193, 208, 252, 254, 258, 287
singer-priestess 99
singers 78, 92, 99, 222, 258, 259
Sirius 42, 43, 44, 117
sistrum ... 21, 23, 37, 57, 70, 71, 72, 73, 74, 75, 76, 77, 78, 83, 84, 91, 97, 98, 119, 149, 186, 190, 194, 202, 225, 234, 235, 240, 242, 257, 259, 265
skull 25
sky .. 12, 14, 18, 21, 23, 27, 28, 35, 36, 37, 40, 41, 42, 43, 44, 45, 48, 49, 60, 68, 78, 81, 84, 86, 98, 117, 121, 125, 130, 134, 136, 137, 138, 146, 147, 150, 151, 155, 157, 163, 166, 167, 173, 182, 184, 187, 199, 201, 207, 235, 241, 243, 265, 270
snake 25, 160, 169, 174, 182, 225
soapstone 93
Sobek 184, 185, 251
Sokar 203, 246
solar 12, 16, 19, 25, 27, 36, 41, 46, 48, 49, 57, 58, 76, 78, 81, 114, 124, 125, 127, 130, 133, 136, 138, 139, 156, 157, 163, 164, 166, 167, 174, 181, 184, 185, 188, 189, 194, 203, 205, 206, 207, 217, 233, 237, 238, 243, 251, 263, 265, 270, 271
Solar Eye 53, 128, 194, 217, 266
Sonebi 78
Sopdet 43, 44
Sothis 43, 44, 192, 197
Speos Artemidos 253, 287
spoons 61, 82, 83
star 24, 34, 36, 39, 41, 43, 44, 165
stars 34, 35, 36, 37, 40, 41, 42, 43, 44, 98, 137, 142, 148
state deities 48
stelae .. 130, 131, 143, 178, 218, 236, 257, 260
stellar 35, 43

Storm in the sky
   One of the Seven Hathors............. 162
Sudan 30, 34, 61, 187, 247
sun. 12, 14, 16, 20, 22, 23, 24, 25, 26, 32, 35, 36, 37, 38, 40, 41, 42, 43, 44, 46, 47, 48, 49, 50, 51, 52, 53, 56, 57, 58, 59, 62, 78, 79, 81, 82, 84, 86, 89, 106, 113, 114, 119, 124, 126, 127, 128, 129, 133, 134, 136, 137, 139, 140, 142, 146, 148, 150, 152, 153, 157, 160, 164, 165, 166, 175, 176, 179, 184, 185, 186, 194, 201, 203, 205, 207, 208, 216, 227, 233, 235, 236, 237, 238, 240, 241, 249, 250, 259, 263, 265, 266, 271, 280, 281, 282
sycamore.... 16, 20, 25, 60, 61, 62, 63, 64, 65, 66, 67, 68, 198, 234, 244, 249, 265
Syria.. 140, 192

T

Tale of the Doomed Prince 160
Tale of the Two Brothers 160
tamarisk 61, 67, 68
tambourine 97, 98, 252
Tammuz 117
Tausert 190
Taweret 207, 209, 216
Tefnut 52, 53, 56, 104, 128, 194, 207, 275
Tell Basta 195, 287
Tell el-Far'in 287
Tell el-Muqdan 287
Tell Hisn 287
Tell Nabasha 287
Tell-Muqdon 193
Tep-ihu 32
textile 154, 214, 234
Texts of the Sarcophagus 143
The Beautiful Hely 19
The Great One 18
The Hand of Atum 18, 101
The Ruler-Goddess 18

Theban 24, 38, 77, 83, 141, 143, 146, 147, 150, 180, 185, 195, 205, 207, 211
Thebes . 24, 32, 38, 48, 58, 62, 67, 94, 95, 98, 105, 115, 132, 134, 136, 143, 148, 176, 180, 192, 211, 216, 221, 222, 224, 249, 250, 286
Thoth..... 16, 44, 52, 56, 57, 65, 101, 104, 109, 124, 127, 128, 137, 144, 146, 149, 153, 157, 160, 174, 187, 189, 190, 196, 205, 206, 208, 223, 224, 226, 244, 253, 263, 265, 268, 271
Thutmose III 102, 108, 126, 172, 181, 208, 239, 245, 249, 250, 253, 265
Timna 78, 254, 287
Trajan 240, 242
travellers 12, 254
tree .12, 25, 26, 27, 60, 61, 62, 63, 64, 65, 66, 67, 68, 85, 135, 143, 147, 152, 161, 167, 182, 199, 217, 236, 244, 249, 265, 270
tree cults 64
Triumph of Horus 174, 187
turquoise. 21, 68, 119, 129, 131, 134, 137
Tutankhamun 37, 67, 77
Typhon 74

U

ukh 21
unguents 111, 113, 114
Upper Egypt 38, 133, 238
uraeus 46, 52, 53, 56, 57, 58, 124, 164, 165, 173, 175, 179, 180, 181, 182, 189, 194, 217, 245
Userhet 67

V

Venus 44
vulture 19, 23, 148, 180, 247, 259

W

wadi 131, 181, 253

Wadi Abbad 254, 287
Wadi el-Hudi 131, 255, 287
Wadi el-Subua 24, 287
Wadi Hammamat 134, 238, 287
Wadi Maghara 134, 252, 287
Wadjet 19, 25, 53, 58, 126, 172, 175, 176, 182, 192, 266
water 30, 31, 43, 54, 55, 56, 57, 64, 65, 66, 68, 104, 114, 122, 131, 133, 144, 150, 171, 186, 209, 216, 218, 220, 221, 237, 242, 251, 253, 254, 262
Wedjat Eye 127
Wepwawet 99
Weret 36, 39, 52, 217, 258
Weret-Hekau 52, 217
Westcar Papyrus 119

Western Desert 30
Western Mountains 130, 143, 215
wig 21, 165, 175, 179, 213
Wine 105, 106, 107, 108, 109, 177
winter solstice 57, 93
Womb of Horus 14
World Tree 68
Wst.t Hr 222

Y

yellow 136, 251

Z

zebu 30

PUBLISHED BY AVALONIA
WWW.AVALONIABOOKS.CO.UK

Printed in October 2021
by Rotomail Italia S.p.A., Vignate (MI) - Italy